Penguin & House vol.1

Akiho Ieda

Penguin & House
Contents

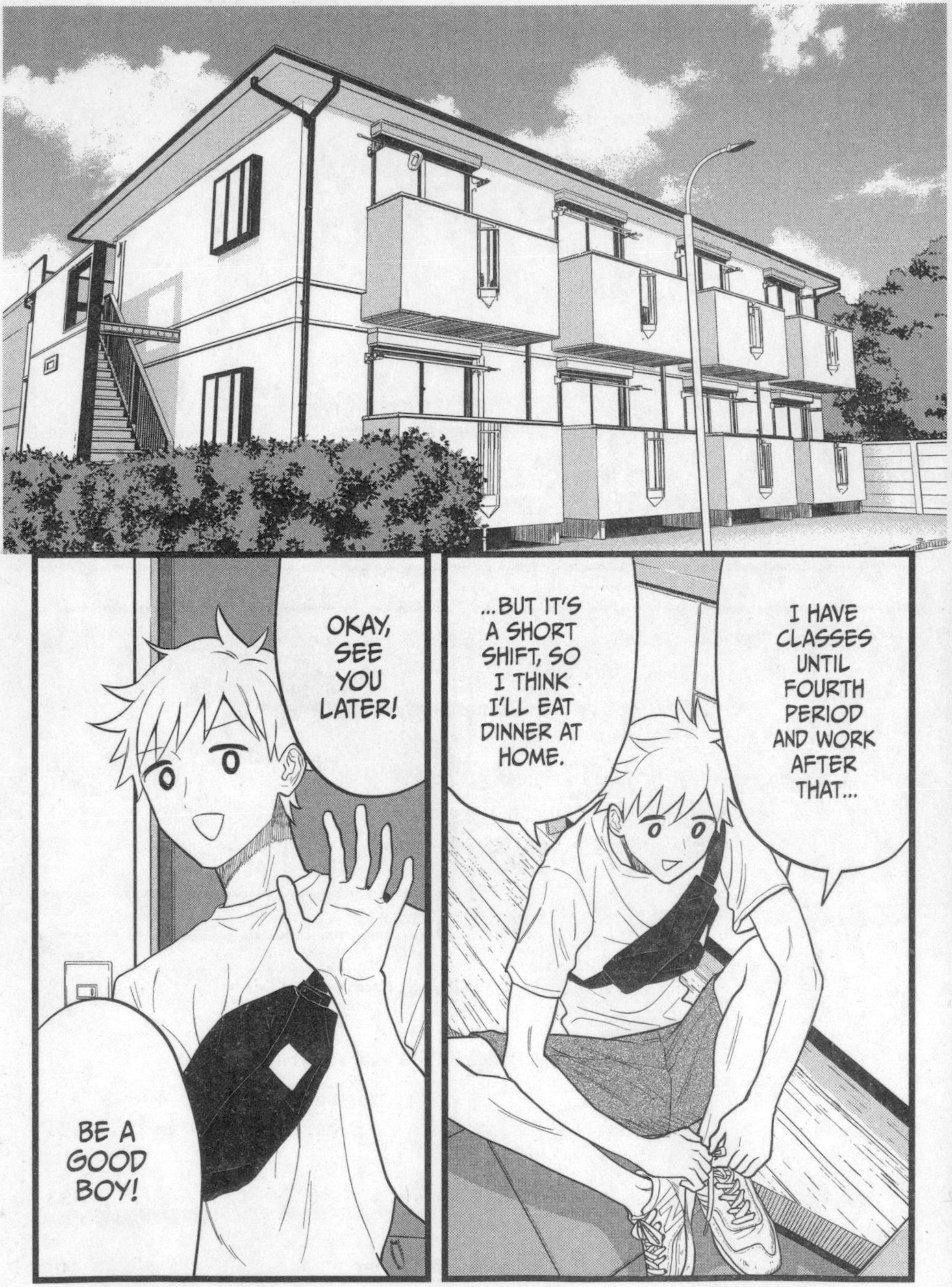
I HAVE CLASSES UNTIL FOURTH PERIOD AND WORK AFTER THAT...
...BUT IT'S A SHORT SHIFT, SO I THINK I'LL EAT DINNER AT HOME.
OKAY, SEE YOU LATER!
BE A GOOD BOY!

Pen 1 The Penguin Grills Steak for His Owner

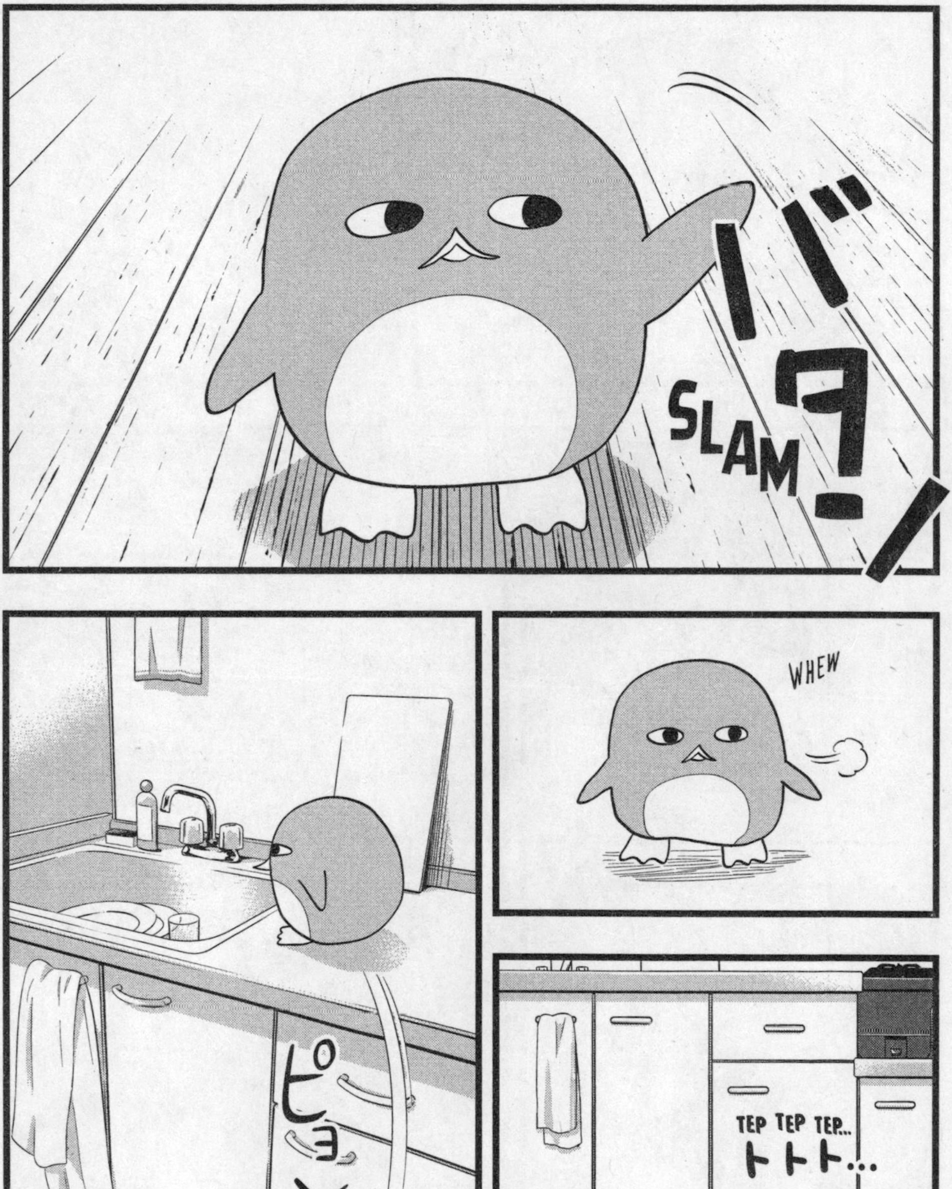
バタ!
SLAM
WHEW
TEP TEP TEP...
トトト...
ピョン
POING

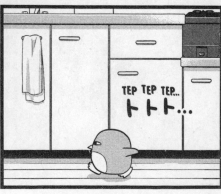

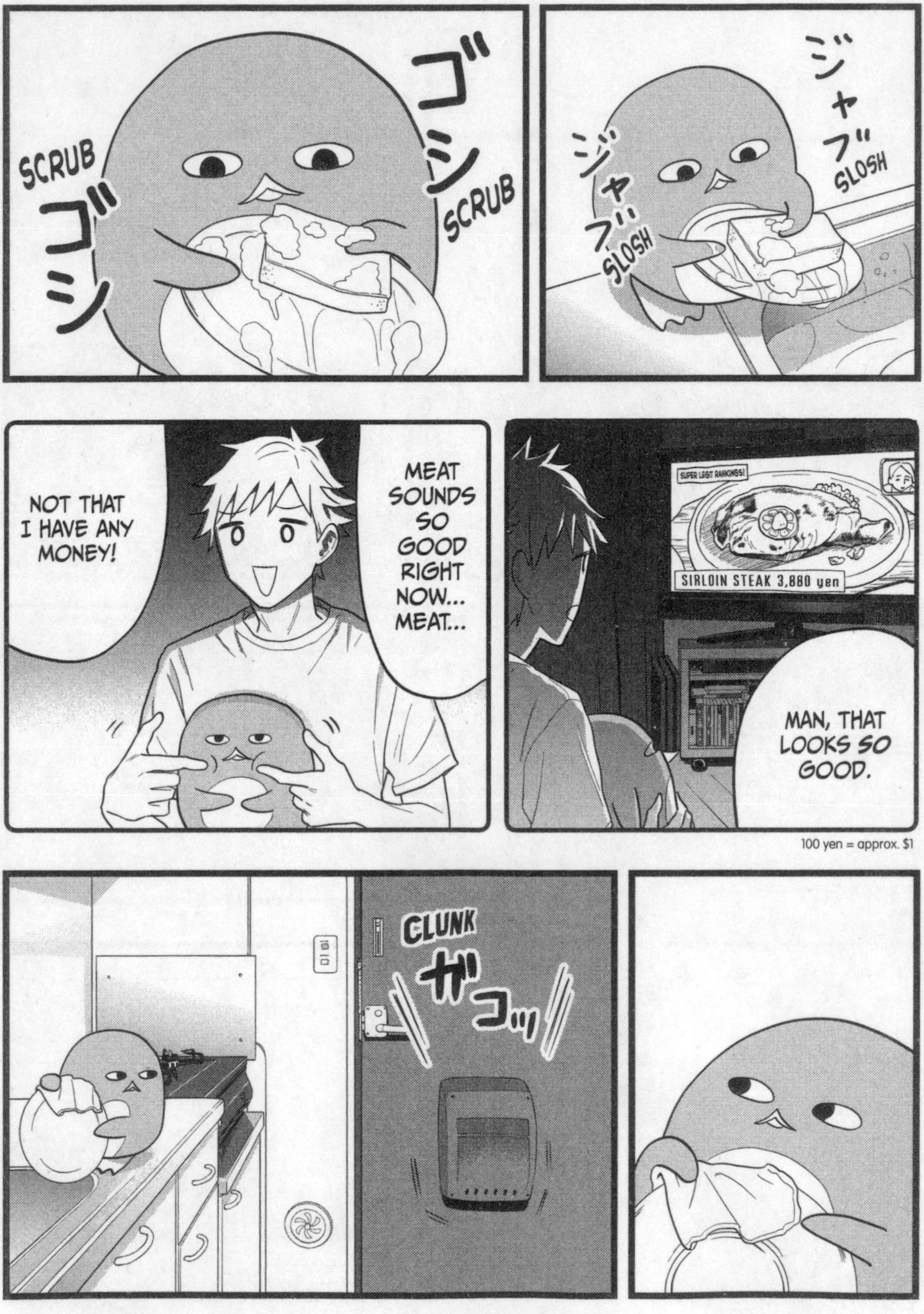
ジャブ
SLOSH
ジャブ
SLOSH
ゴシ
SCRUB
SCRUB
ゴシ
SUPER LEGIT RANKINGS!
SIRLOIN STEAK 3,880 yen
MAN, THAT LOOKS SO GOOD.
MEAT SOUNDS SO GOOD RIGHT NOW... MEAT...
NOT THAT I HAVE ANY MONEY!
CLUNK
ガコッ

100 yen = approx. $1

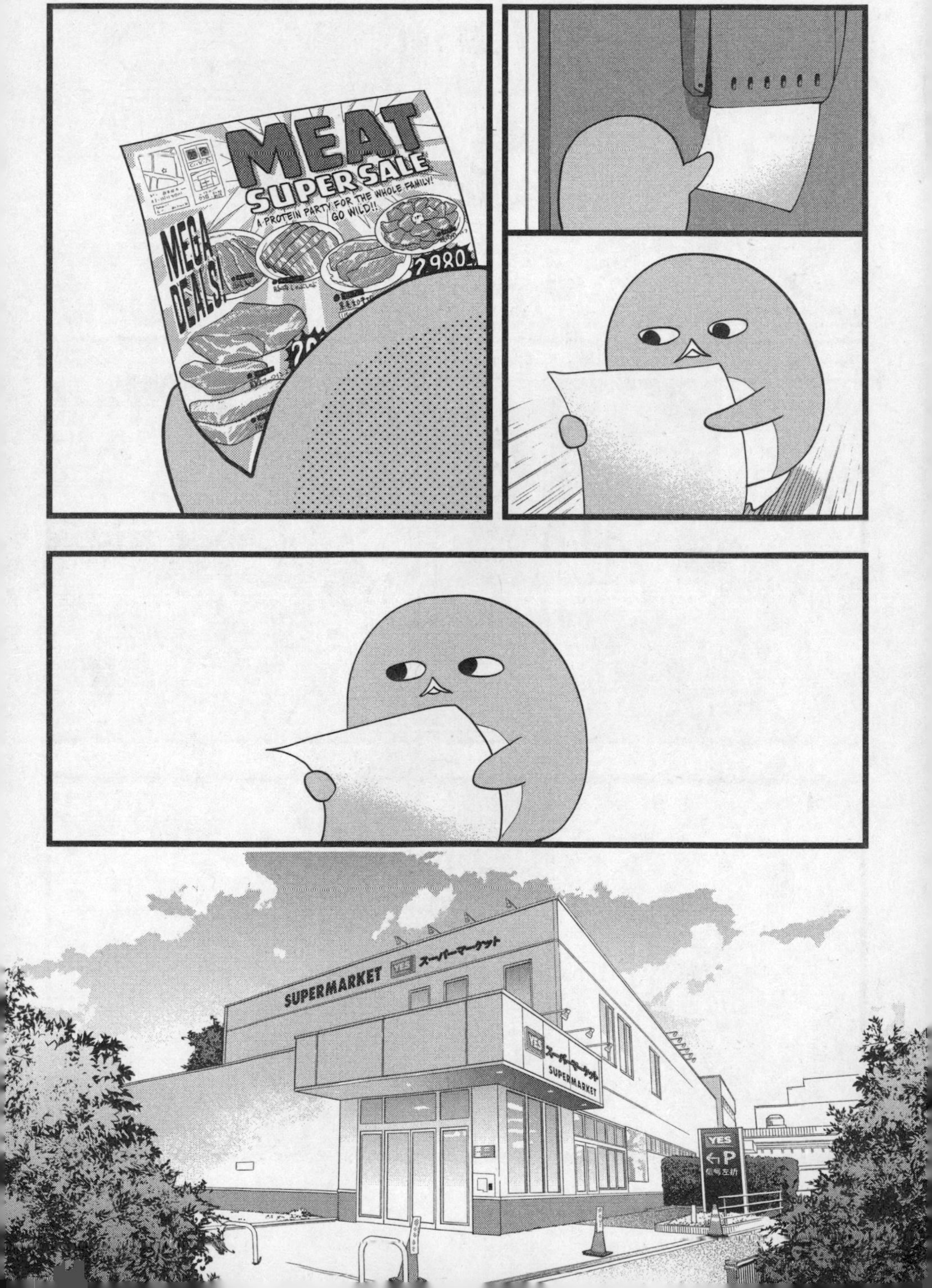
MEAT
SUPER SALE
A PROTEIN PARTY FOR THE WHOLE FAMILY! GO WILD!!
MEGA DEALS!
2,980
SUPERMARKET
YES
スーパーマーケット
YES
スーパーマーケット
SUPERMARKET
YES
P

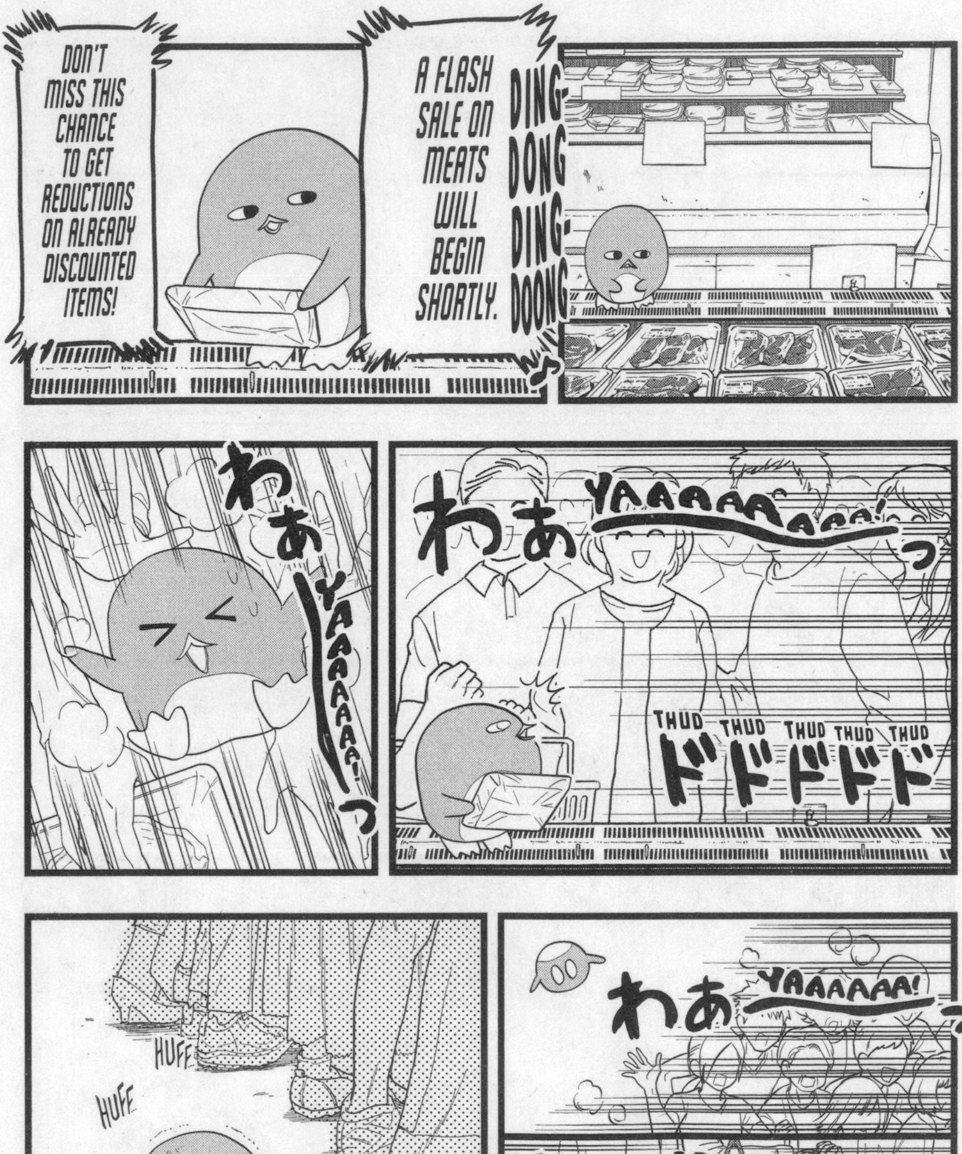
DING-DONG DING-DOONG
A FLASH SALE ON MEATS WILL BEGIN SHORTLY.
DON'T MISS THIS CHANCE TO GET REDUCTIONS ON ALREADY DISCOUNTED ITEMS!
わあ YAAAAAAAA!
THUD THUD THUD THUD THUD
ドドドドド
わあ YAAAAAAAAA!
わあ YAAAAAA!
わあ YAAAAAAAAA!
HUFF
HUFF
ヨロ…
HOBBLE...

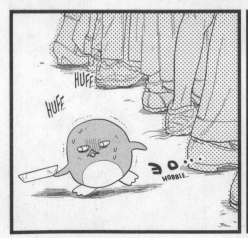

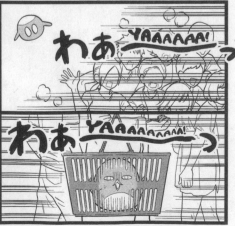

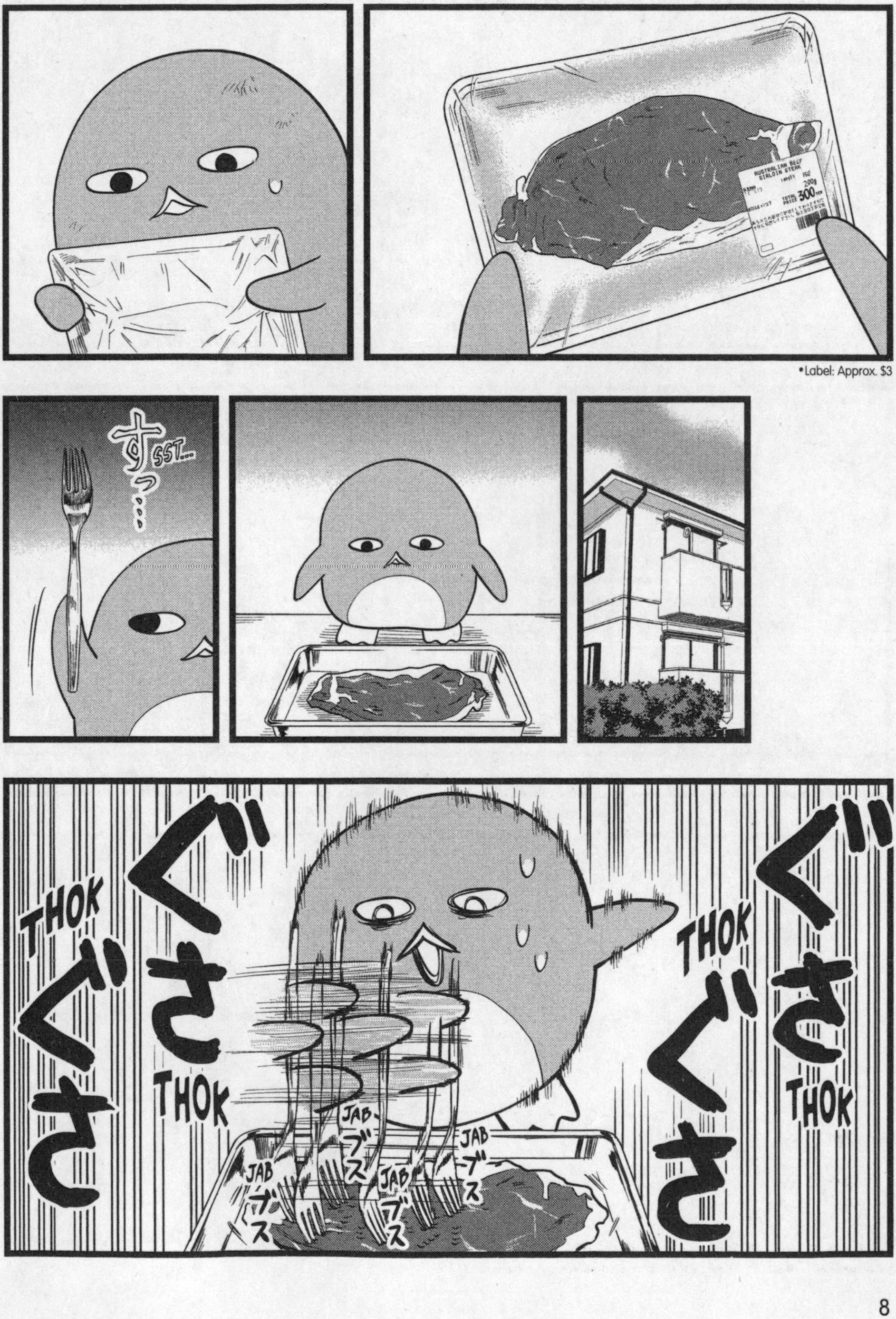
AUSTRALIAN BEEF SIRLOIN STEAK
200g
TOTAL PRICE 300 YEN
すっ...
SST...
ぐさぐさ
THOK
THOK
ぐさぐさ
THOK
THOK
JAB
ブス
JAB
ブス
JAB
ブス
JAB
ブス

*Label: Approx. $3

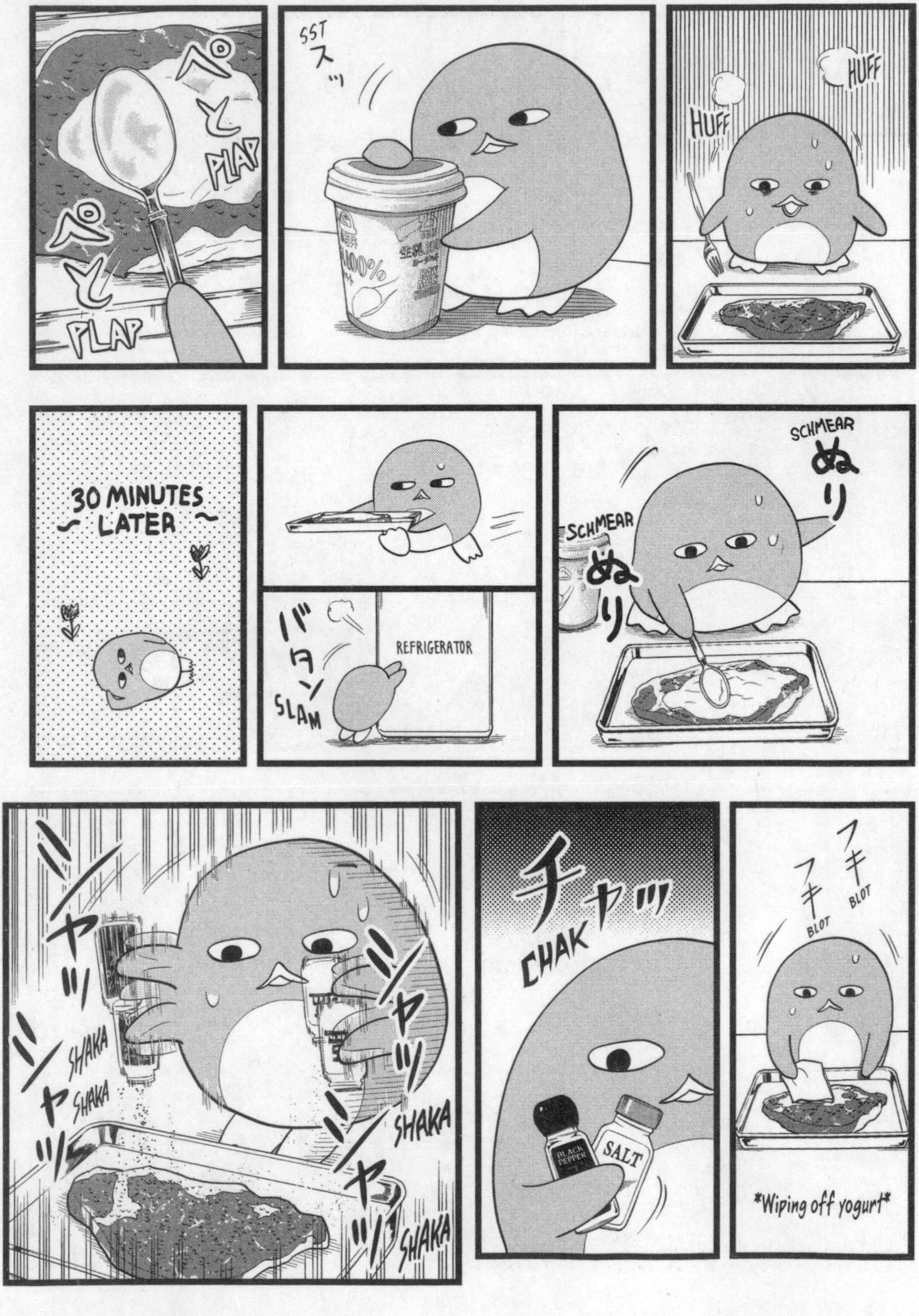
HUFF
HUFF
SST スッ
ペと PLAP
ペと PLAP
ぬり SCHMEAR
ぬり SCHMEAR
バタン SLAM
REFRIGERATOR
~30 MINUTES LATER~
フキ BLOT
フキ BLOT
Wiping off yogurt
チャッ CHAK
BLACK PEPPER
SALT
シャッ SHAKA
シャッ SHAKA
シャッ SHAKA
シャッ SHAKA

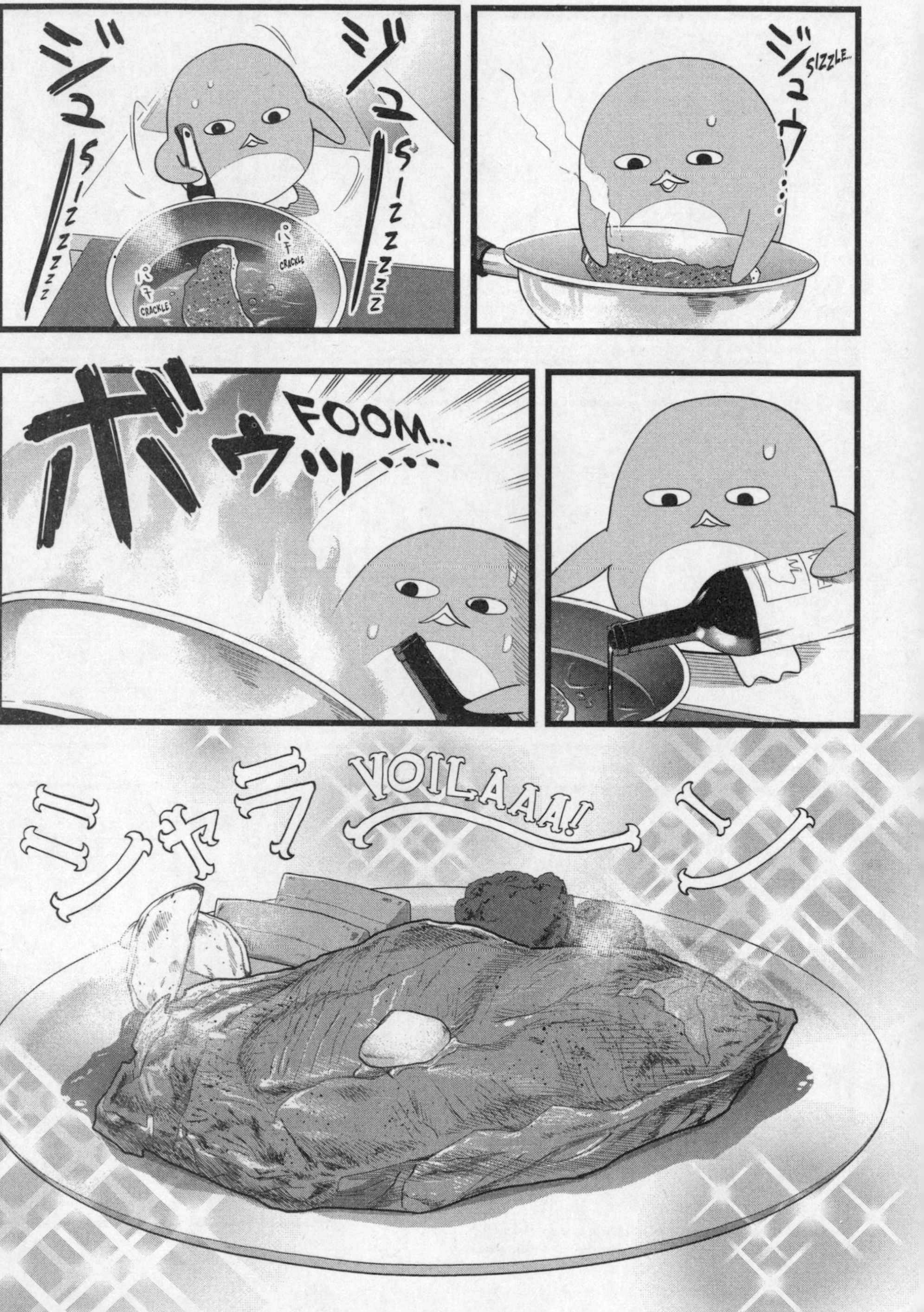
ジュウ…
SIZZLE...
ジュ
SIZZZZZZ
ジュ
SIZZZZZZ
パチ
CRACKLE
パチ
CRACKLE
ボウッ…
FOOM...
シャラ〜ン
VOILAAA!

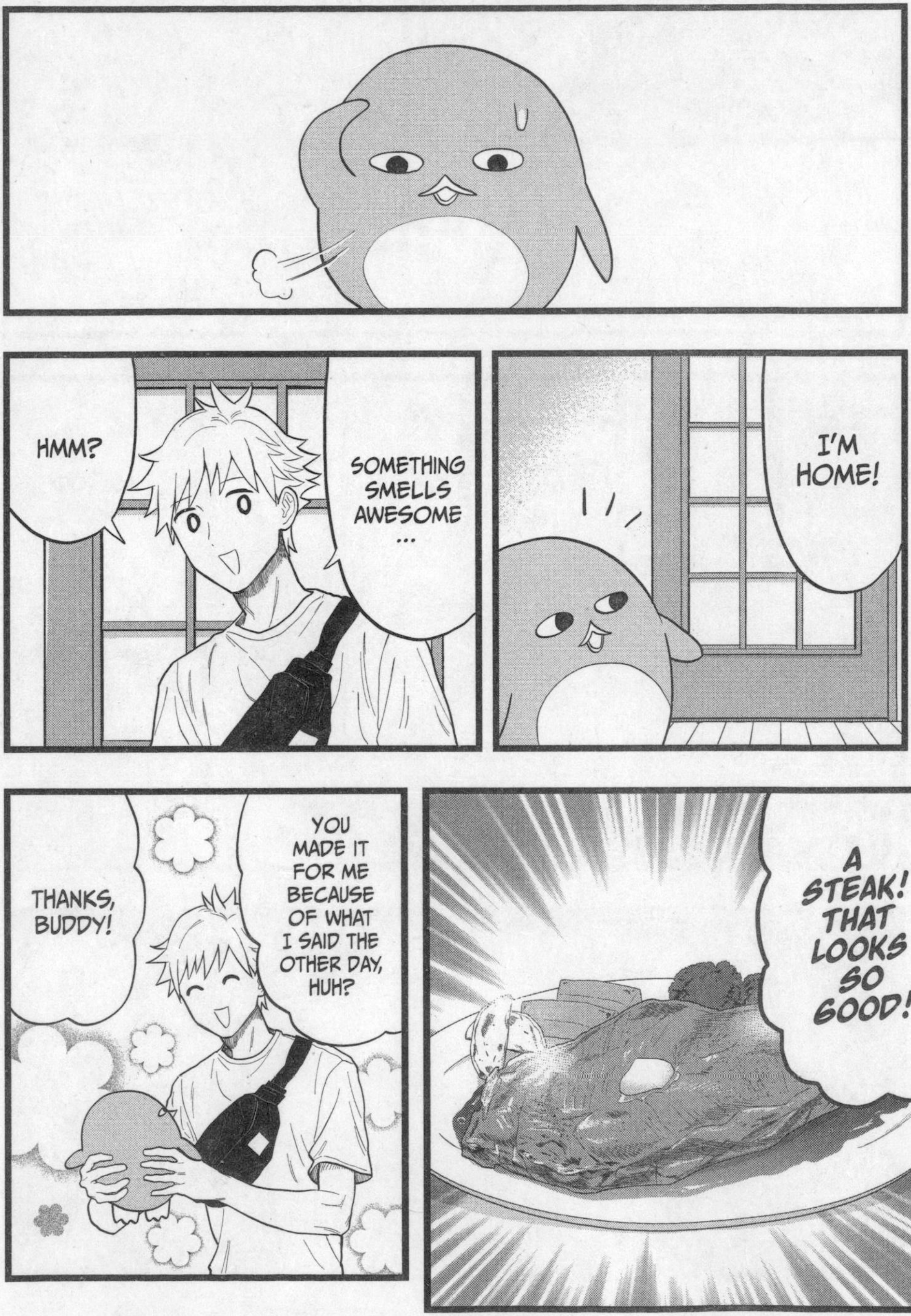
I'M HOME!
SOMETHING SMELLS AWESOME ...
HMM?
A STEAK! THAT LOOKS SO GOOD!
YOU MADE IT FOR ME BECAUSE OF WHAT I SAID THE OTHER DAY, HUH?
THANKS, BUDDY!

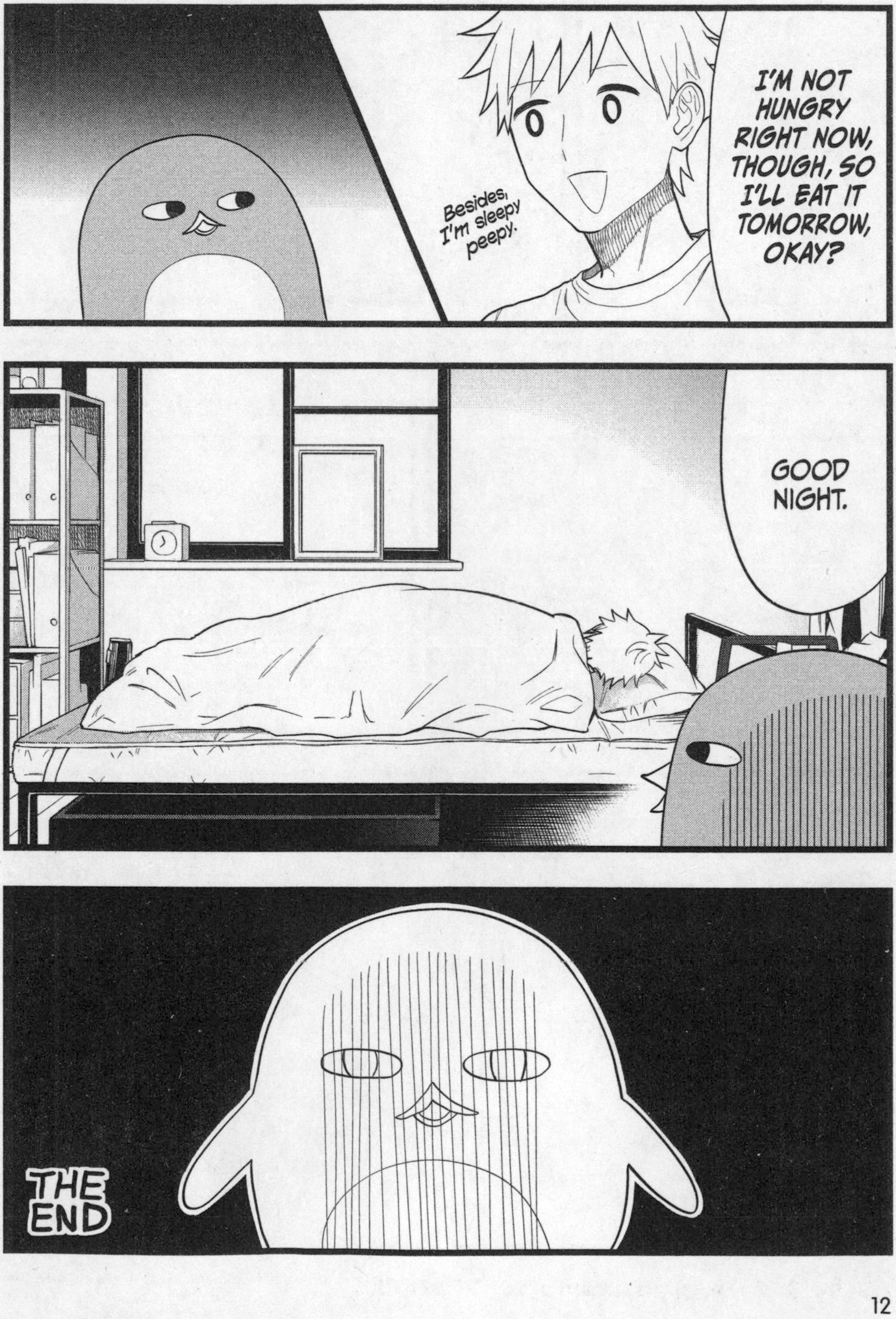
I'M NOT HUNGRY RIGHT NOW, THOUGH, SO I'LL EAT IT TOMORROW, OKAY?
Besides, I'm sleepy peepy.
GOOD NIGHT.
THE END

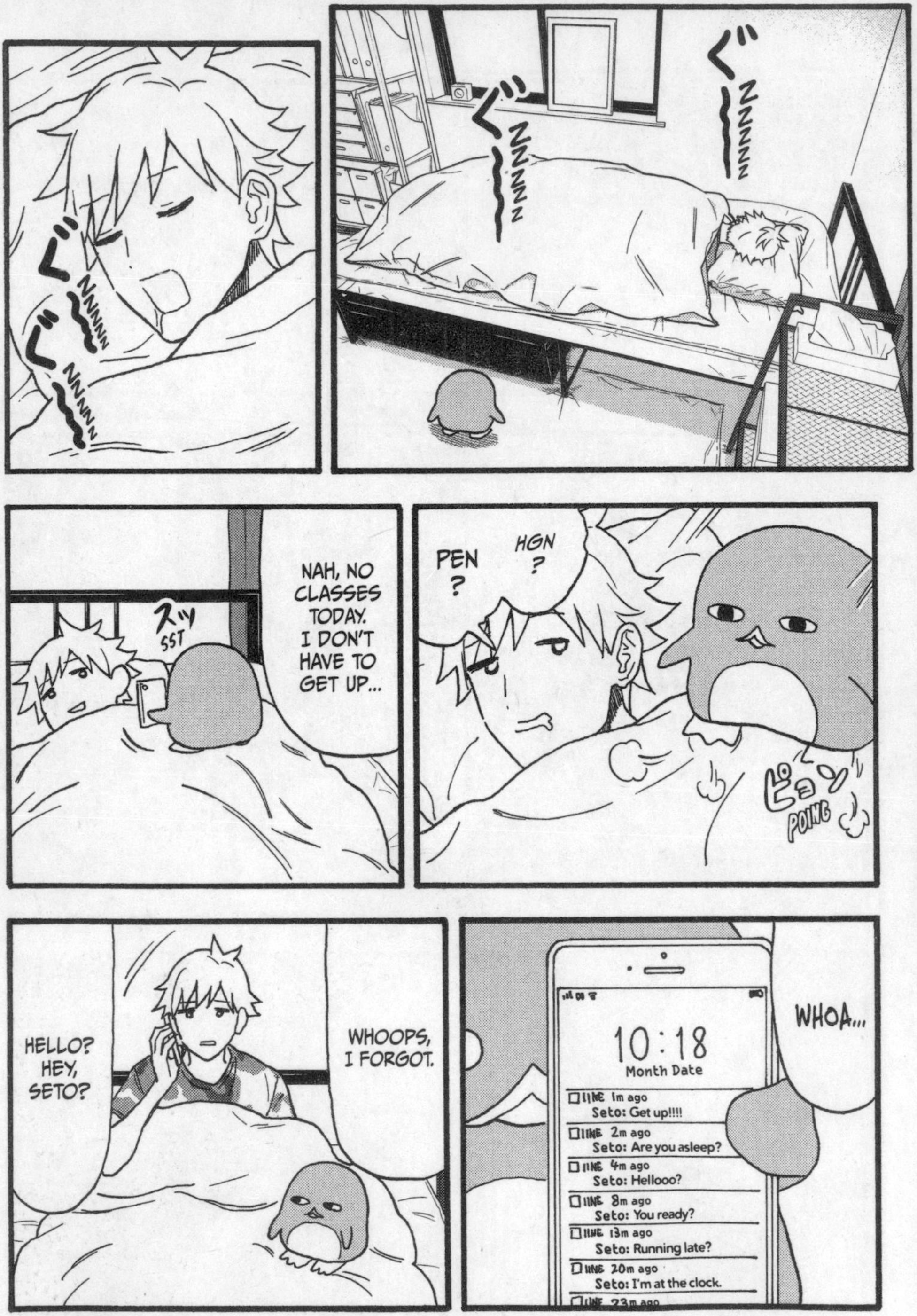
ぐ〜ZZZZZ
ぐ〜ZZZZZ
ぐ〜ZZZZZ
ぐ〜ZZZZZ
HGN?
PEN?
ピョン
POING
NAH, NO CLASSES TODAY. I DON'T HAVE TO GET UP...
スッ
SST
WHOA...
10:18
Month Date
LINE 1m ago
Seto: Get up!!!!
LINE 2m ago
Seto: Are you asleep?
LINE 4m ago
Seto: Hellooo?
LINE 8m ago
Seto: You ready?
LINE 13m ago
Seto: Running late?
LINE 20m ago
Seto: I'm at the clock.
LINE 23m ago
WHOOPS, I FORGOT.
HELLO? HEY, SETO?

Pen 2 The Penguin Is Adored by His Owner's Friend

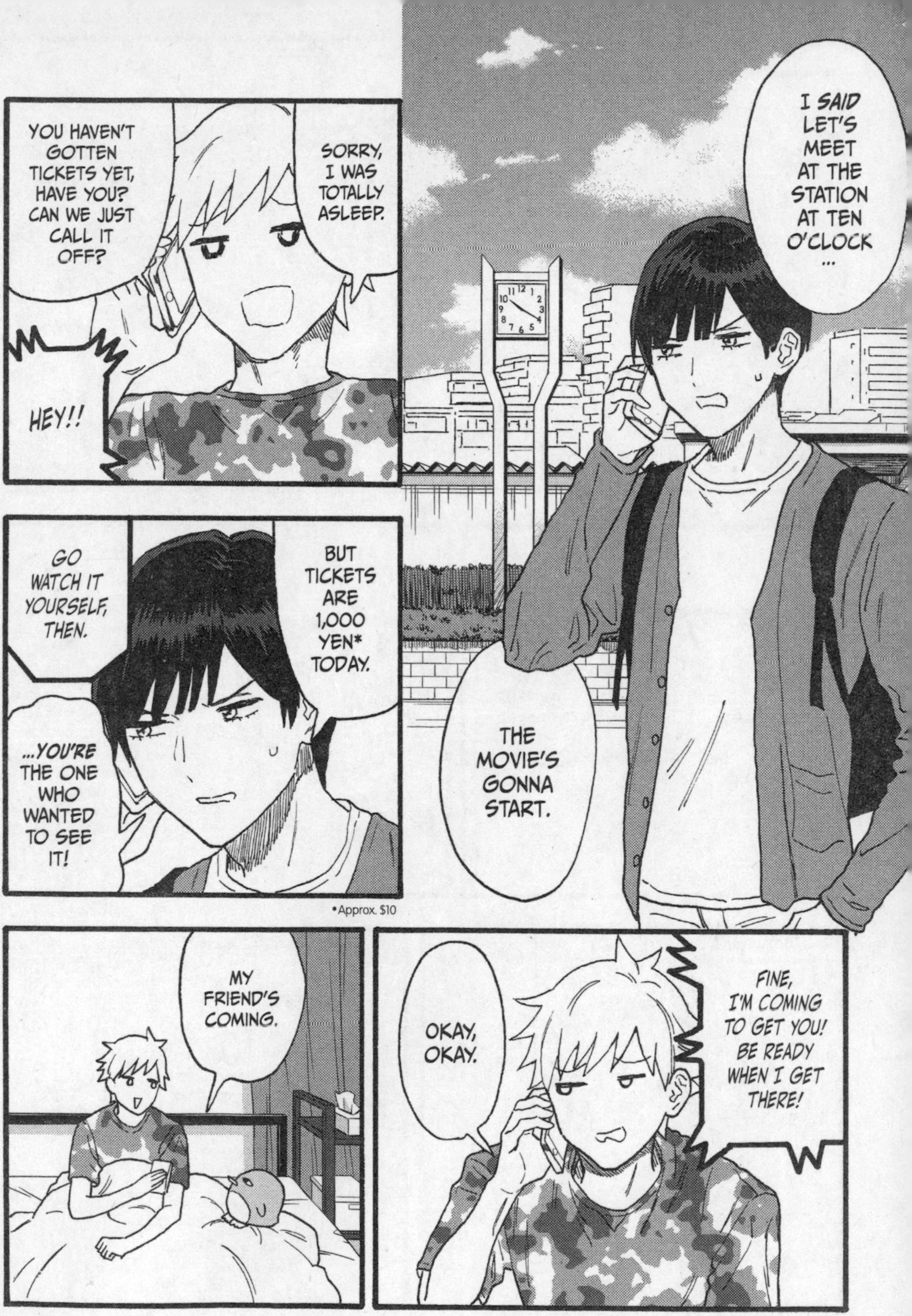
I SAID LET'S MEET AT THE STATION AT TEN O'CLOCK ...
THE MOVIE'S GONNA START.
SORRY, I WAS TOTALLY ASLEEP.
YOU HAVEN'T GOTTEN TICKETS YET, HAVE YOU? CAN WE JUST CALL IT OFF?
HEY!!
BUT TICKETS ARE 1,000 YEN* TODAY.
GO WATCH IT YOURSELF, THEN.
...YOU'RE THE ONE WHO WANTED TO SEE IT!
FINE, I'M COMING TO GET YOU! BE READY WHEN I GET THERE!
OKAY, OKAY.
MY FRIEND'S COMING.

*Approx. $10

COMING!

DING-DOOONG ♪

GA-CHK GA-CHK

THIS IS IT.

I GUESS THIS IS THE FIRST TIME I'VE BEEN TO HAYAKAWA'S PLACE...

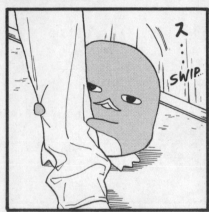

SWIP.

I'M NOT READY YET. COME ON IN FOR A SEC.

...UH, WHO'S THIS?
OH, DIDN'T I TELL YOU?
MY PENGUIN.
YOU'RE ALLOWED TO HAVE PETS HERE?
DUNNO. PROBABLY NOT? BUT HE DOESN'T SQUAWK.
UHHH...
I'M GONNA GO TAKE A SHOWER, SO MAKE YOURSELF AT HOME.
OKAY.
...
...A PENGUIN? ARE YOU EVEN ALLOWED TO KEEP PENGUINS AS PETS?
DID PENGUINS ALWAYS LOOK LIKE THIS?
WELL...
ALL THAT ASIDE...

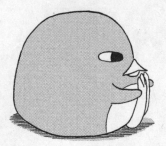

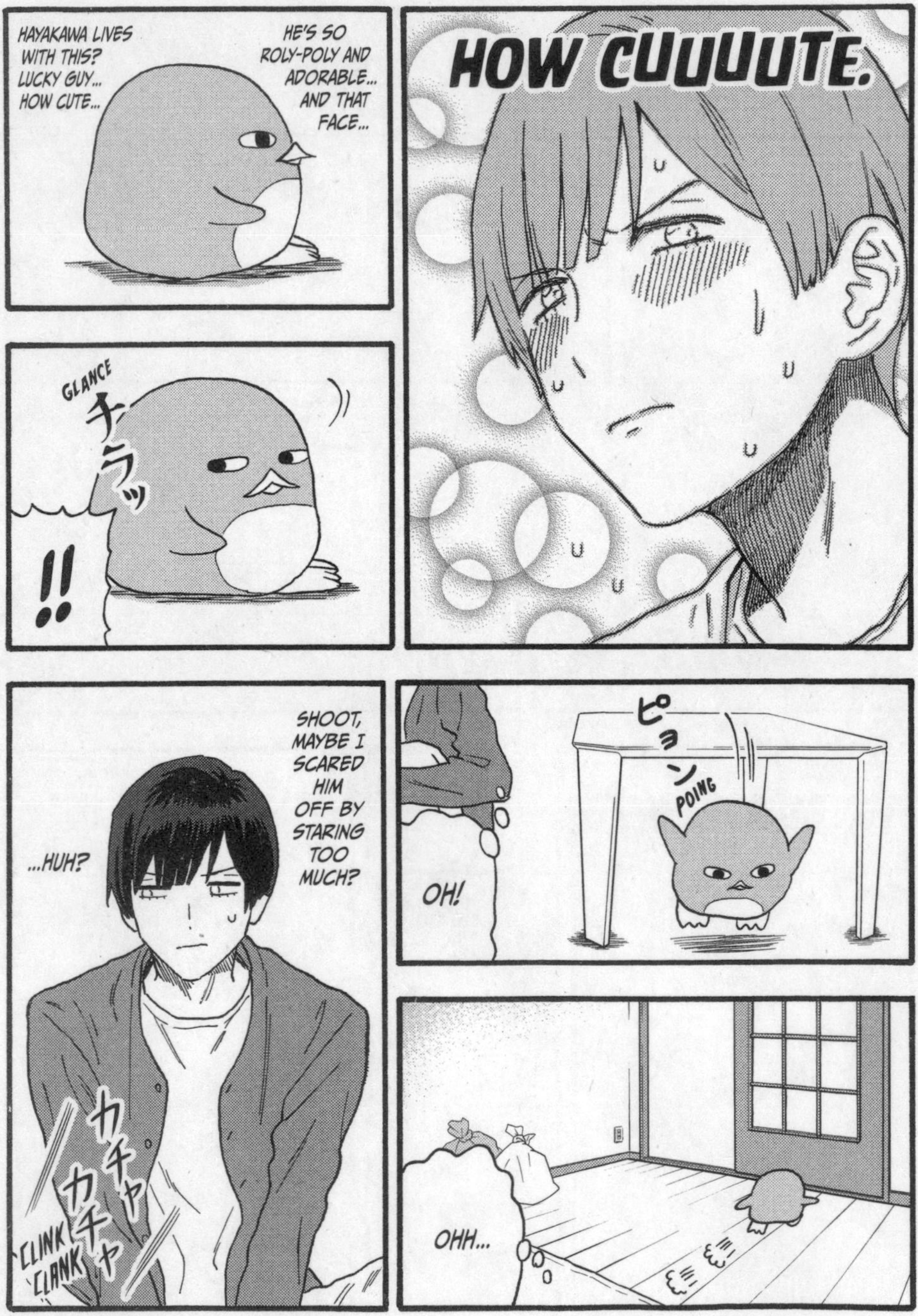
HOW CUUUUTE.
HE'S SO ROLY-POLY AND ADORABLE... AND THAT FACE...
HAYAKAWA LIVES WITH THIS? LUCKY GUY... HOW CUTE...
GLANCE
チラッ
!!
ピョン
POING
OH!
OHH...
SHOOT, MAYBE I SCARED HIM OFF BY STARING TOO MUCH?
...HUH?
カチャ
カチャ
CLINK
CLANK

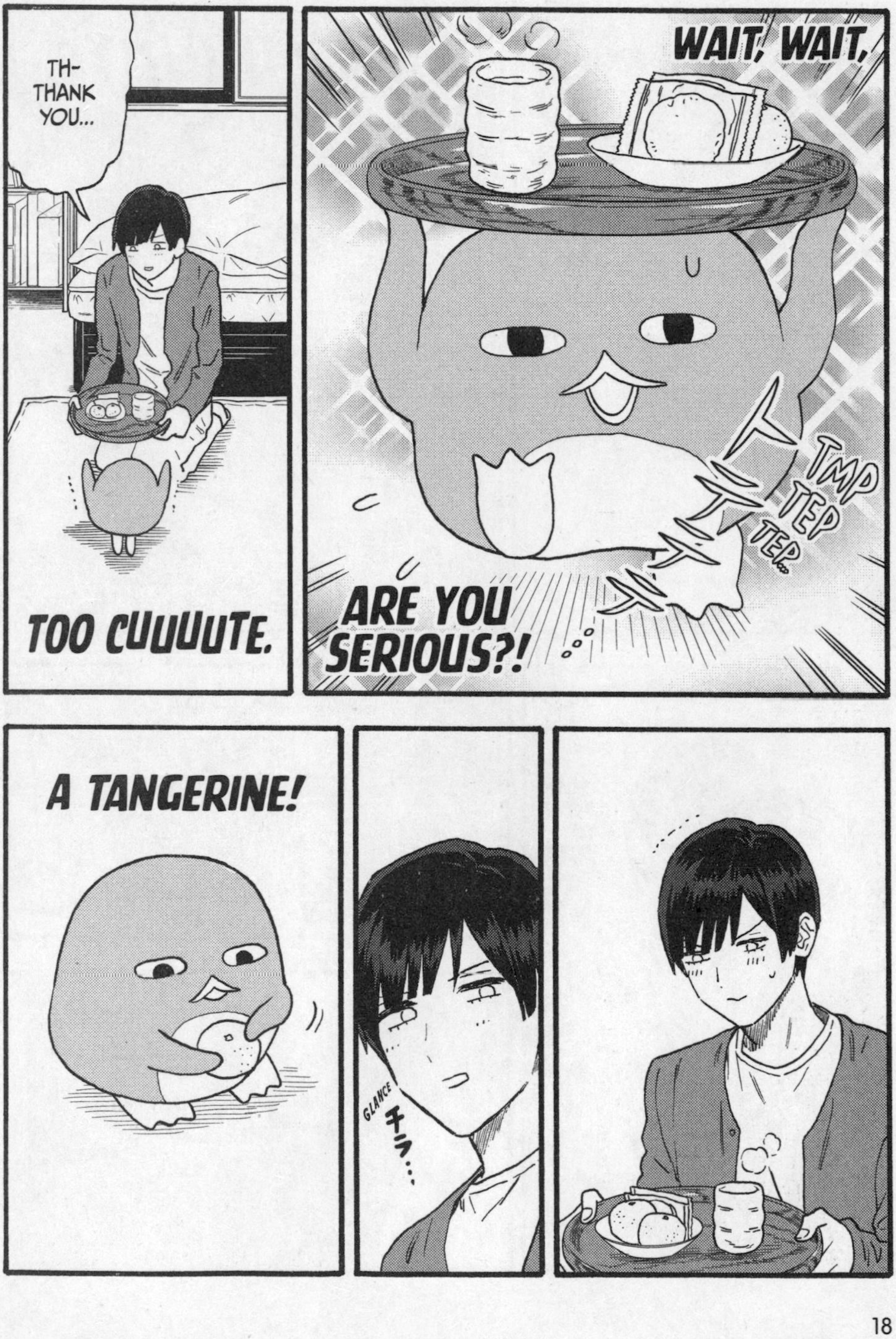
WAIT, WAIT,
TMP TEP TEP...
ARE YOU SERIOUS?!
TH-THANK YOU...
TOO CUUUUTE.
GLANCE
チラ…
A TANGERINE!

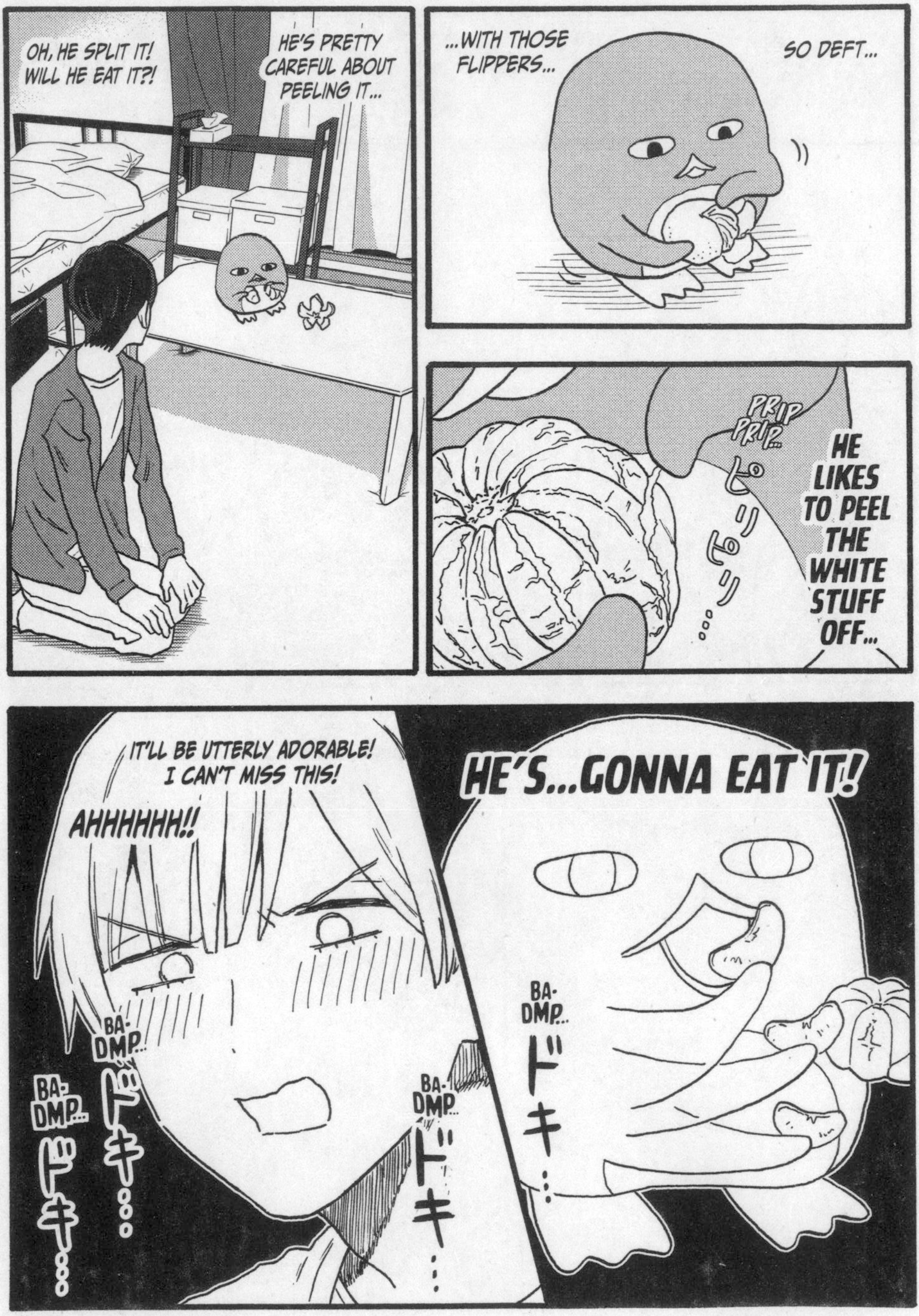

SO DEFT...
...WITH THOSE FLIPPERS...
PRIP PRIP...
ピリピリ...
HE LIKES TO PEEL THE WHITE STUFF OFF...
HE'S PRETTY CAREFUL ABOUT PEELING IT...
OH, HE SPLIT IT! WILL HE EAT IT?!
HE'S...GONNA EAT IT!
BA-DMP...
ドキ...
IT'LL BE UTTERLY ADORABLE! I CAN'T MISS THIS!
AHHHHHH!!
BA-DMP...
ドキ...
BA-DMP...
ドキ...
BA-DMP...
ドキ...

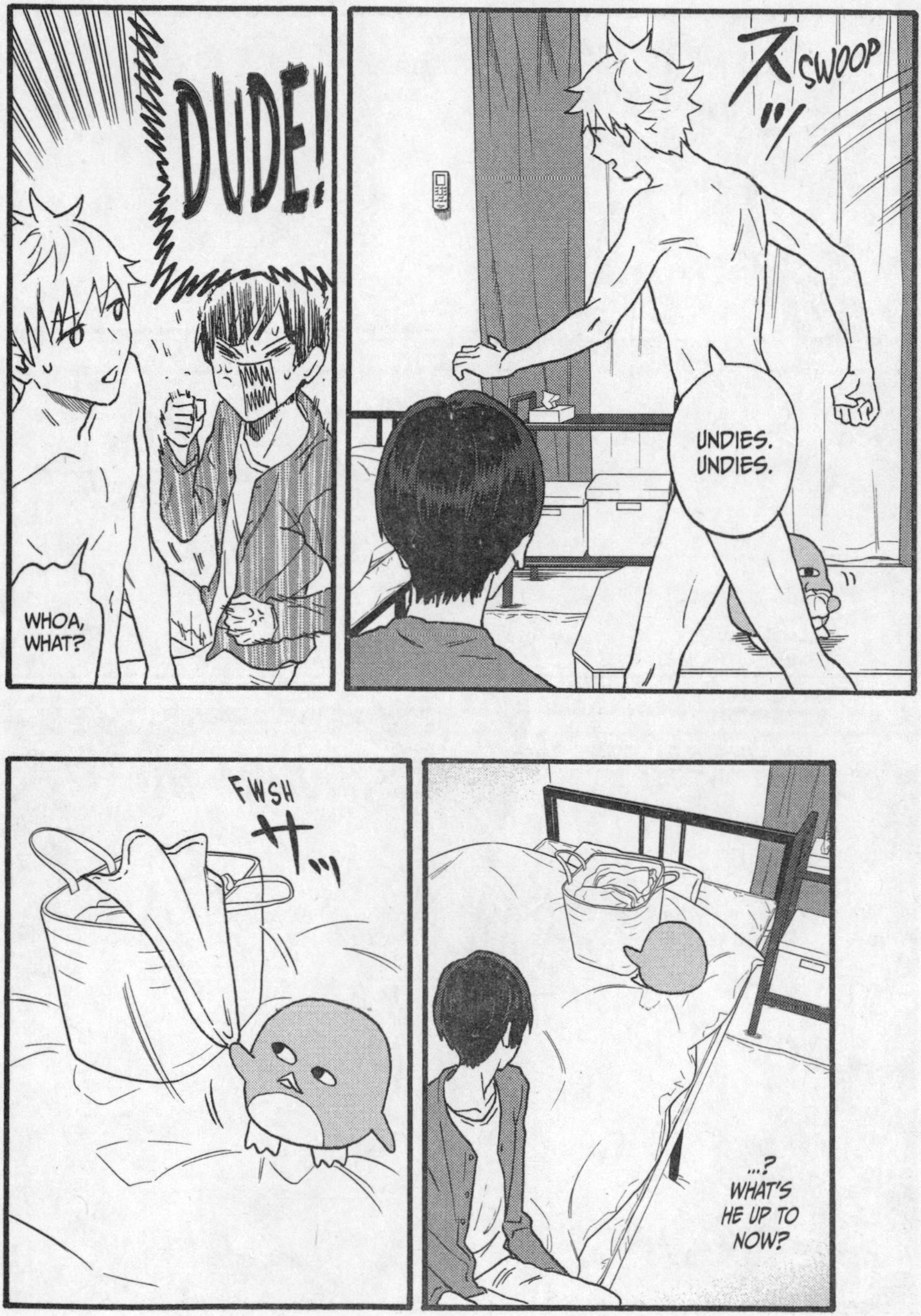
スッ
SWOOP
UNDIES. UNDIES.
DUDE!
WHOA, WHAT?
...? WHAT'S HE UP TO NOW?
サッ
FWSH

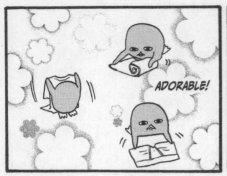

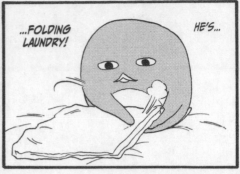

HE'S...
...FOLDING LAUNDRY!
ADORABLE!
HEY...
クイッ GWIP
SWIP SWIP サッサッ
FLAP シュバ
IT'S THE THREE-SECOND FOLDING HACK!
HE'S SUCH A GOOD PENGUIN...
LOOK AT THAT CAREFUL FOLDING...

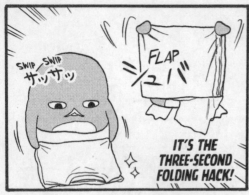

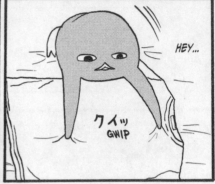

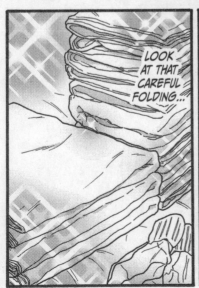

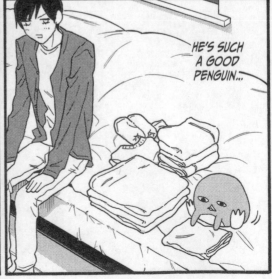

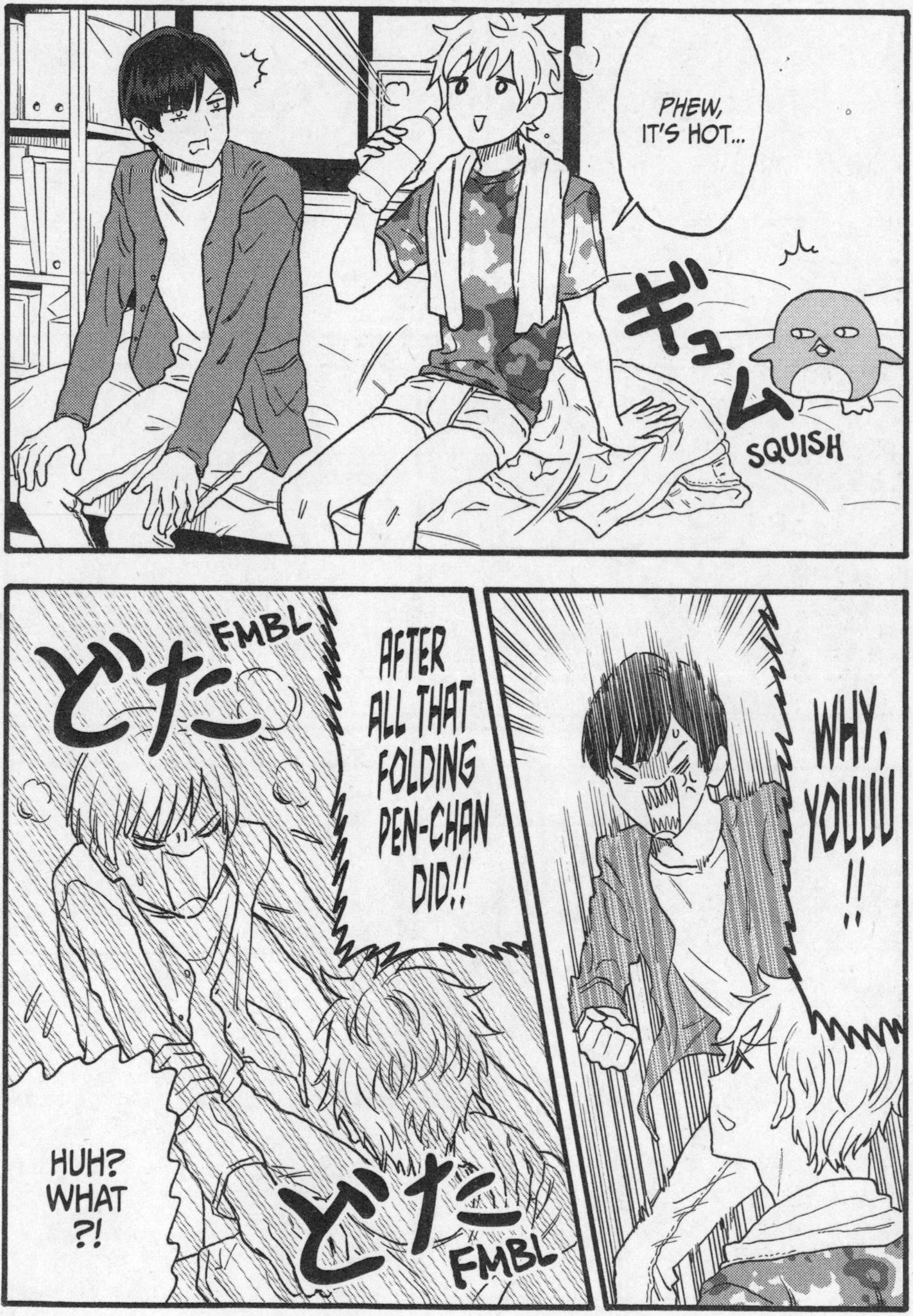
PHEW, IT'S HOT...
ギュム
SQUISH
WHY, YOUUU!!
AFTER ALL THAT FOLDING PEN-CHAN DID!!
どたー
FMBL
HUH? WHAT?!
どたー
FMBL

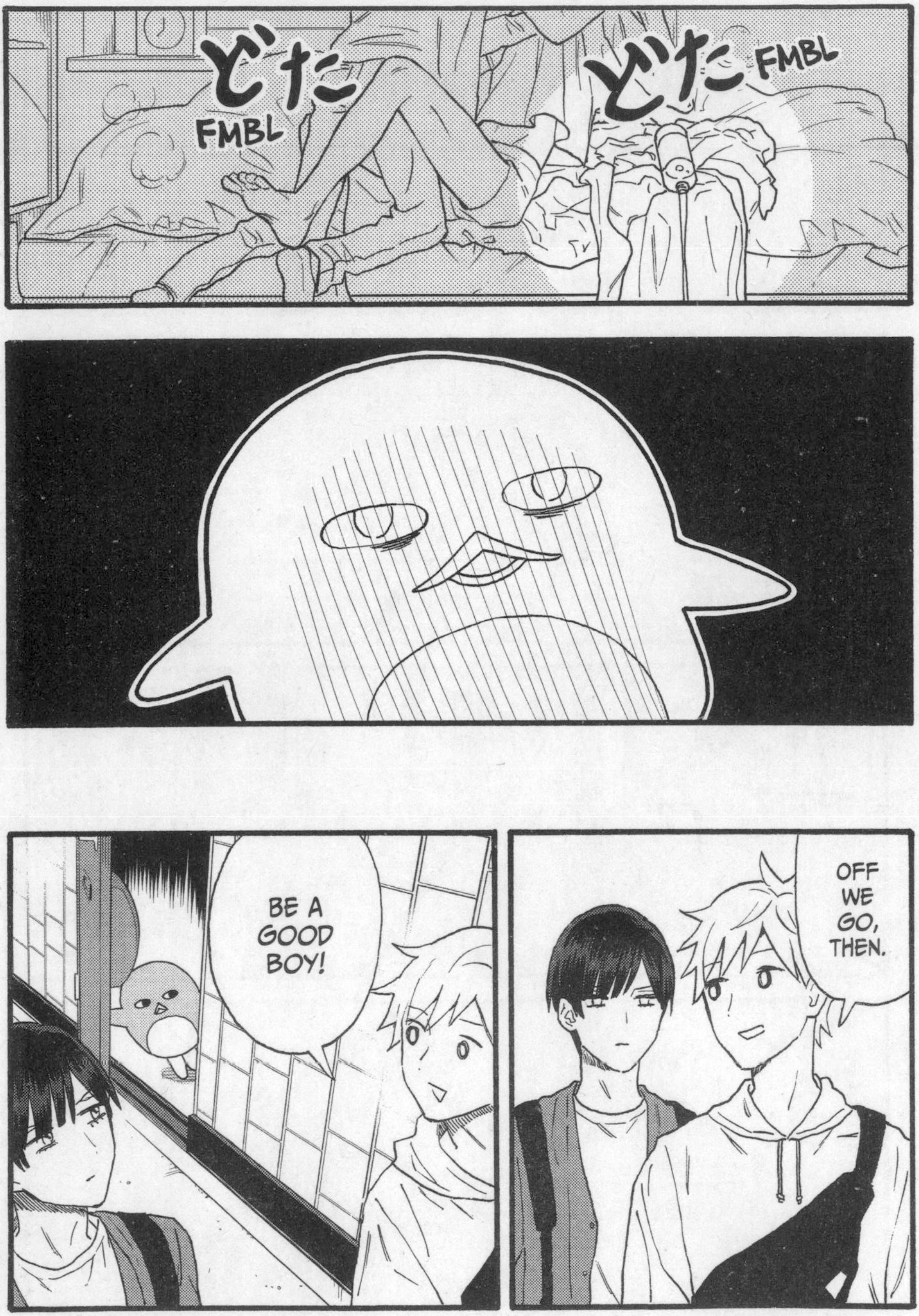
どた
FMBL
どた
FMBL
OFF WE GO, THEN.
BE A GOOD BOY!

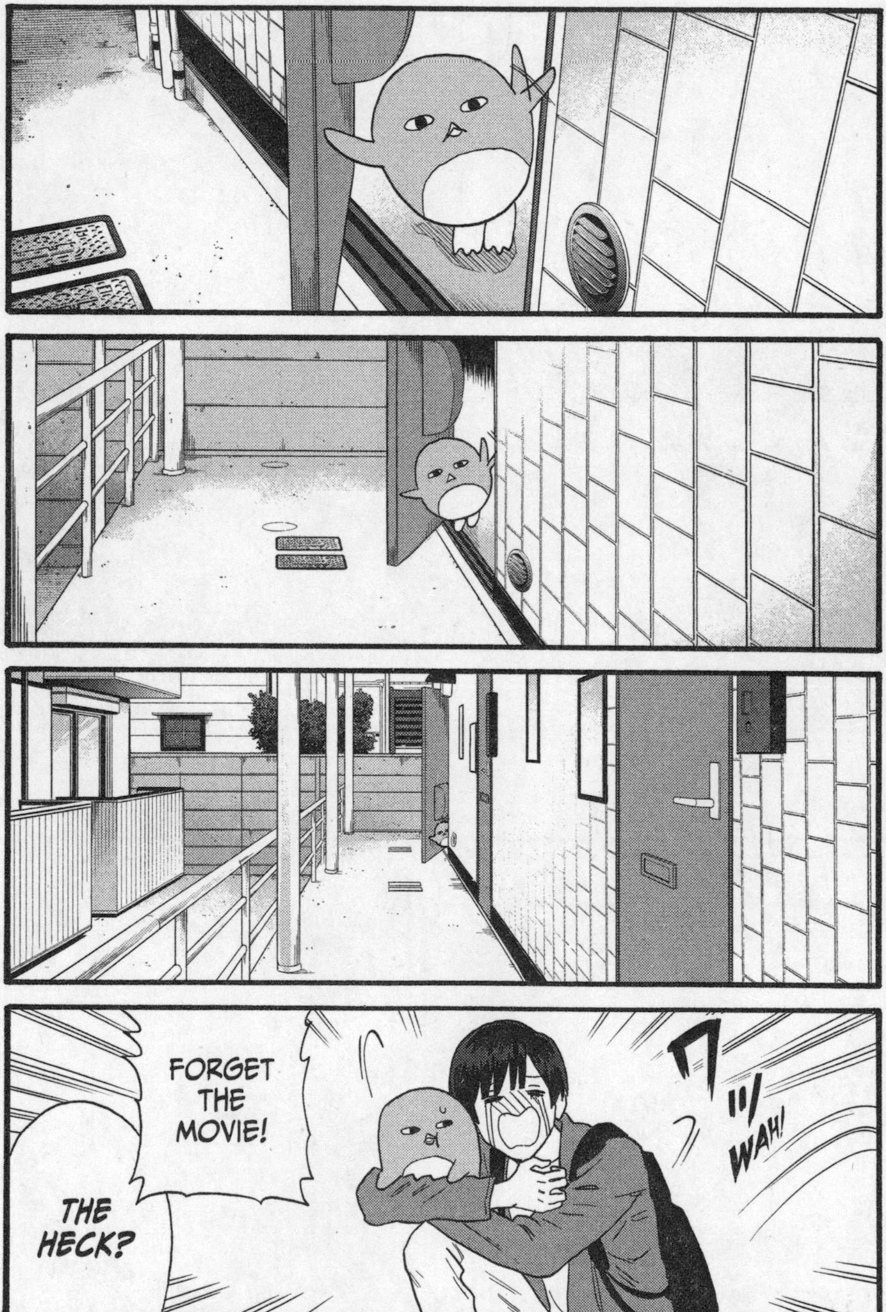
ワッ
WAH!
FORGET THE MOVIE!
THE HECK?

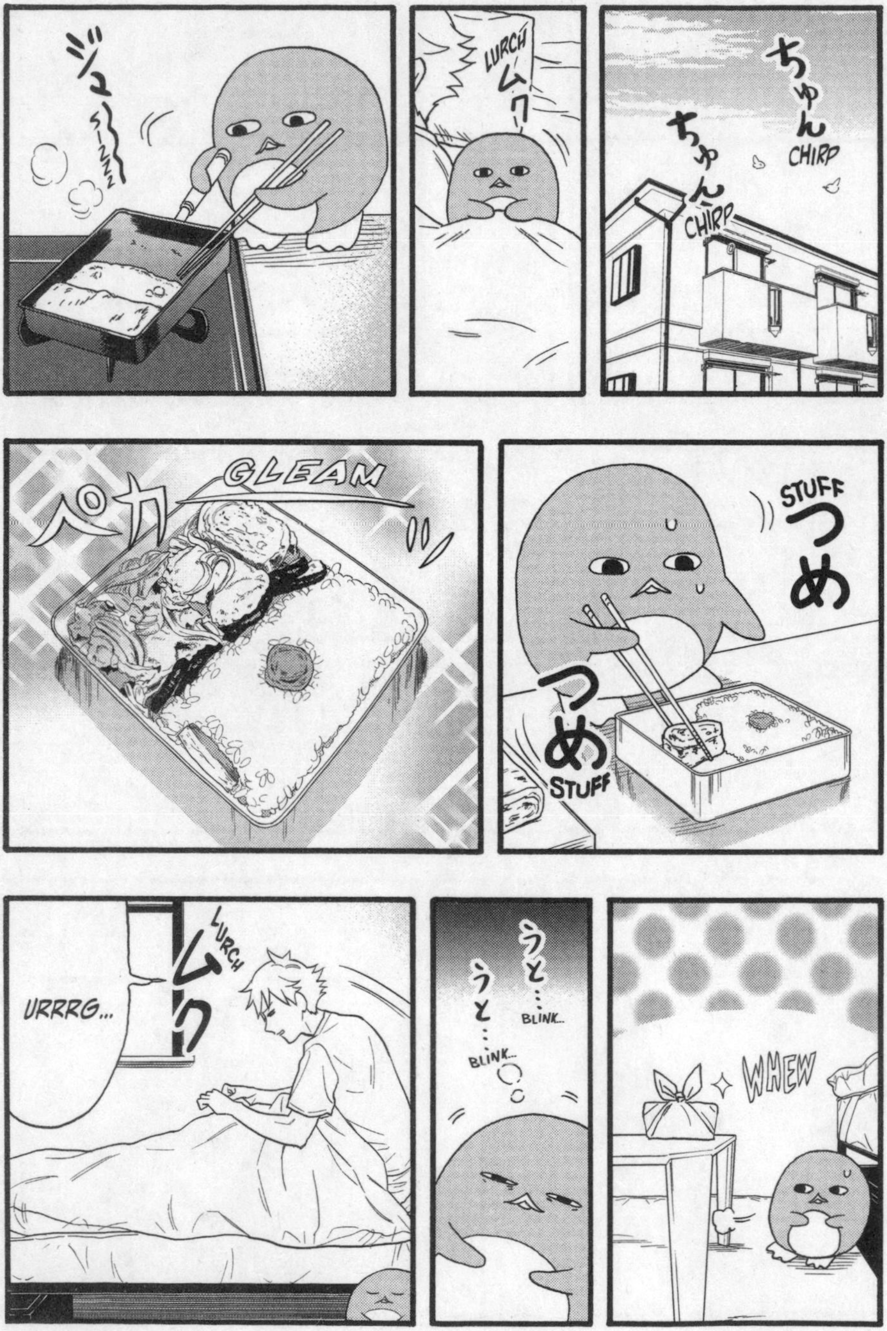
ちゅん
CHIRP
ちゅん
CHIRP
LURCH
ムクー
ジュ〜
SIZZZZ
STUFF
つめ
つめ
STUFF
パカ
GLEAM
WHEW
うと…
BLINK...
うと…
BLINK...
URRRG...
LURCH
ムク

Pen 3 The Penguin Delivers Lunch for His Owner

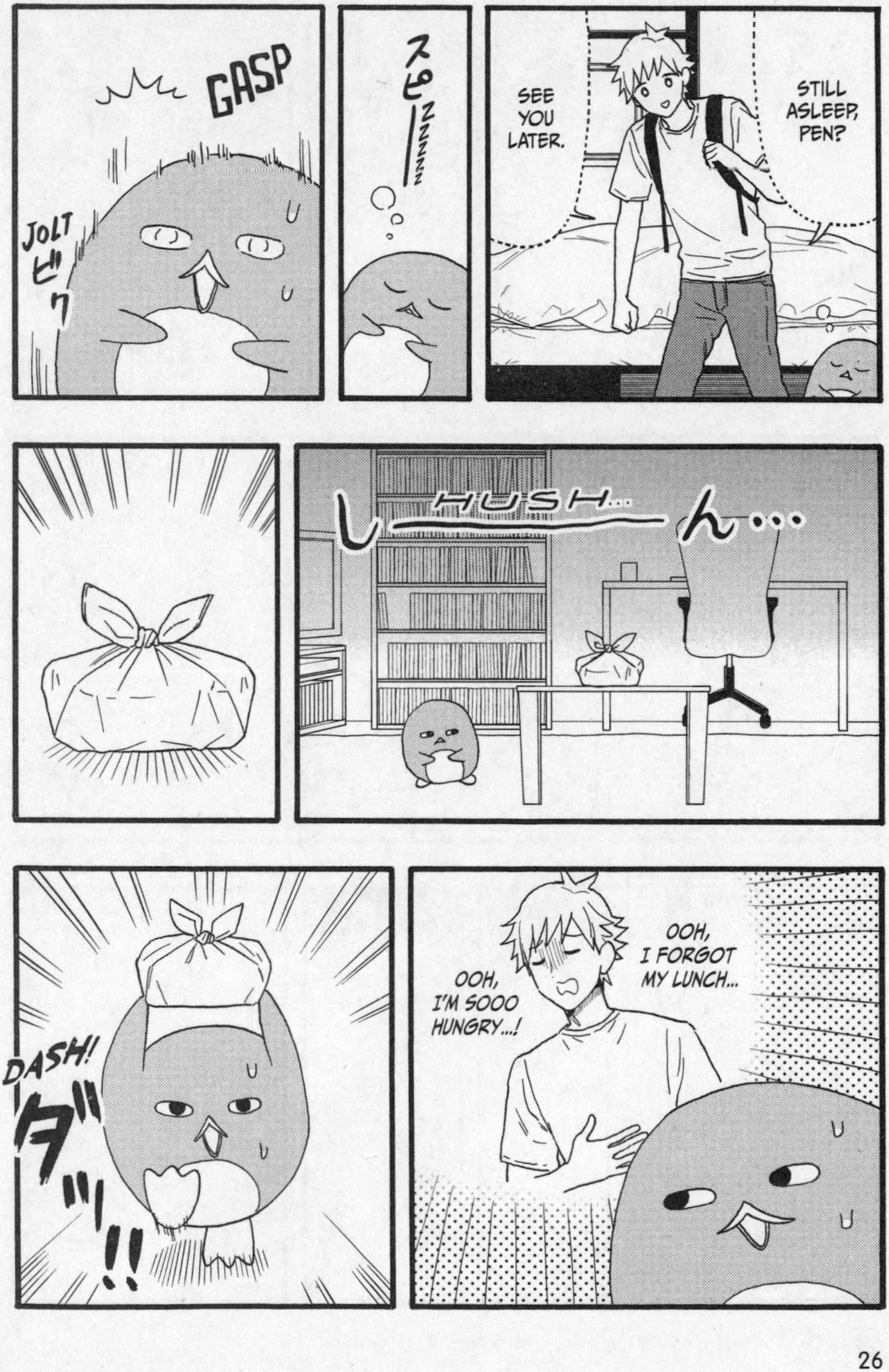
STILL ASLEEP, PEN?
SEE YOU LATER.
スピーZZZZZ
GASP
JOLT
ビク
HUSH...
し——ん…
OOH, I FORGOT MY LUNCH...
OOH, I'M SOOO HUNGRY...!
DASH!
ダッ!!

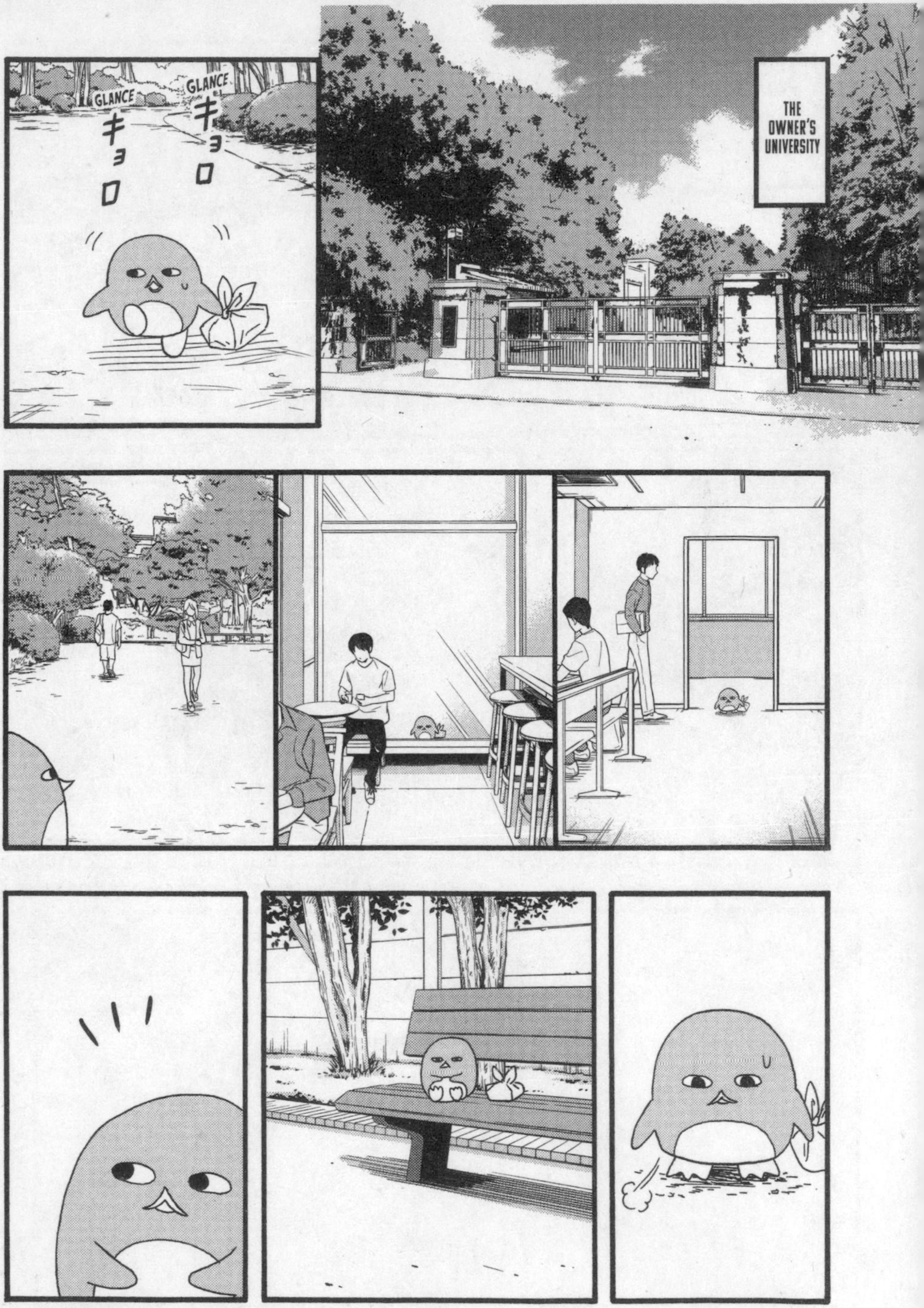
THE OWNER'S UNIVERSITY
GLANCE
キョロ
GLANCE
キョロ

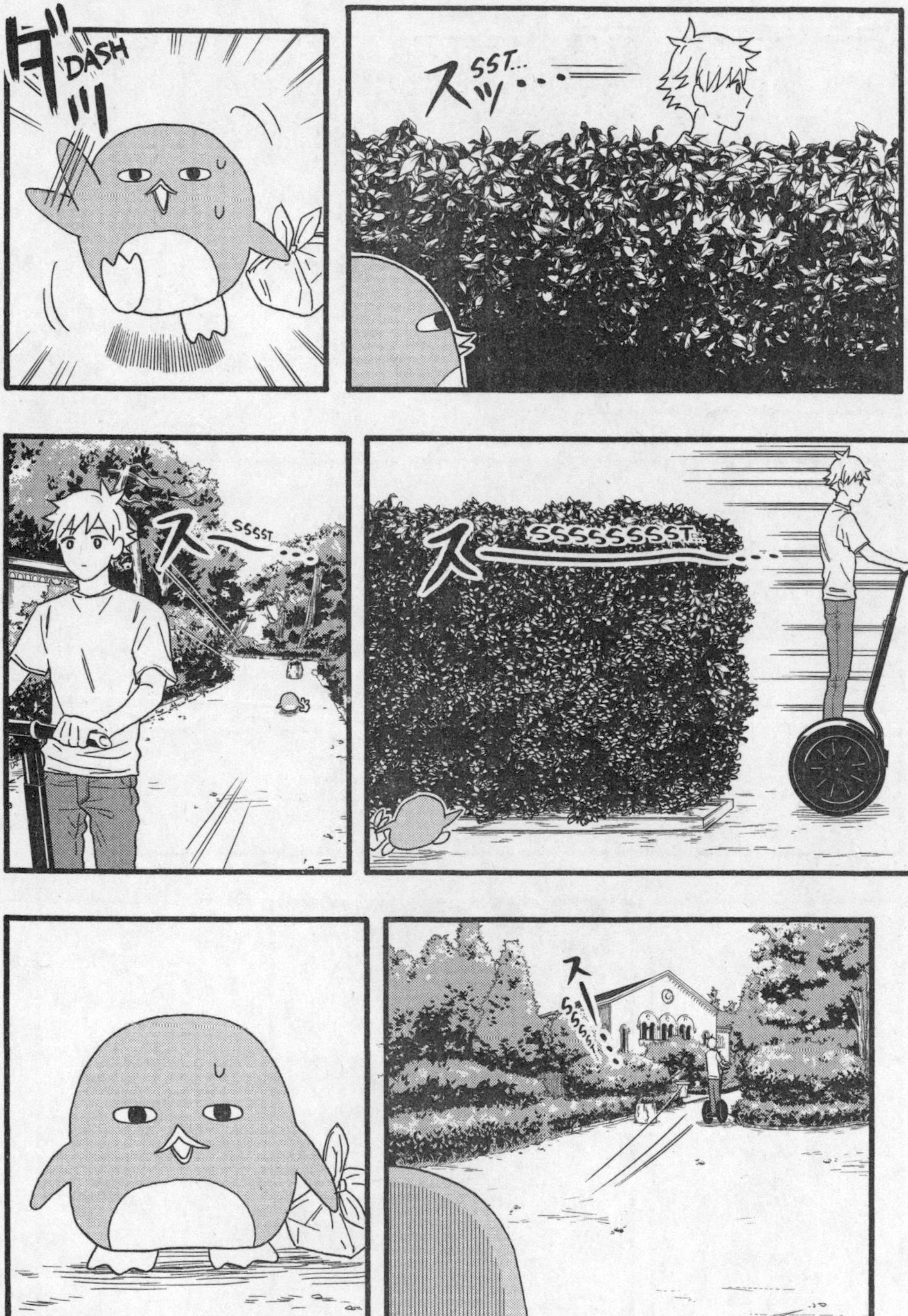
スッ
SST...
ダッ
DASH
ス
SSSSSSSSST...
ス
SSSST...
ス
SSSSST...

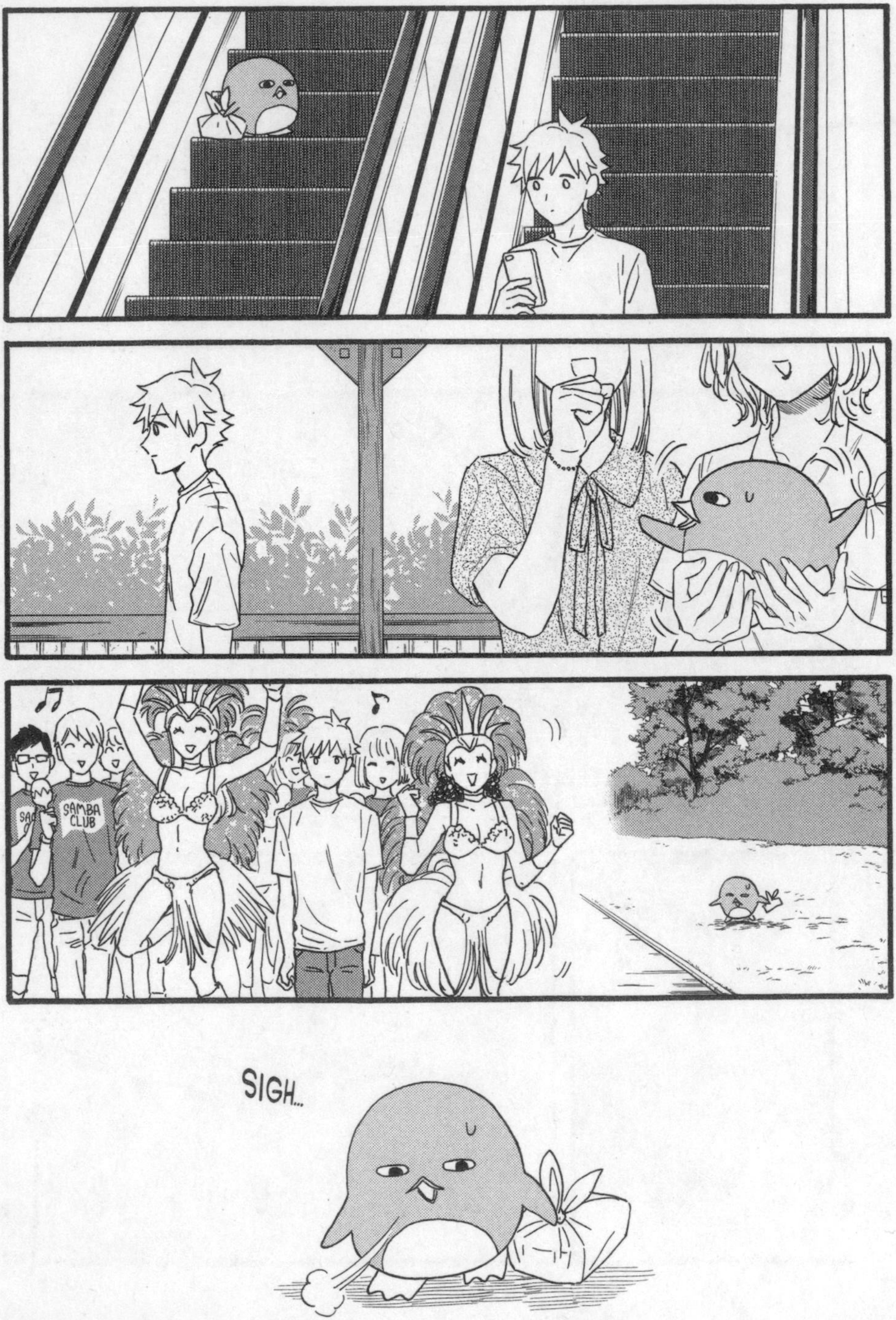
SAMBA CLUB
SIGH...

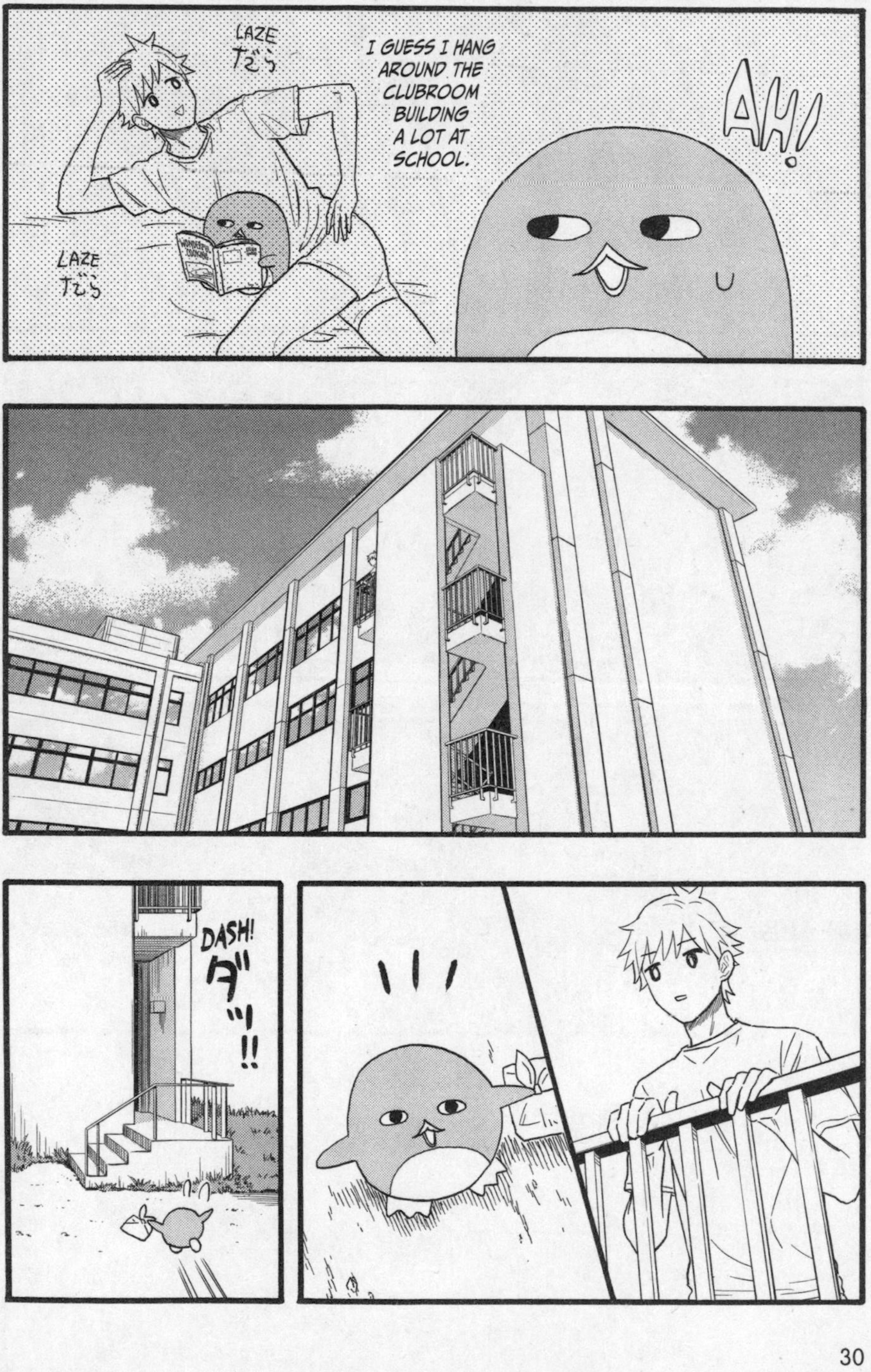
AH!
I GUESS I HANG AROUND THE CLUBROOM BUILDING A LOT AT SCHOOL.
LAZE
だら
LAZE
だら
DASH!
ダッ!!

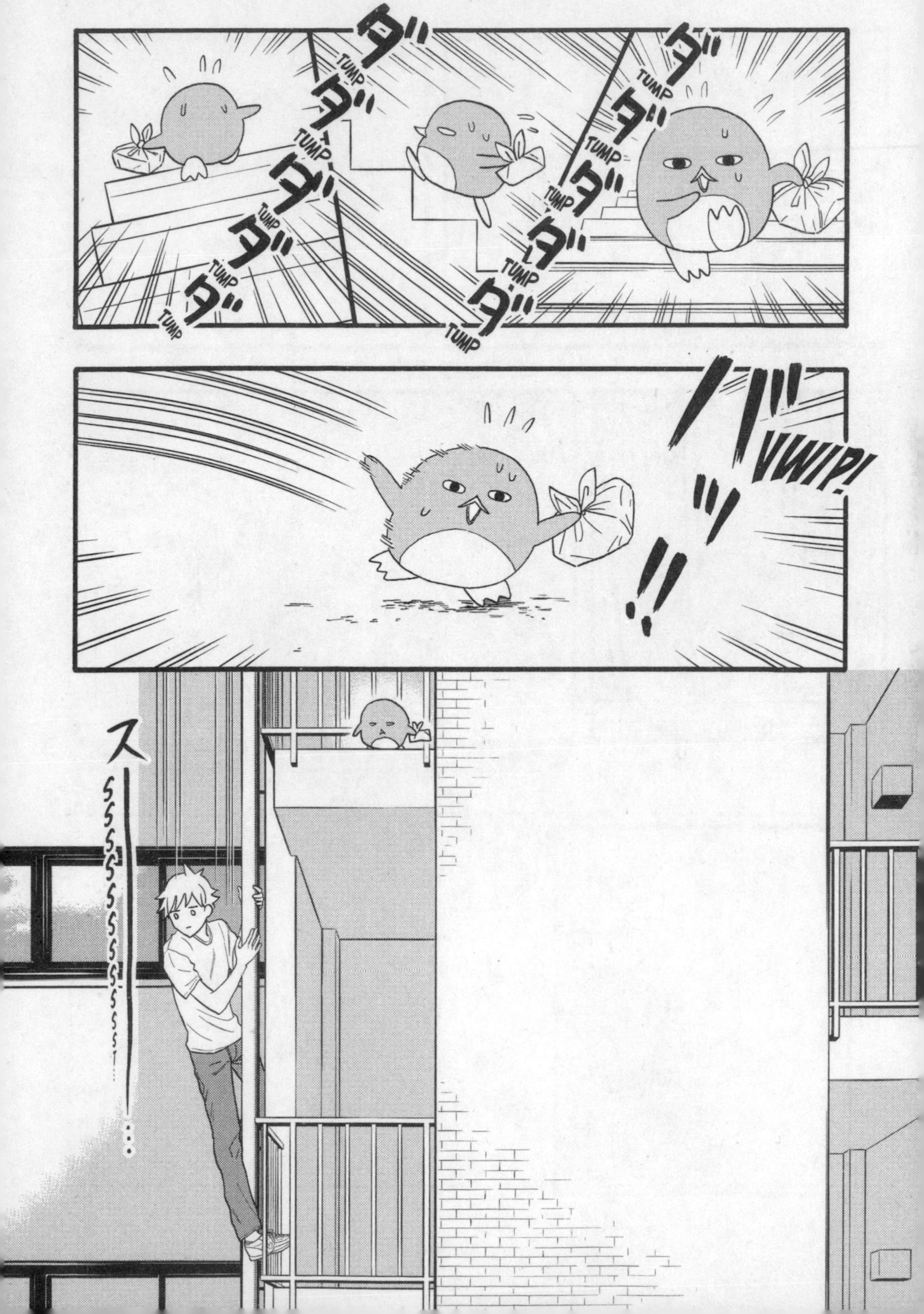
ダ TUMP ダ TUMP ダ TUMP ダ TUMP ダ TUMP
ダ TUMP ダ TUMP ダ TUMP ダ TUMP ダ TUMP
バッ!! VWIP!
ス———… SSSSSSSSSSSSST…

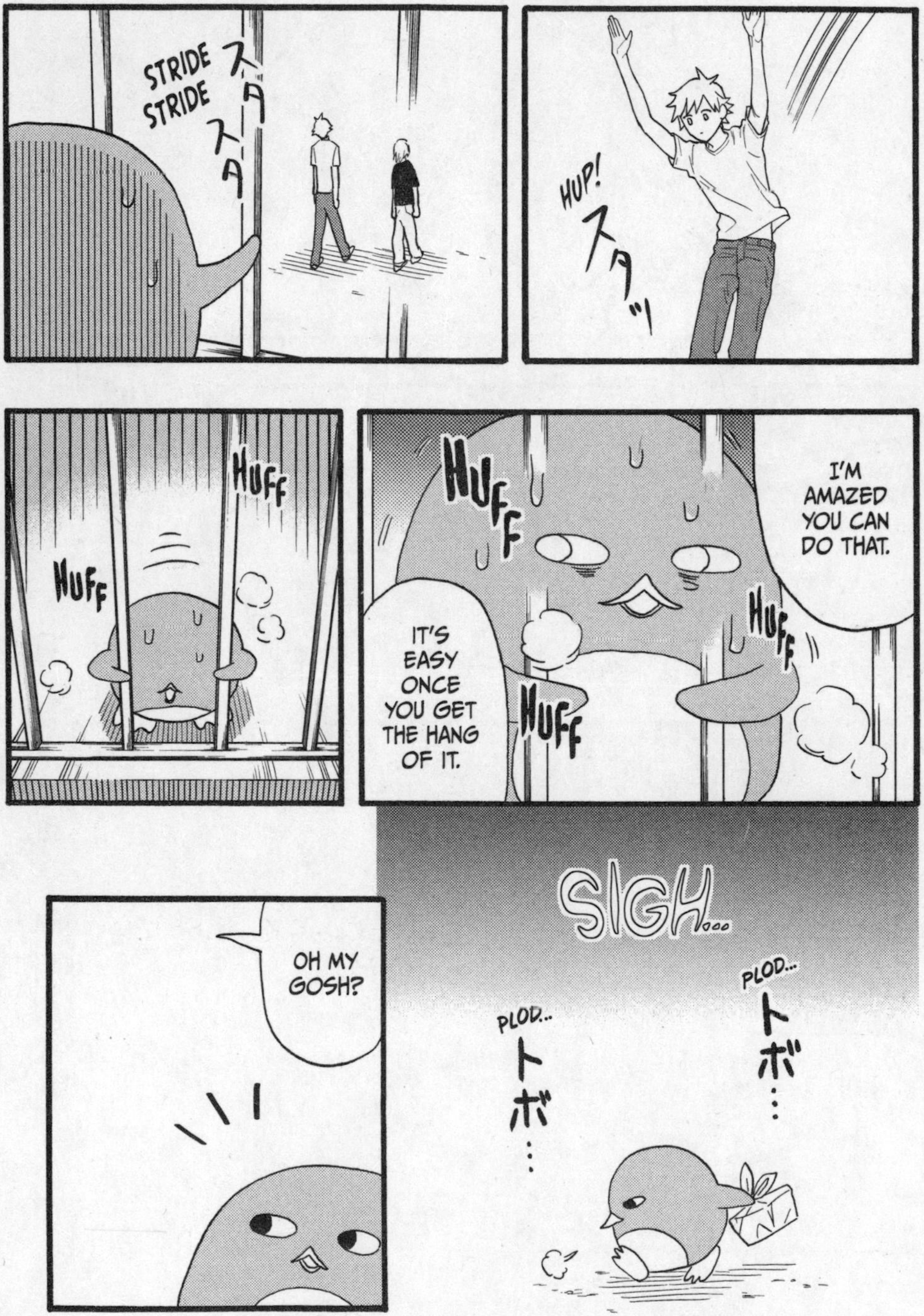
HUP!
スタッ
STRIDE STRIDE
スタスタ
I'M AMAZED YOU CAN DO THAT.
HUFF
HUFF
IT'S EASY ONCE YOU GET THE HANG OF IT.
HUFF
HUFF
HUFF
SIGH...
PLOD...
トボ…
PLOD...
トボ…
OH MY GOSH?

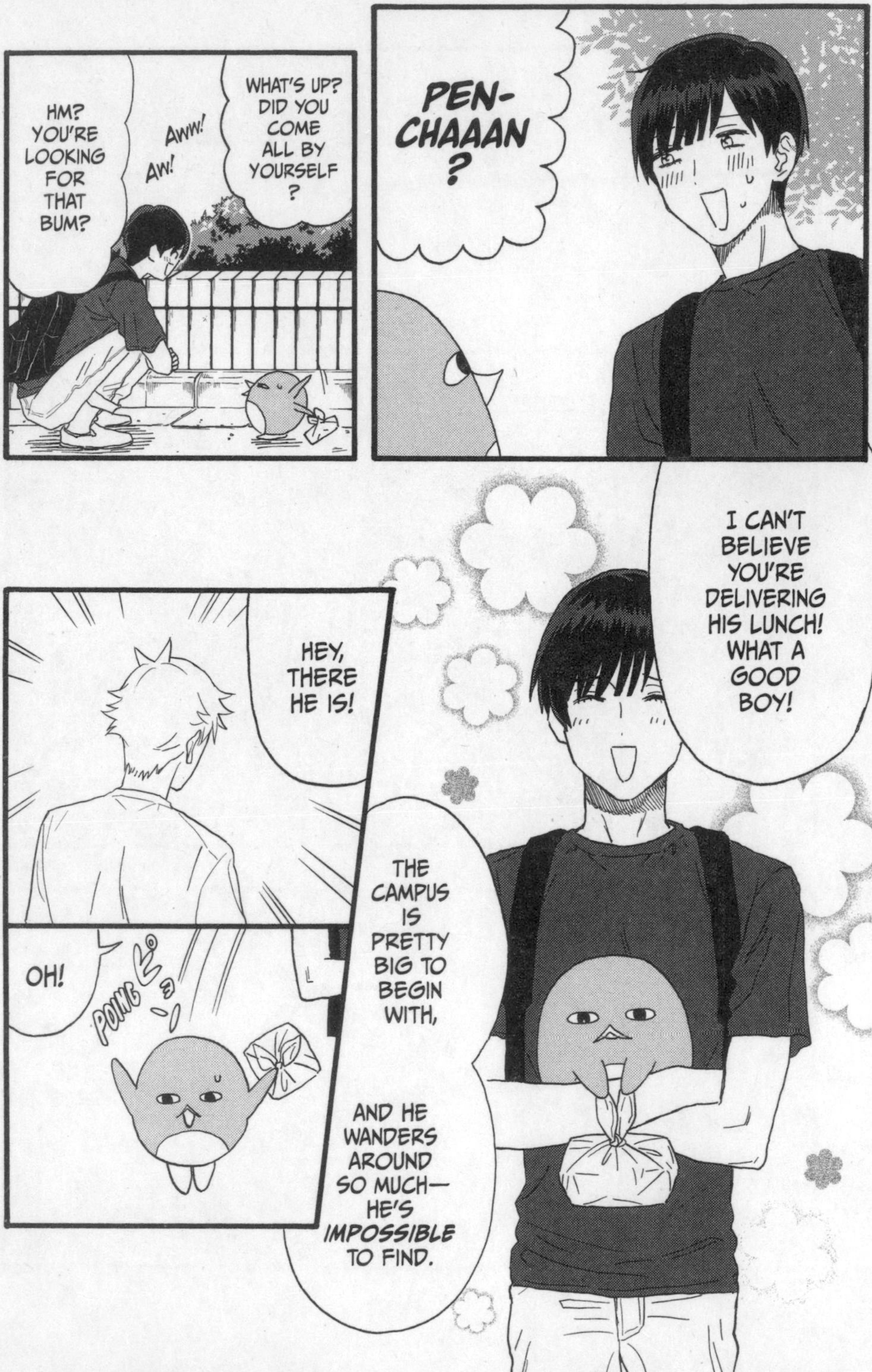
PEN-CHAAAN?
WHAT'S UP? DID YOU COME ALL BY YOURSELF?
AWW!
AW!
HM? YOU'RE LOOKING FOR THAT BUM?
I CAN'T BELIEVE YOU'RE DELIVERING HIS LUNCH! WHAT A GOOD BOY!
THE CAMPUS IS PRETTY BIG TO BEGIN WITH,
AND HE WANDERS AROUND SO MUCH— HE'S *IMPOSSIBLE* TO FIND.
HEY, THERE HE IS!
OH!
POING

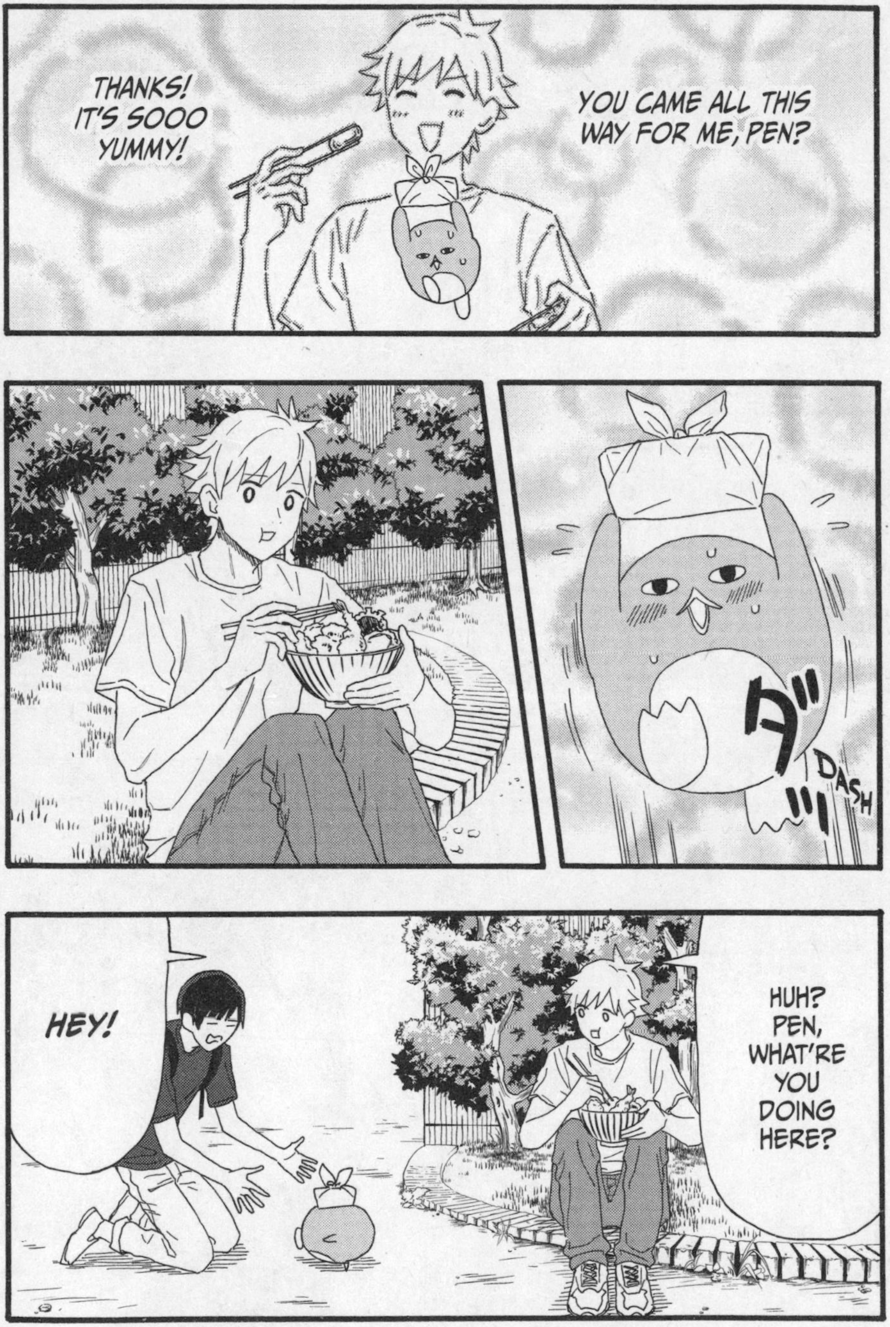
YOU CAME ALL THIS WAY FOR ME, PEN?
THANKS! IT'S SOOO YUMMY!
ダ
DASH
HUH? PEN, WHAT'RE YOU DOING HERE?
HEY!

Spot the Difference

THERE ARE THREE PENS HIDING IN THE ROWS OF LINE-DANCING PENGUINS THAT ARE NOT LIKE THE OTHERS. CAN YOU SPOT THEM?

Answer on next page!

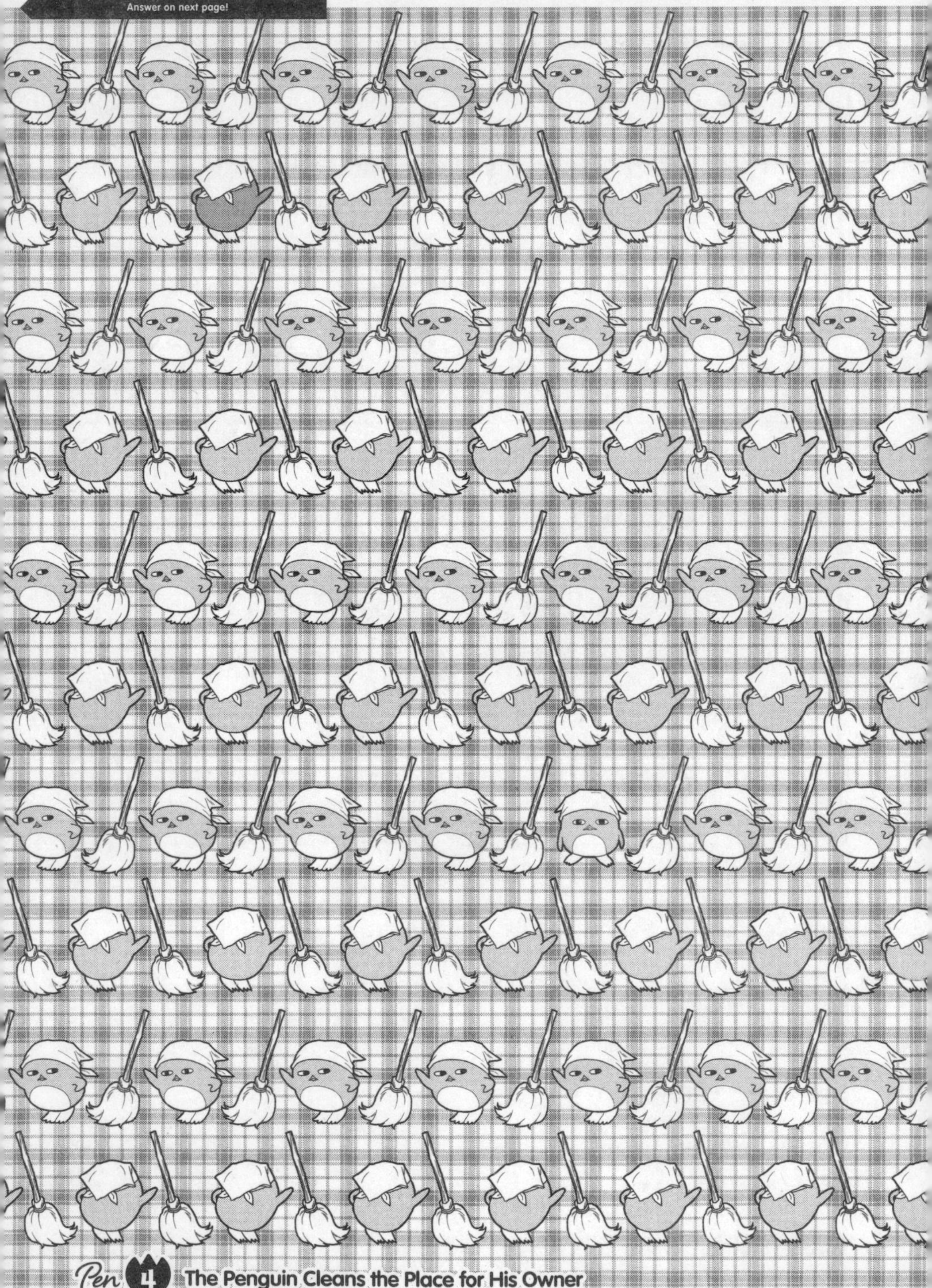

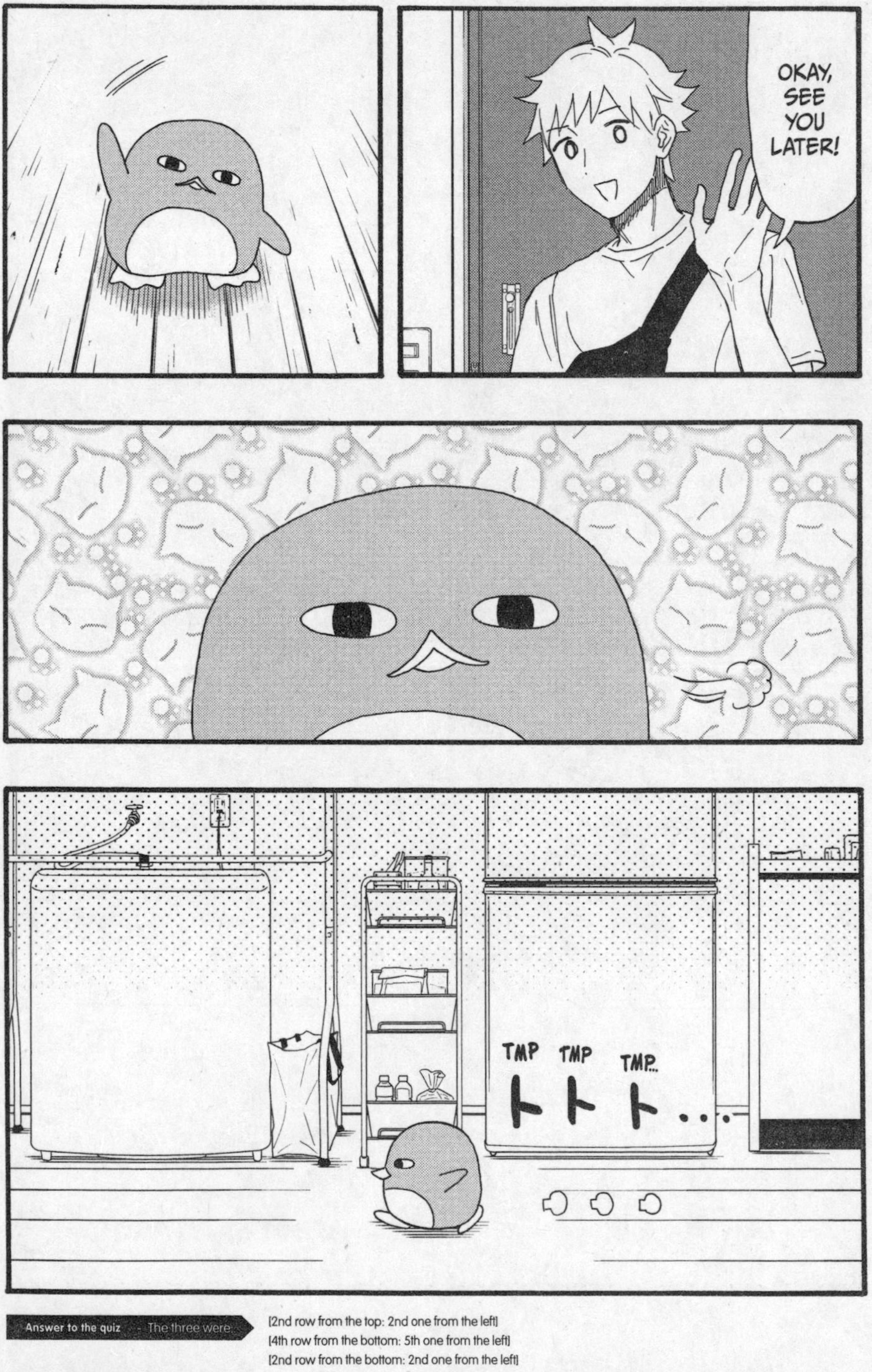
OKAY, SEE YOU LATER!
TMP TMP TMP...
トトト…

Answer to the quiz - - The three were:

[2nd row from the top: 2nd one from the left]
[4th row from the bottom: 5th one from the left]
[2nd row from the bottom: 2nd one from the left]

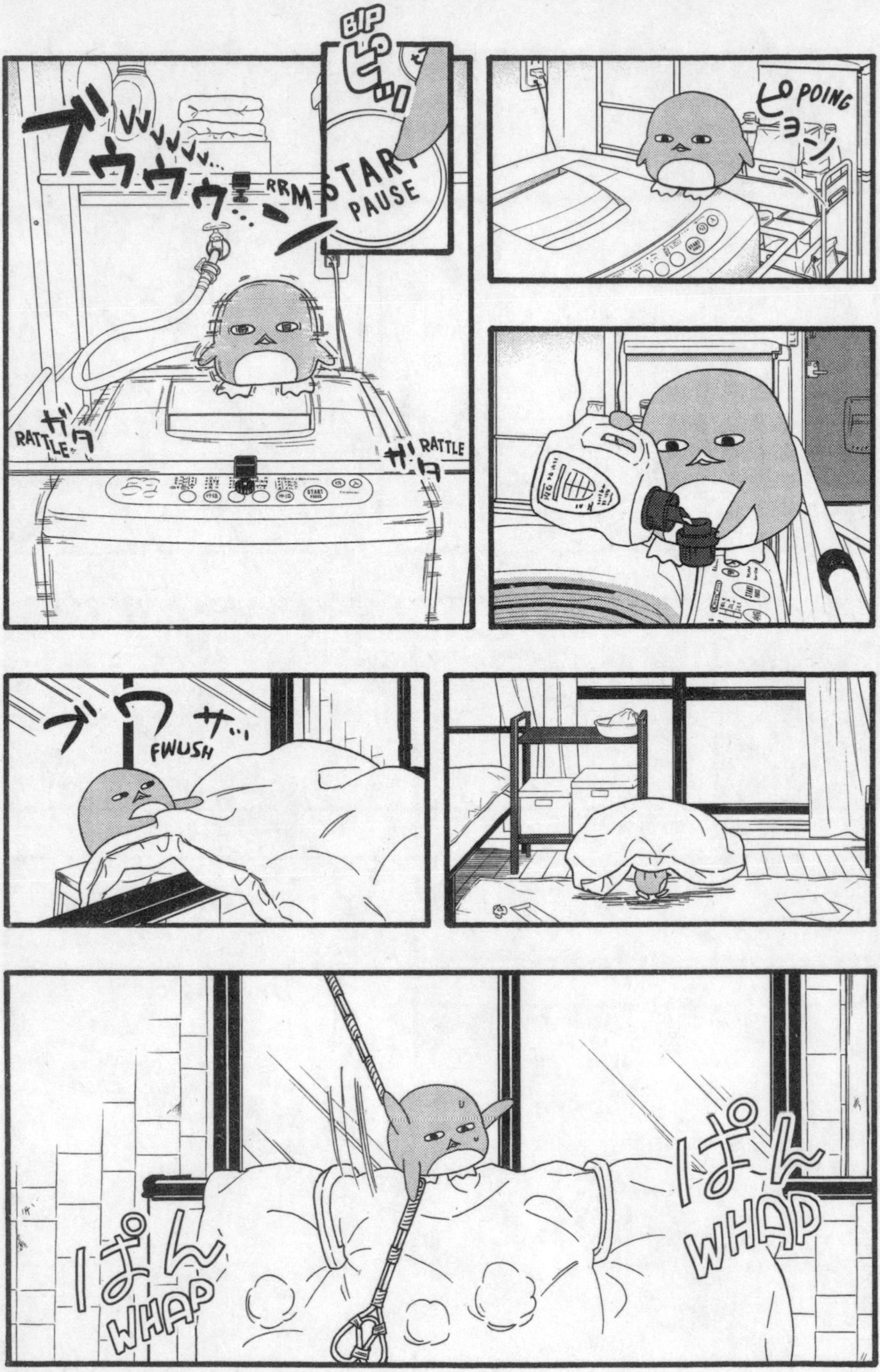

ピョン
POING
BIP
ピッ
START
PAUSE
ブウウウ…
VVVVVV…
RRM
ガタ
RATTLE
ガタ
RATTLE
ブワ
サッ
FWUSH
ぱん
WHAP
ぱん
WHAP

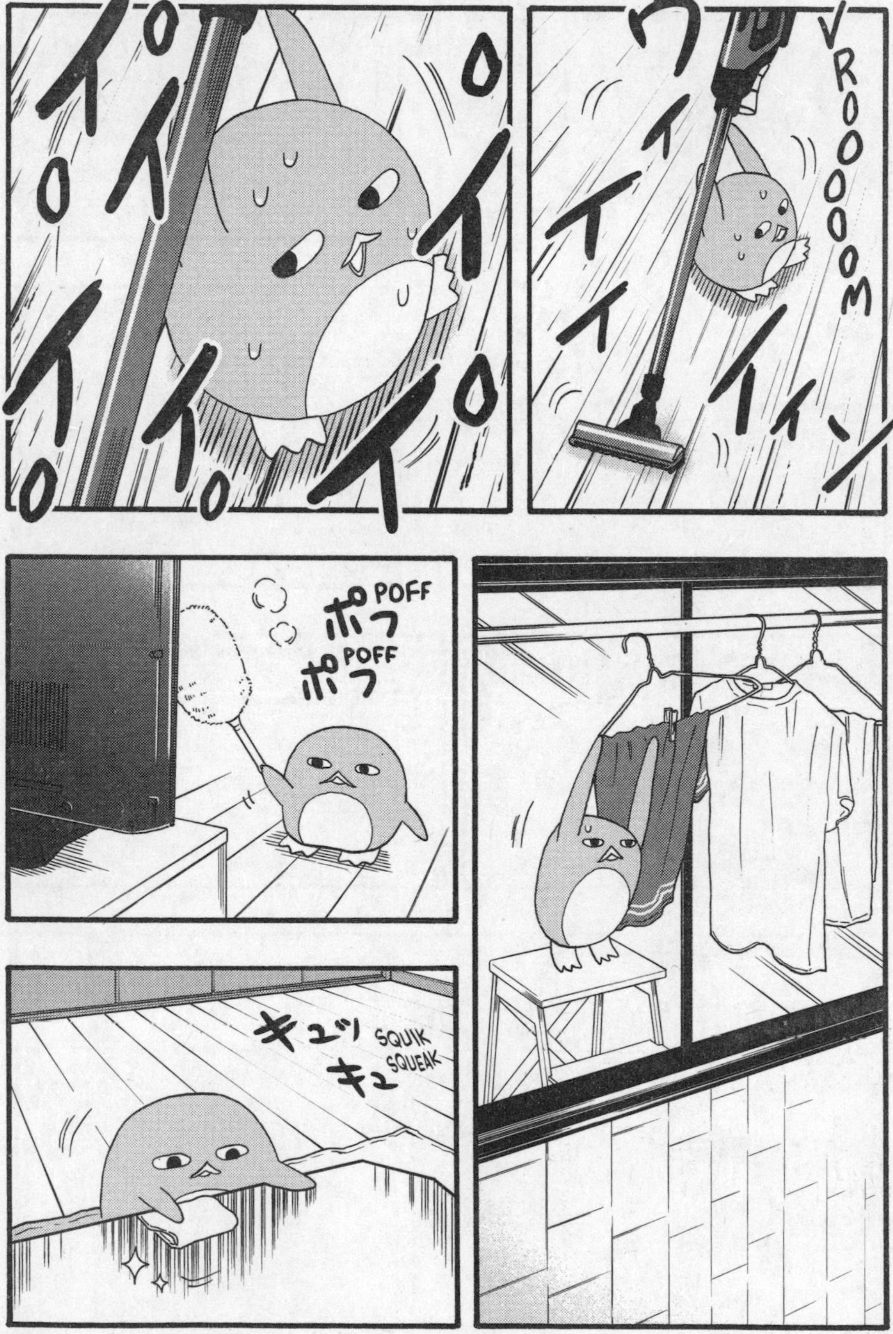
ウィイイイイン
VROOOOOOM
ポフ POFF
ポフ POFF
キュッ SQUIK
キュ SQUEAK

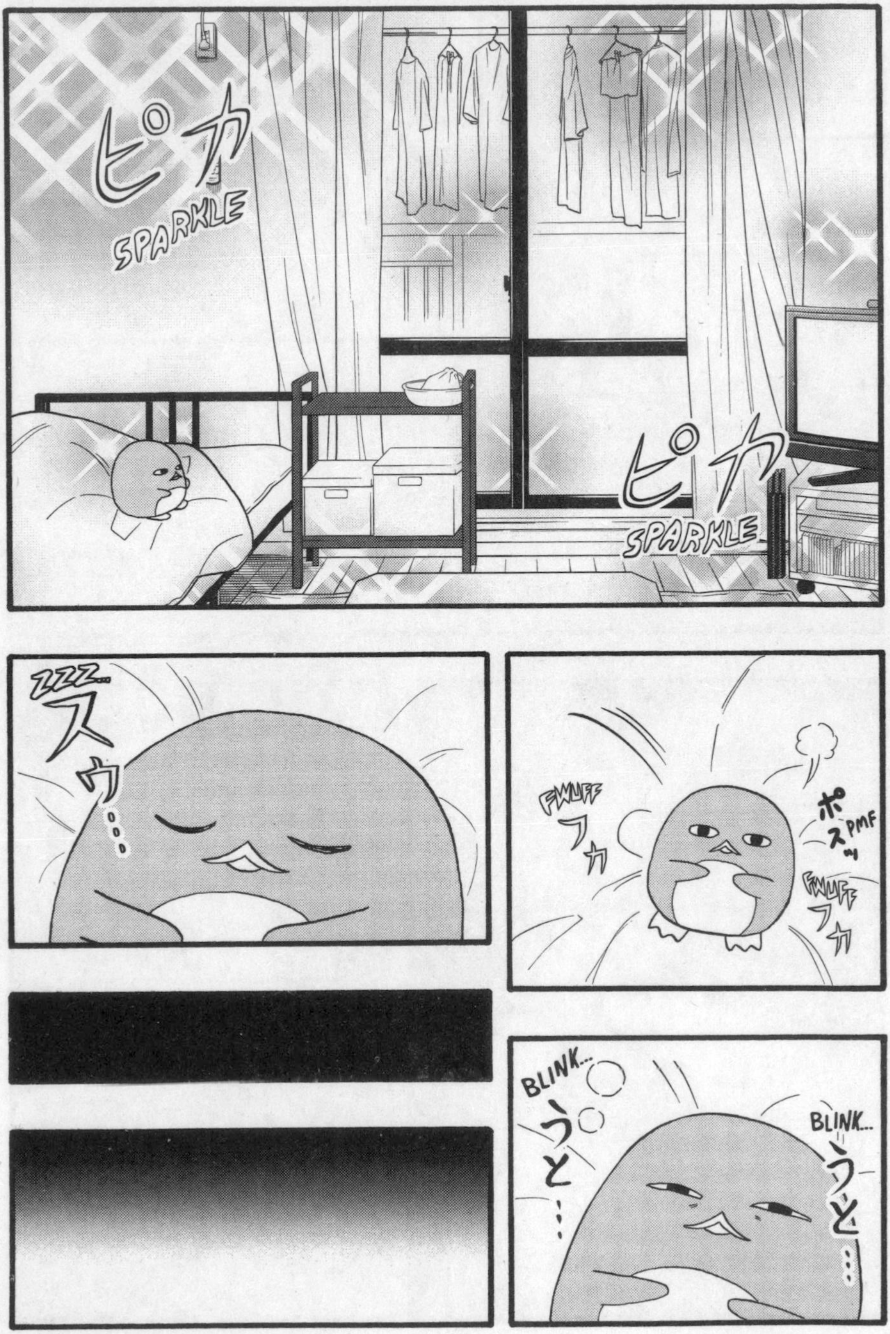
ピカ
SPARKLE
ピカ
SPARKLE
ポスッ
PMF
FWUFF
フカ
FWUFF
フカ
ZZZ...
スゥ...
BLINK...
うと...
BLINK...
うと...

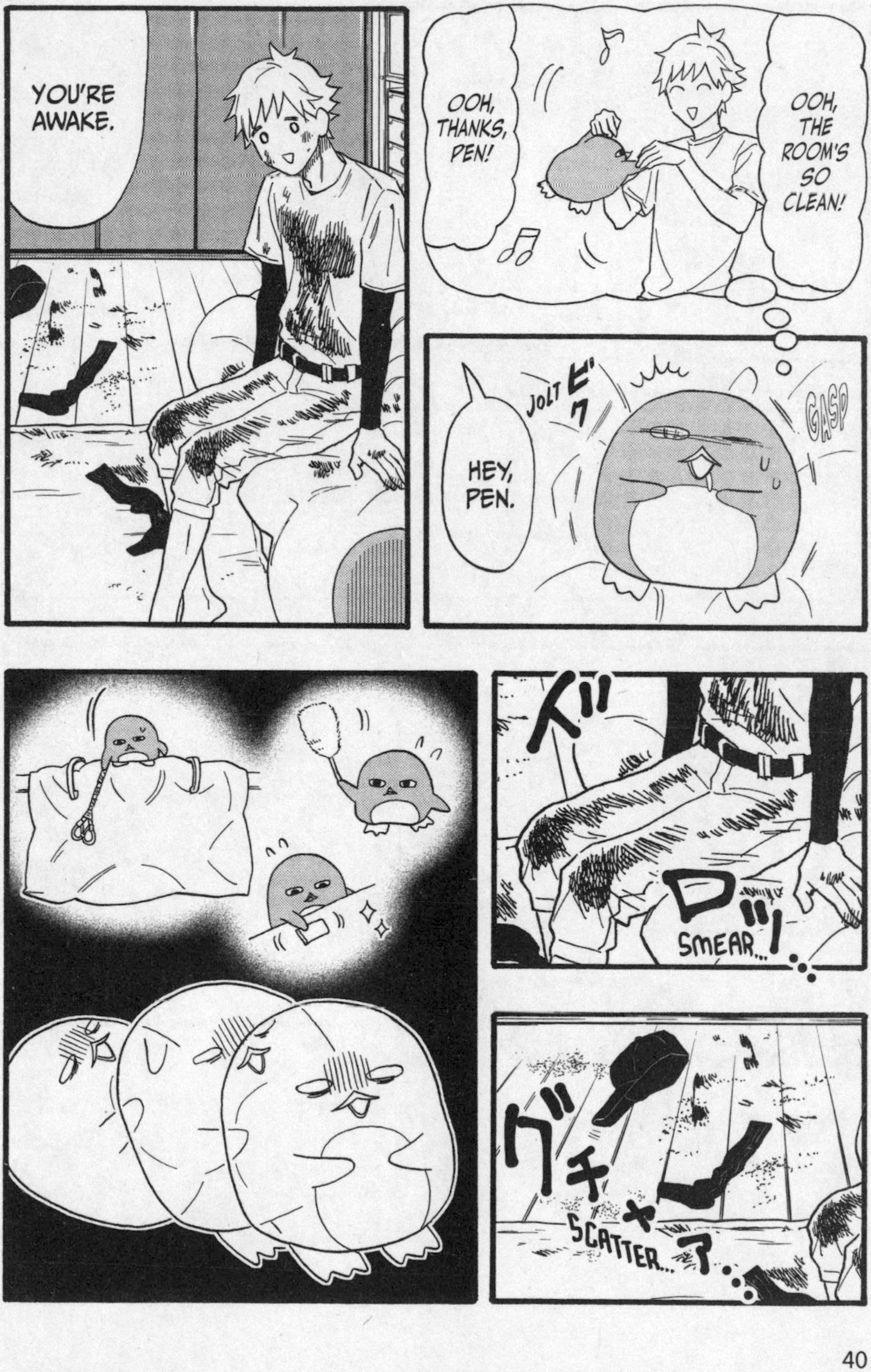
OOH, THE ROOM'S SO CLEAN!
OOH, THANKS, PEN!
GASP
JOLT
HEY, PEN.
YOU'RE AWAKE.
SMEAR...
SCATTER...

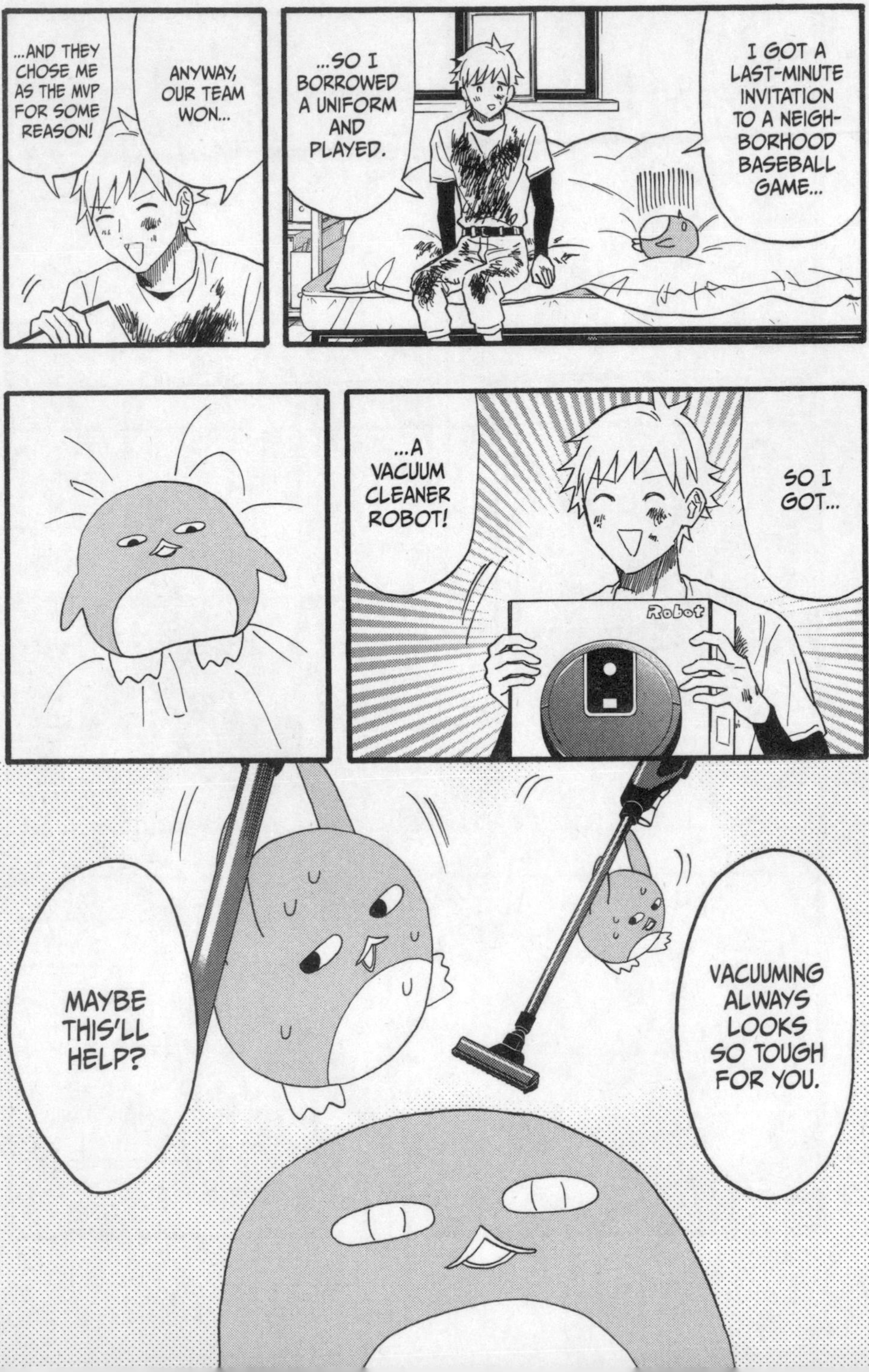
I GOT A LAST-MINUTE INVITATION TO A NEIGH-BORHOOD BASEBALL GAME...
...SO I BORROWED A UNIFORM AND PLAYED.
ANYWAY, OUR TEAM WON...
...AND THEY CHOSE ME AS THE MVP FOR SOME REASON!
SO I GOT...
...A VACUUM CLEANER ROBOT!
Robot
VACUUMING ALWAYS LOOKS SO TOUGH FOR YOU.
MAYBE THIS'LL HELP?

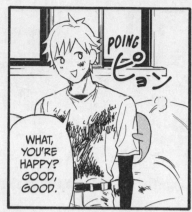

YOU MIGHT NOT GET MUCH USE OUT OF IT IN SUCH A SMALL ROOM...
...BUT I HOPE IT'LL MAKE THINGS EASIER!
Robot
POING ピョン
WHAT, YOU'RE HAPPY? GOOD, GOOD.
LET'S GIVE IT A WHIRL.
BIP ピッ
ウィーン VREEEN ♪
WOW, THERE IT GOES.
ウィーン VREEN

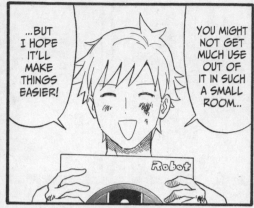

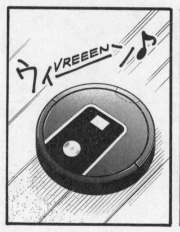

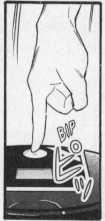

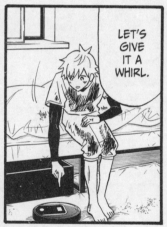

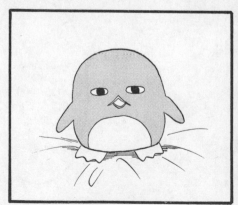

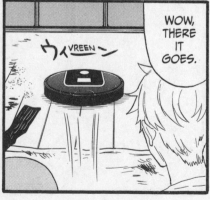

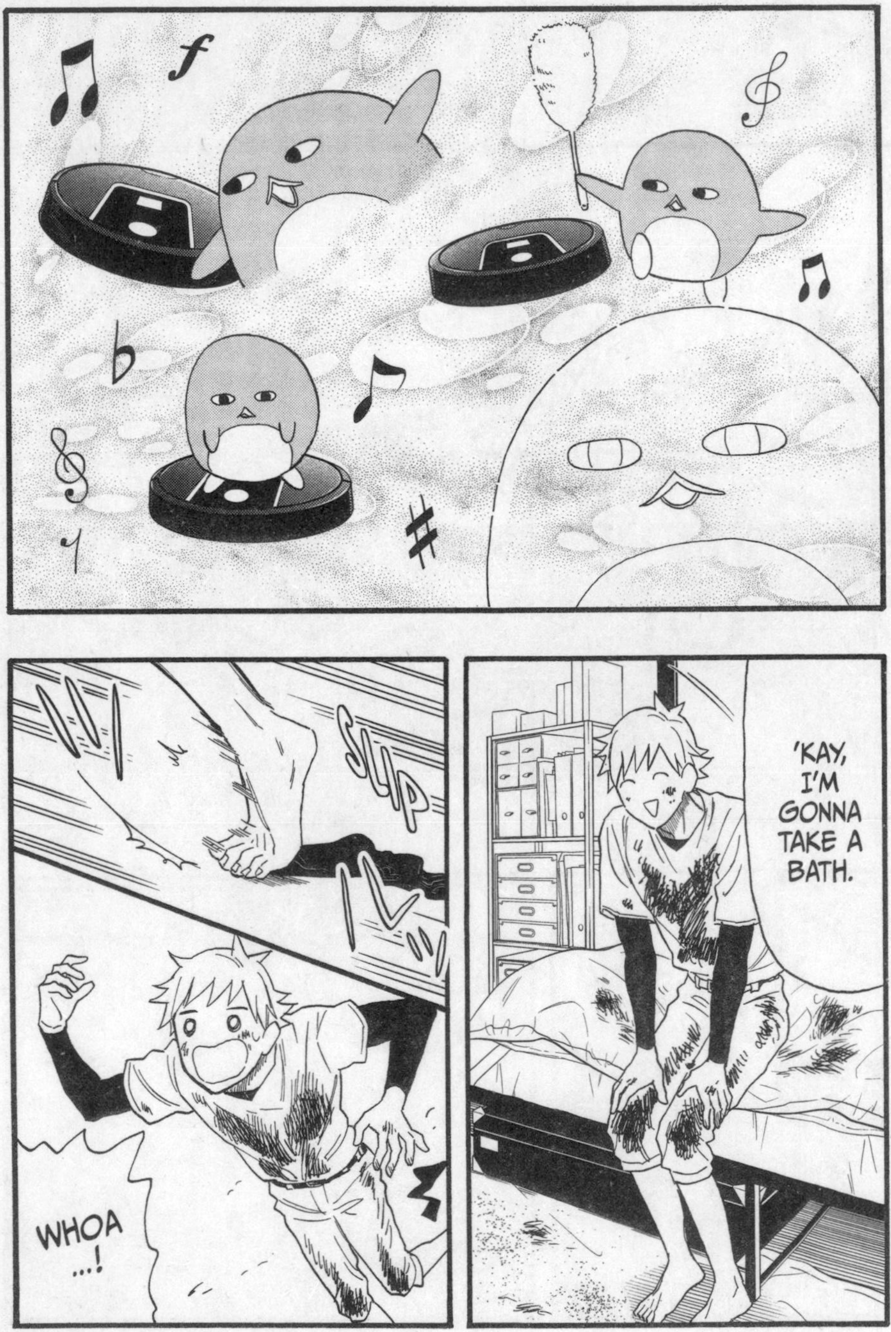
'KAY, I'M GONNA TAKE A BATH.
SLIP
WHOA ...!

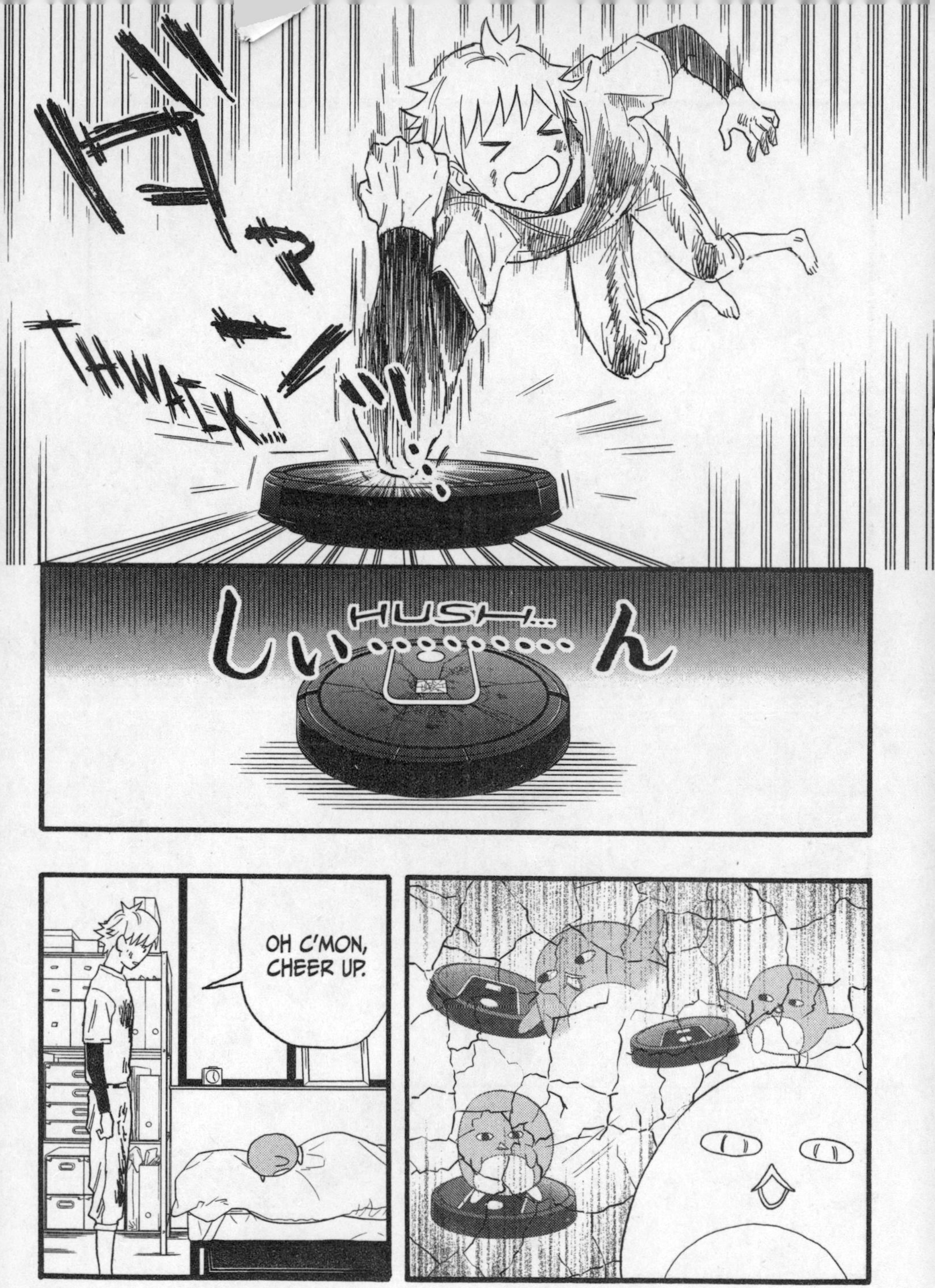
THWACK..!!
HUSH...
しい…………ん
OH C'MON, CHEER UP.

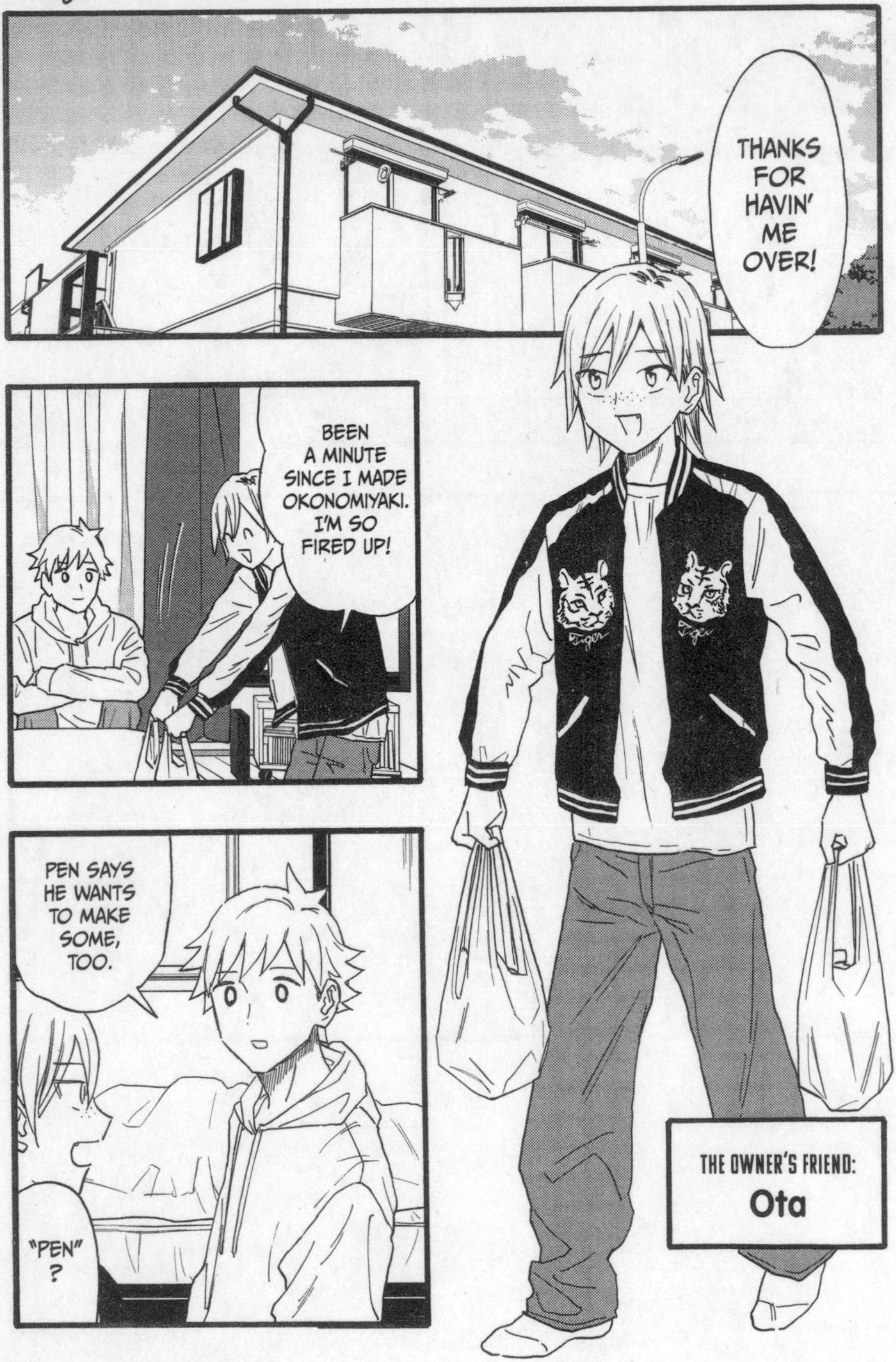
THANKS FOR HAVIN' ME OVER!
THE OWNER'S FRIEND:
Ota
BEEN A MINUTE SINCE I MADE OKONOMIYAKI. I'M SO FIRED UP!
PEN SAYS HE WANTS TO MAKE SOME, TOO.
"PEN"?

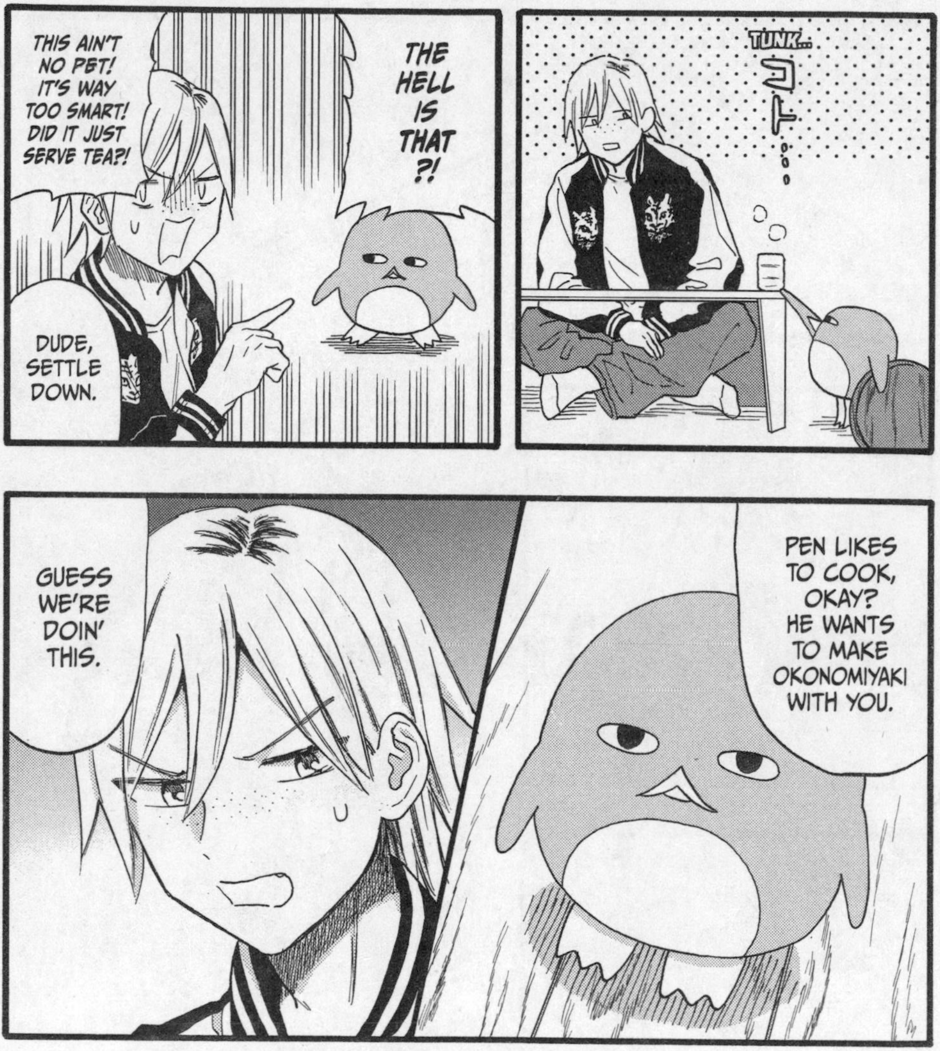
TUNK...
コト...
THE HELL IS THAT?!
THIS AIN'T NO PET! IT'S WAY TOO SMART! DID IT JUST SERVE TEA?!
DUDE, SETTLE DOWN.
PEN LIKES TO COOK, OKAY? HE WANTS TO MAKE OKONOMIYAKI WITH YOU.
GUESS WE'RE DOIN' THIS.

Pen 5 The Penguin Makes Okonomiyaki With His Owner's Friend

ALRIGHTY THEN, PENTARO...
WE'LL START WITH THE BATTER!
FIRST, WE CUT THE CABBAGE!
MIX COARSELY-CHOPPED CABBAGE RIGHT IN—KANSAI STYLE!
BUT YA KNOW, IN HIRO-SHIMA, THEY GENERALLY SHRED THE CABBAGE.
Today, it's Kansai style.
NEXT, WE MINCE THE SCALLIONS!
YA GOTTA GET THE SWEET GREEN SCALLIONS!
NEXT, THE DRY STUFF! MIX FLOUR, POWDERED BROTH, EGG, AN' WATER REAAAL GOOD, 'TIL ALL THE CLUMPS ARE GONE!
OH, SIFT THE DRY STUFF FIRST FOR LESS CLUMPS!
THEN YA MIX IN THE CABBAGE AN' SCALLIONS!
ADDIN' TEMPURA CRUMBS OR RED PICKLED GINGER'S MIGHTY TASTY, TOO.

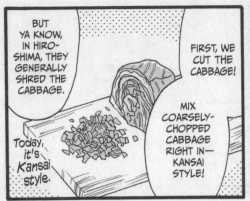

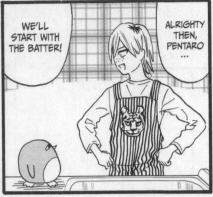

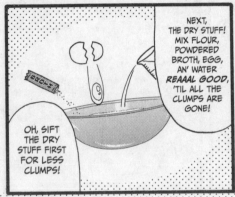

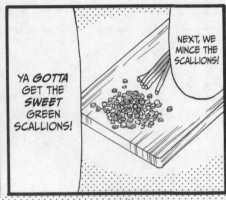

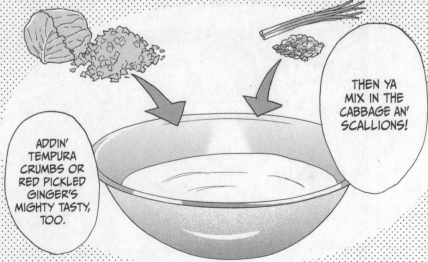

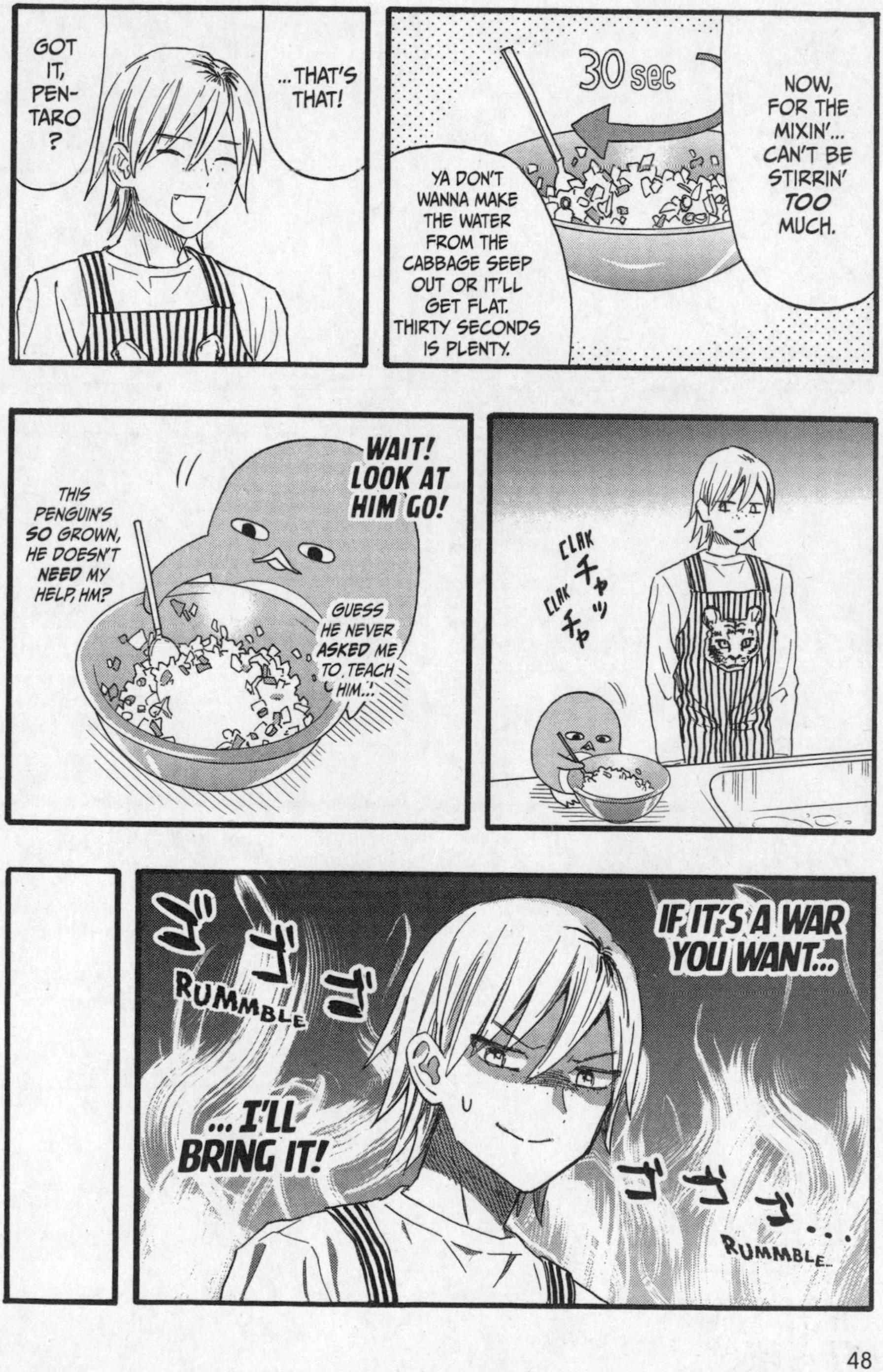
30 sec
NOW, FOR THE MIXIN'... CAN'T BE STIRRIN' *TOO* MUCH.
YA DON'T WANNA MAKE THE WATER FROM THE CABBAGE SEEP OUT OR IT'LL GET FLAT. THIRTY SECONDS IS PLENTY.
...THAT'S THAT!
GOT IT, PEN-TARO?
CLAK チャッ
CLAK チャ
WAIT! LOOK AT HIM GO!
GUESS HE NEVER ASKED ME TO TEACH HIM...
THIS PENGUIN'S SO GROWN, HE DOESN'T NEED MY HELP, HM?
IF IT'S A WAR YOU WANT...
ゴゴゴ
RUMMBLE
...I'LL BRING IT!
ゴゴゴ...
RUMMBLE...

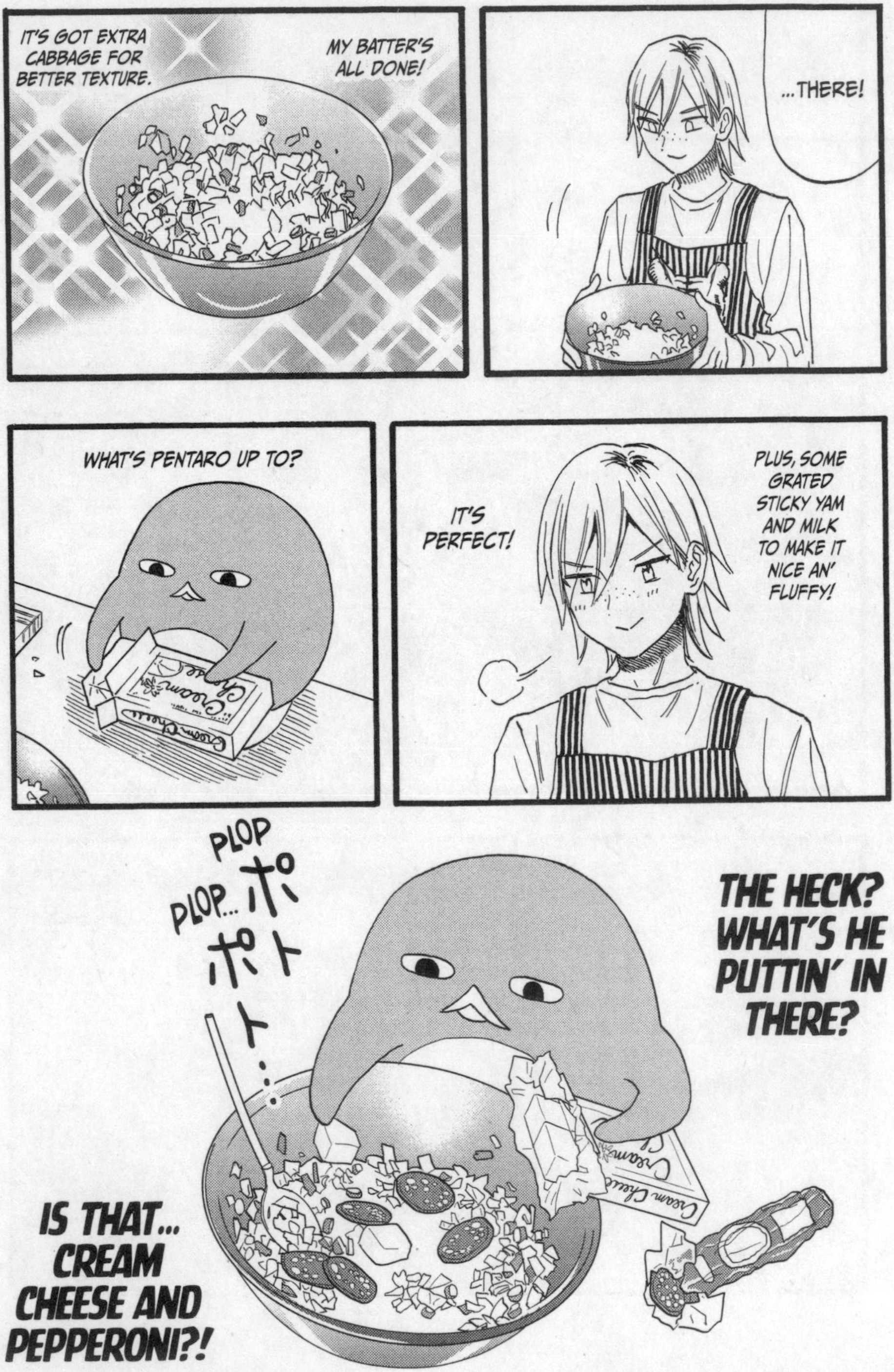
...THERE!
MY BATTER'S ALL DONE!
IT'S GOT EXTRA CABBAGE FOR BETTER TEXTURE.
PLUS, SOME GRATED STICKY YAM AND MILK TO MAKE IT NICE AN' FLUFFY!
IT'S PERFECT!
WHAT'S PENTARO UP TO?
THE HECK? WHAT'S HE PUTTIN' IN THERE?
PLOP PLOP... ポトポト...
IS THAT... CREAM CHEESE AND PEPPERONI?!

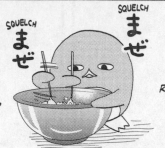

WHAT'RE YOU, A FOODIE?!
CREAM CHEESE, RIGHT OFF THE BAT...?
SQUELCH
まぜ
SQUELCH
まぜ
C'MON, YOU GOTTA START WITH THE CLASSICS—SQUID OR PORK! GUESS IT'S TOO MUCH TO EXPECT SOME BIRD TO KNOW WHAT'S TRIED AN' TRUE! CREAM CHEESE? SHEESH... PEPPERONI...? GETTIN' ALL FANCY...
WHATEVER... THINK YOUR OKONOMIYAKI CAN TOP MINE?
NOT A CHANCE!!
HMPH...
RIGHT, IT'S GRILLIN' TIME!
HEAT THE GRIDDLE TO ABOUT 200°C*...
OIL THE PLATE AND PLOP ON BATTER 'BOUT TWO CENTIMETERS* THICK!
SIZZZZZZ...
ジュ
AND PENTARO...?
HUH, NICE AN' CAREFUL WORK. NOT HALF BAD.
のせ
HEAP
のせ
HEAP

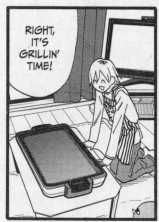

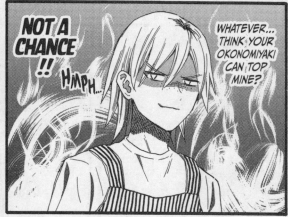

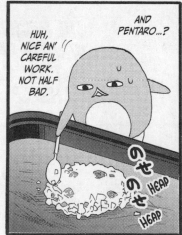

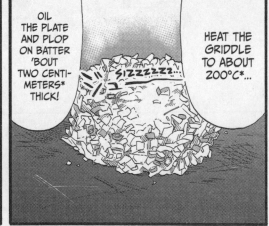

• About 400°F, about 0.79-inches

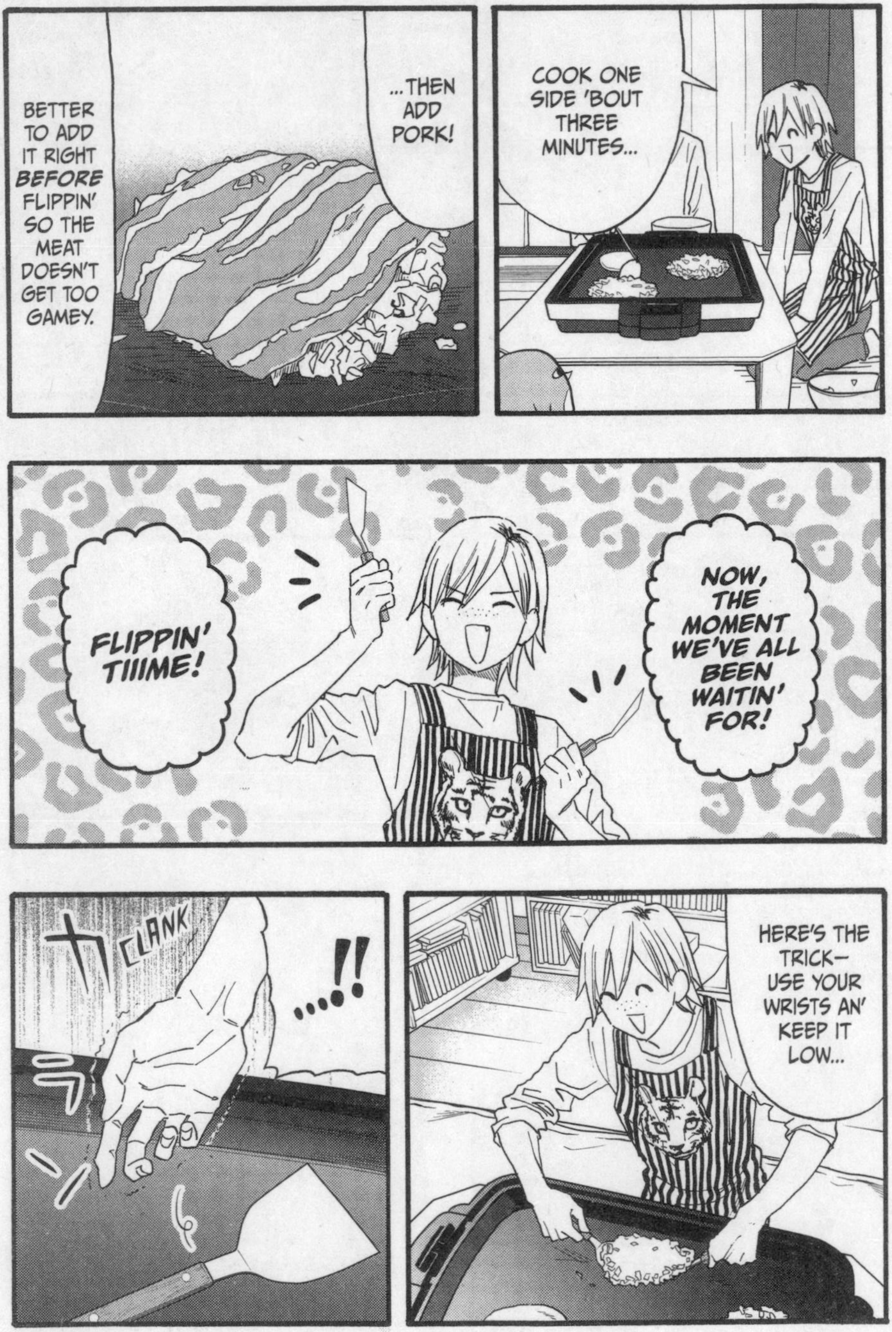
COOK ONE SIDE 'BOUT THREE MINUTES...
...THEN ADD PORK!
BETTER TO ADD IT RIGHT *BEFORE* FLIPPIN' SO THE MEAT DOESN'T GET TOO GAMEY.
NOW, THE MOMENT WE'VE ALL BEEN WAITIN' FOR!
FLIPPIN' TIIIME!
HERE'S THE TRICK— USE YOUR WRISTS AN' KEEP IT LOW...
CLANK
...!!

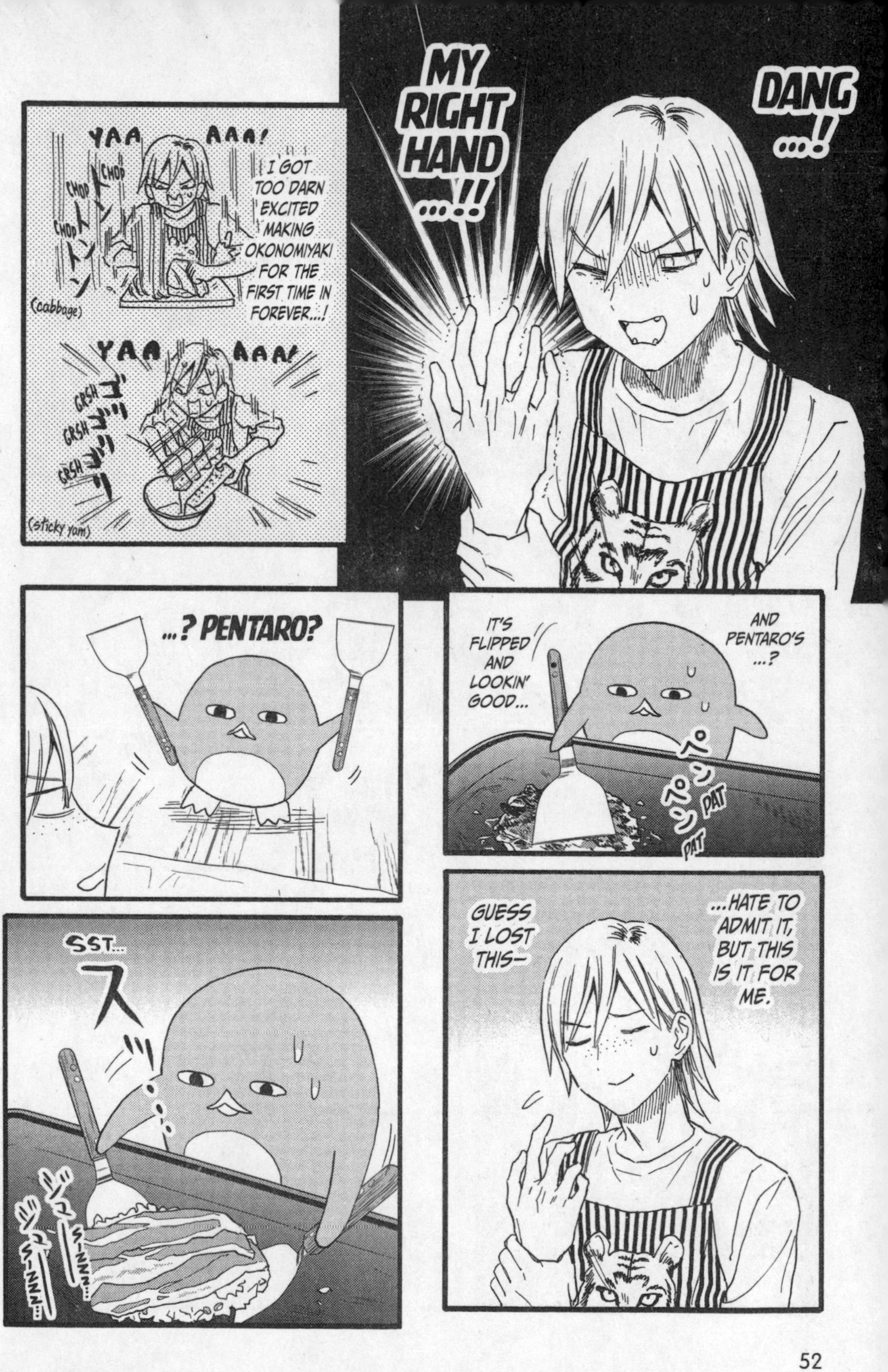
DANG ...!
MY RIGHT HAND ...!!
YAA AAA!
I GOT TOO DARN EXCITED MAKING OKONOMIYAKI FOR THE FIRST TIME IN FOREVER...!
CHOP CHOP CHOP
(cabbage)
YAA AAA!
GRSH GRSH GRSH
(sticky yam)
AND PENTARO'S ...?
IT'S FLIPPED AND LOOKIN' GOOD...
PAT PAT
...? PENTARO?
...HATE TO ADMIT IT, BUT THIS IS IT FOR ME.
GUESS I LOST THIS—
SST...
S-ZZZ... S-ZZZ...

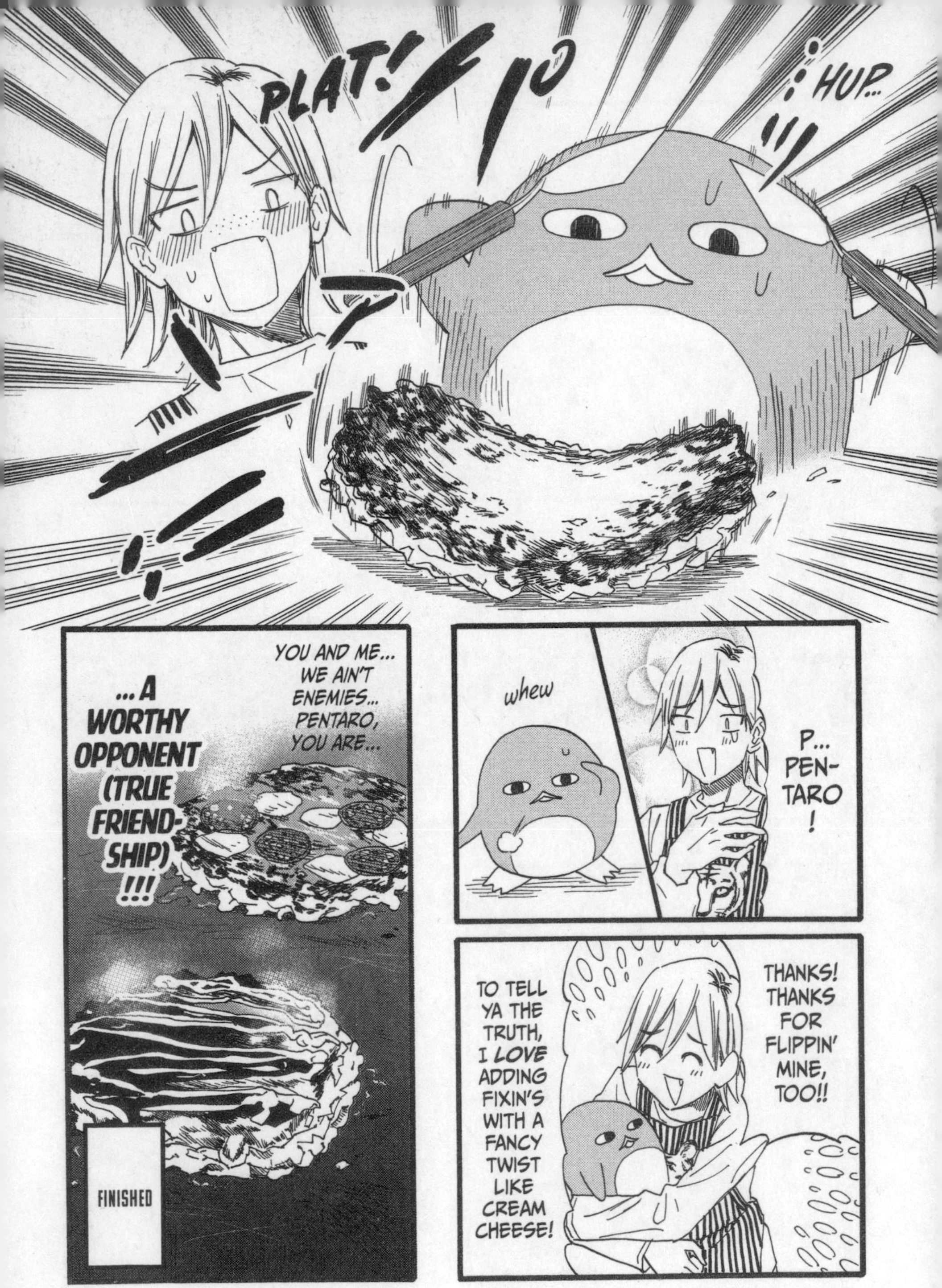
HUP...
PLAT!
P... PEN-TARO!
whew
THANKS! THANKS FOR FLIPPIN' MINE, TOO!!
TO TELL YA THE TRUTH, I LOVE ADDING FIXIN'S WITH A FANCY TWIST LIKE CREAM CHEESE!
YOU AND ME... WE AIN'T ENEMIES... PENTARO, YOU ARE...
...A WORTHY OPPONENT (TRUE FRIEND-SHIP) !!!
FINISHED

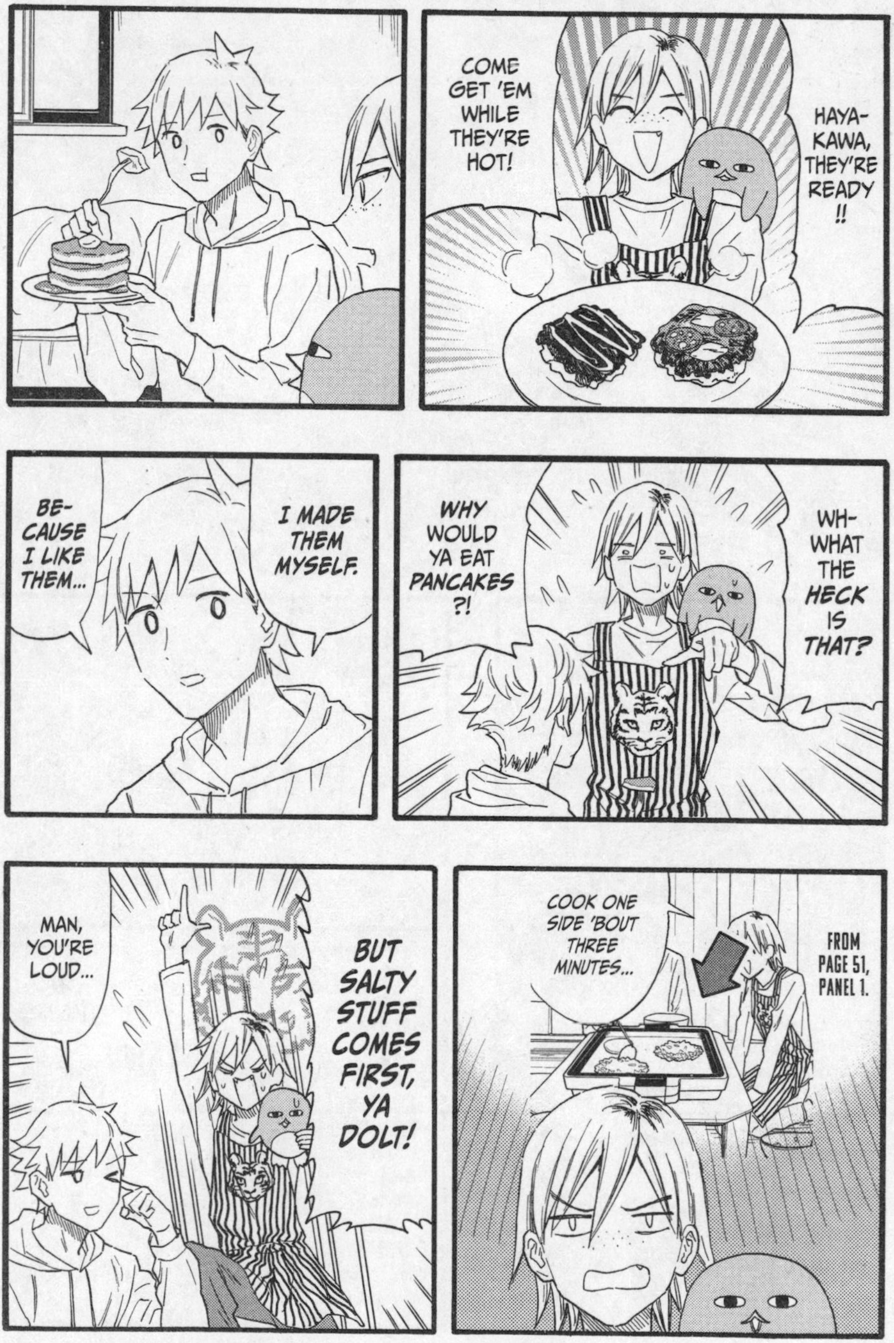
HAYA-KAWA, THEY'RE READY!!
COME GET 'EM WHILE THEY'RE HOT!
WH-WHAT THE HECK IS THAT?
WHY WOULD YA EAT PANCAKES?!
I MADE THEM MYSELF.
BE-CAUSE I LIKE THEM...
FROM PAGE 51, PANEL 1.
COOK ONE SIDE 'BOUT THREE MINUTES...
BUT SALTY STUFF COMES FIRST, YA DOLT!
MAN, YOU'RE LOUD...

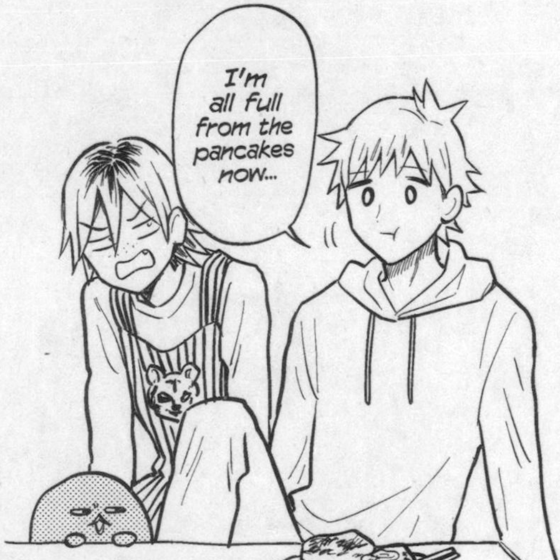
I'm all full from the pancakes now...

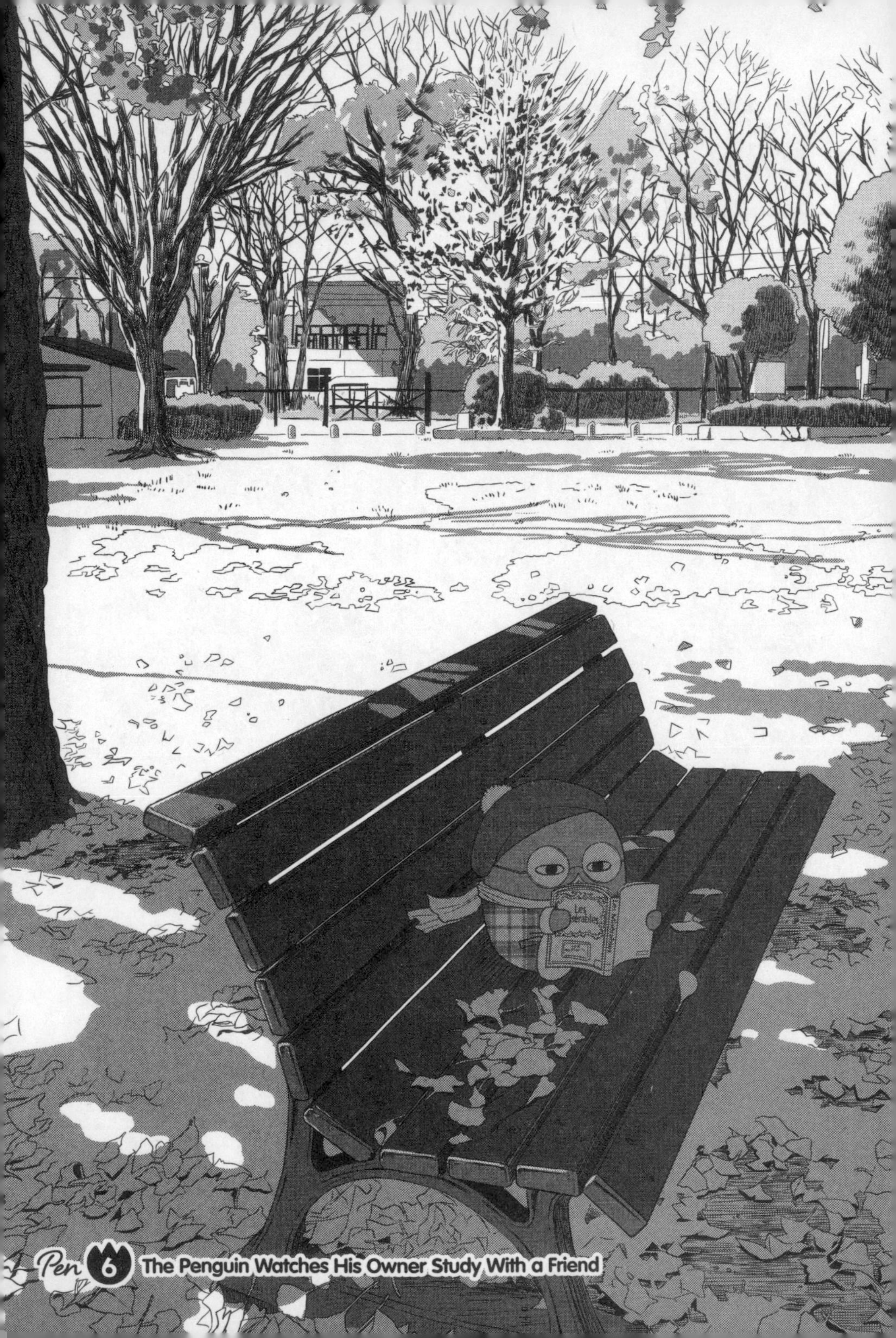

Pen 6 The Penguin Watches His Owner Study With a Friend

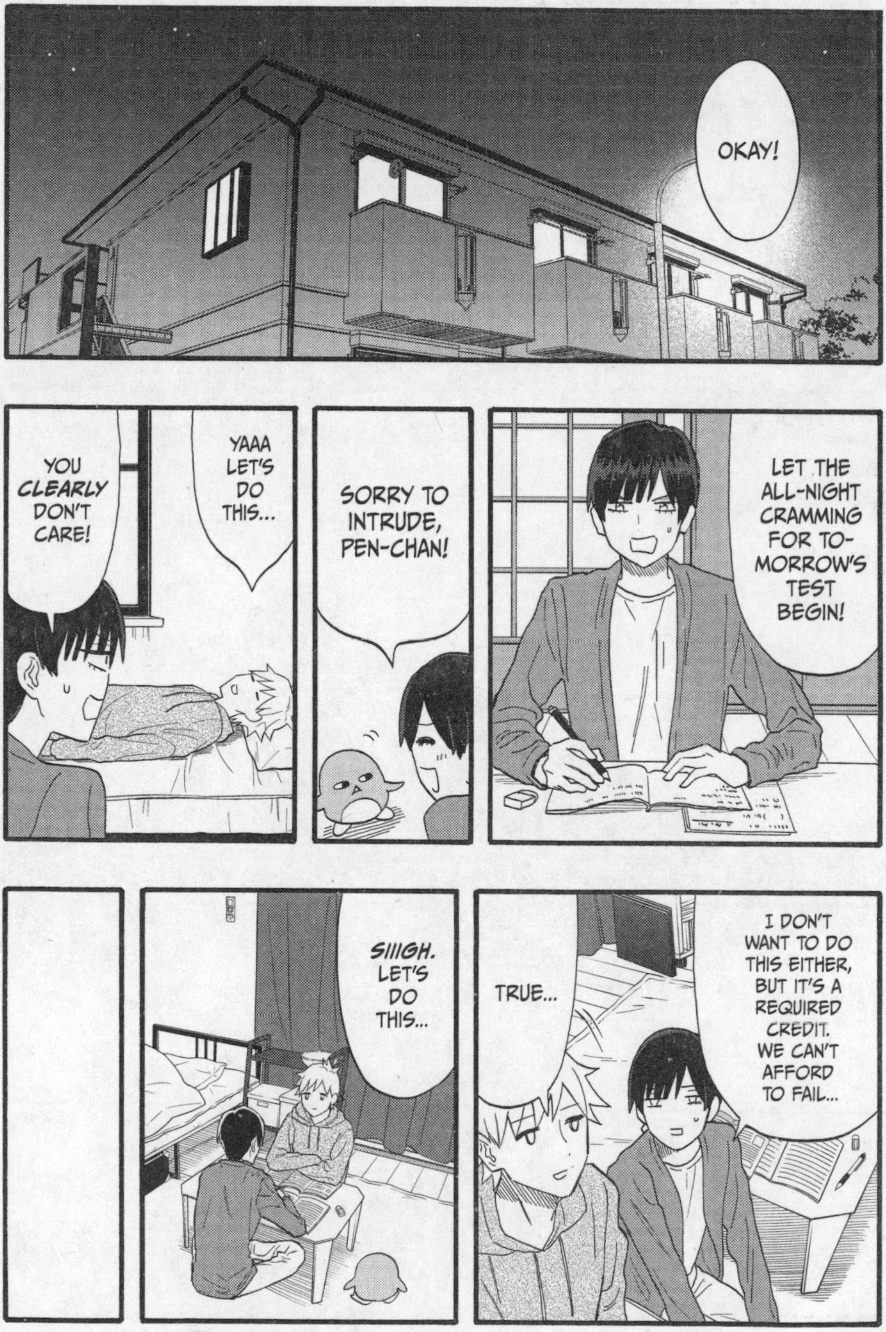
OKAY!
LET THE ALL-NIGHT CRAMMING FOR TO-MORROW'S TEST BEGIN!
SORRY TO INTRUDE, PEN-CHAN!
YAAA LET'S DO THIS...
YOU *CLEARLY* DON'T CARE!
I DON'T WANT TO DO THIS EITHER, BUT IT'S A REQUIRED CREDIT. WE CAN'T AFFORD TO FAIL...
TRUE...
SIIIGH. LET'S DO THIS...

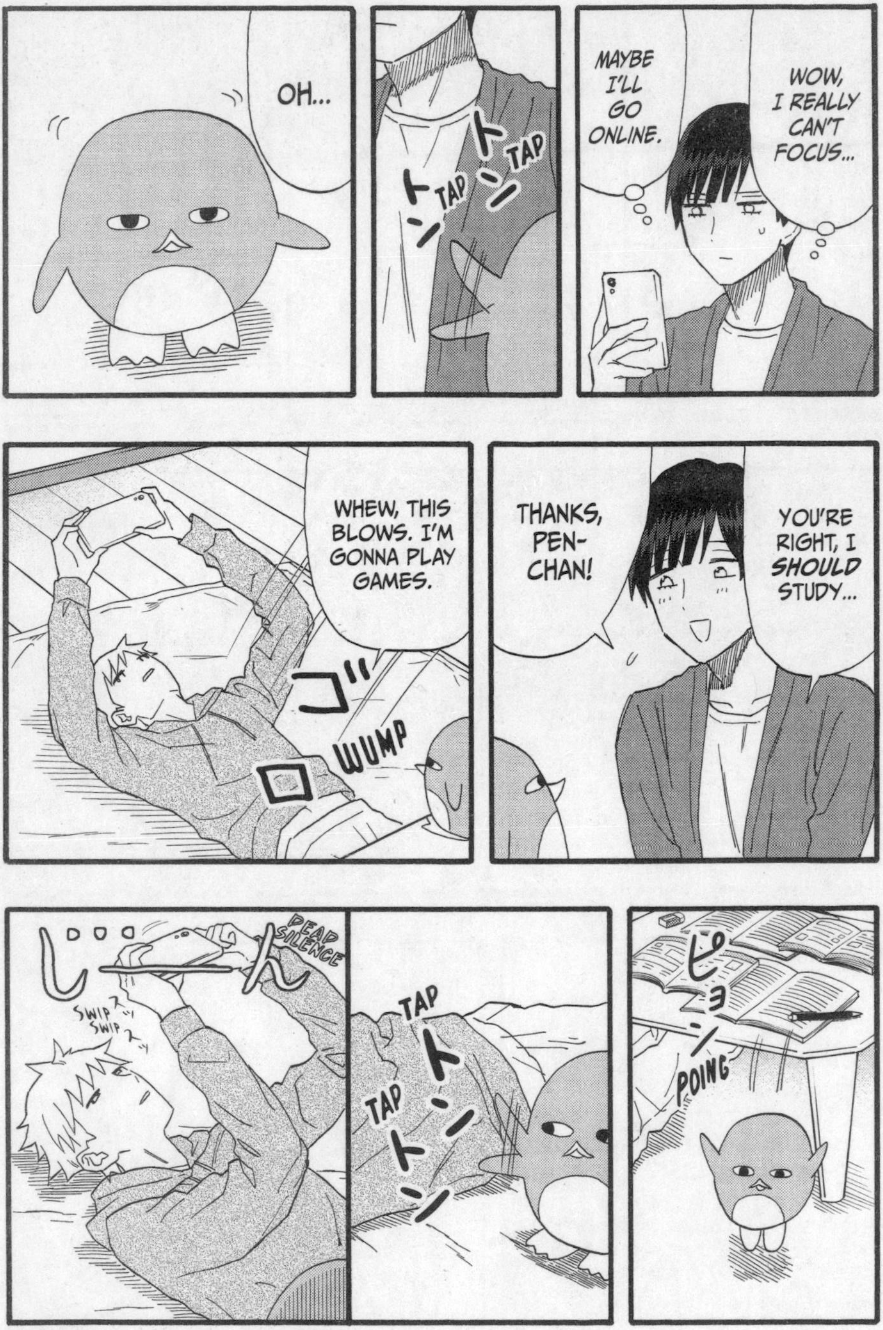
WOW, I REALLY CAN'T FOCUS...
MAYBE I'LL GO ONLINE.
トン
TAP
トン
TAP
OH...
YOU'RE RIGHT, I SHOULD STUDY...
THANKS, PEN-CHAN!
WHEW, THIS BLOWS. I'M GONNA PLAY GAMES.
ゴロ
WUMP
ピョーン
POING
トーン
TAP
トーン
TAP
しーん
DEAD SILENCE
SWIP スッ
SWIP スッ

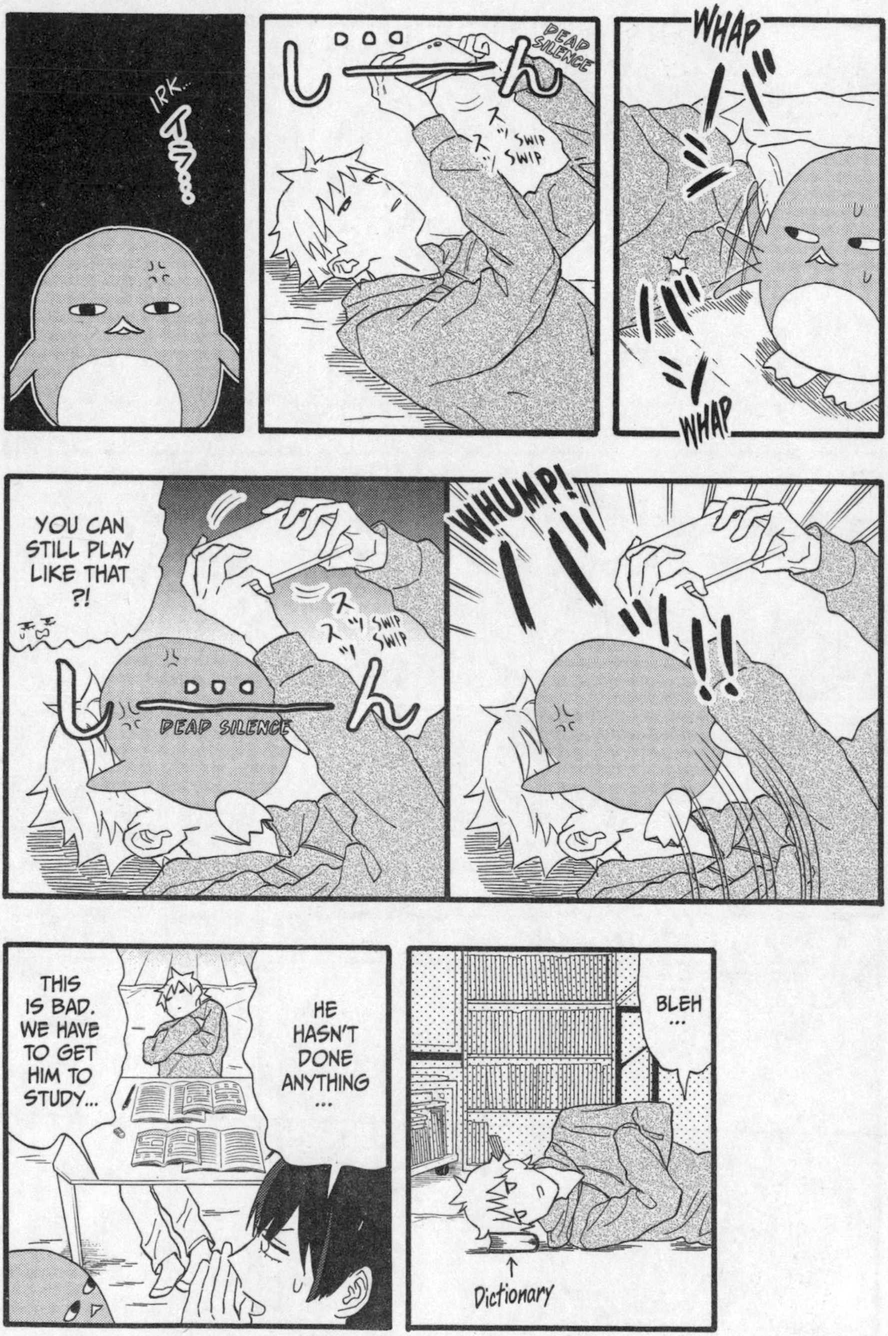

WHAP
WHAP
DEAD SILENCE
SWIP SWIP
IRK...
WHUMP!
YOU CAN STILL PLAY LIKE THAT?!
SWIP SWIP
DEAD SILENCE
BLEH...
↑
Dictionary
HE HASN'T DONE ANYTHING...
THIS IS BAD. WE HAVE TO GET HIM TO STUDY...

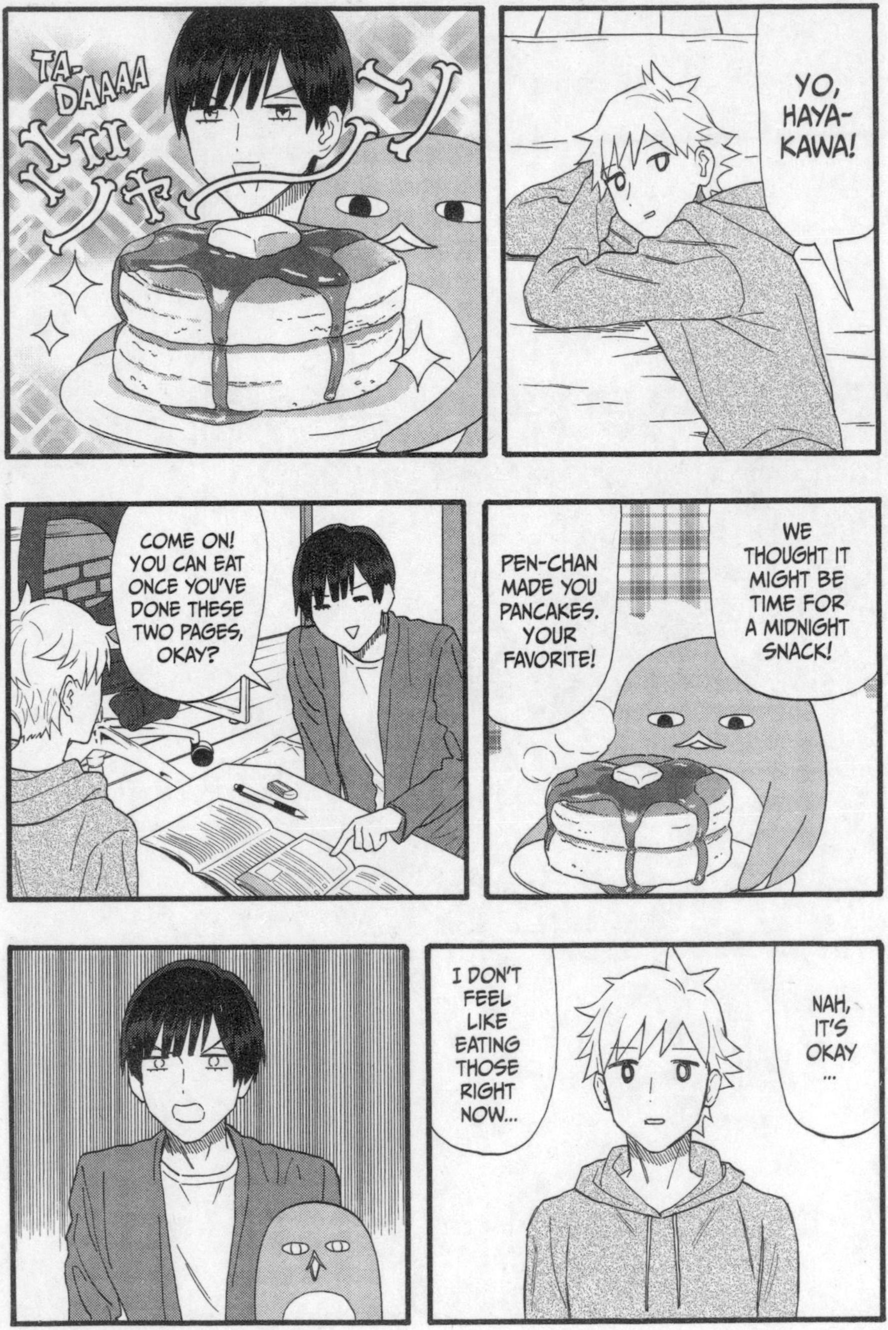
YO, HAYA-KAWA!
TA-DAAAA
WE THOUGHT IT MIGHT BE TIME FOR A MIDNIGHT SNACK!
PEN-CHAN MADE YOU PANCAKES. YOUR FAVORITE!
COME ON! YOU CAN EAT ONCE YOU'VE DONE THESE TWO PAGES, OKAY?
NAH, IT'S OKAY ...
I DON'T FEEL LIKE EATING THOSE RIGHT NOW...

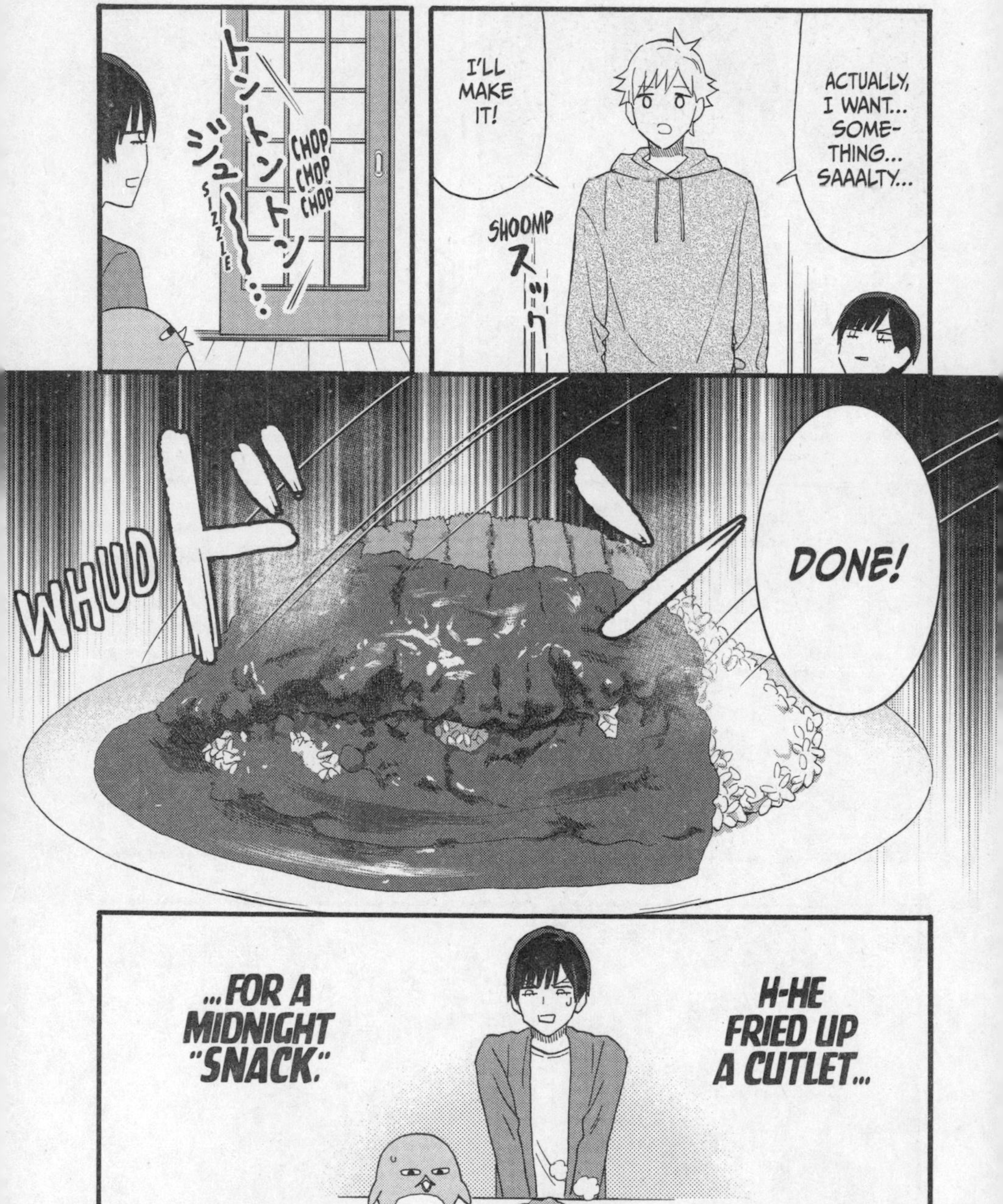
ACTUALLY, I WANT... SOMETHING... SAAALTY...
I'LL MAKE IT!
SHOOMP
スック
トントントン
CHOP CHOP CHOP
ジュ〜〜…
SIZZLE
DONE!
ド
WHUD
H-HE FRIED UP A CUTLET...
...FOR A MIDNIGHT "SNACK."

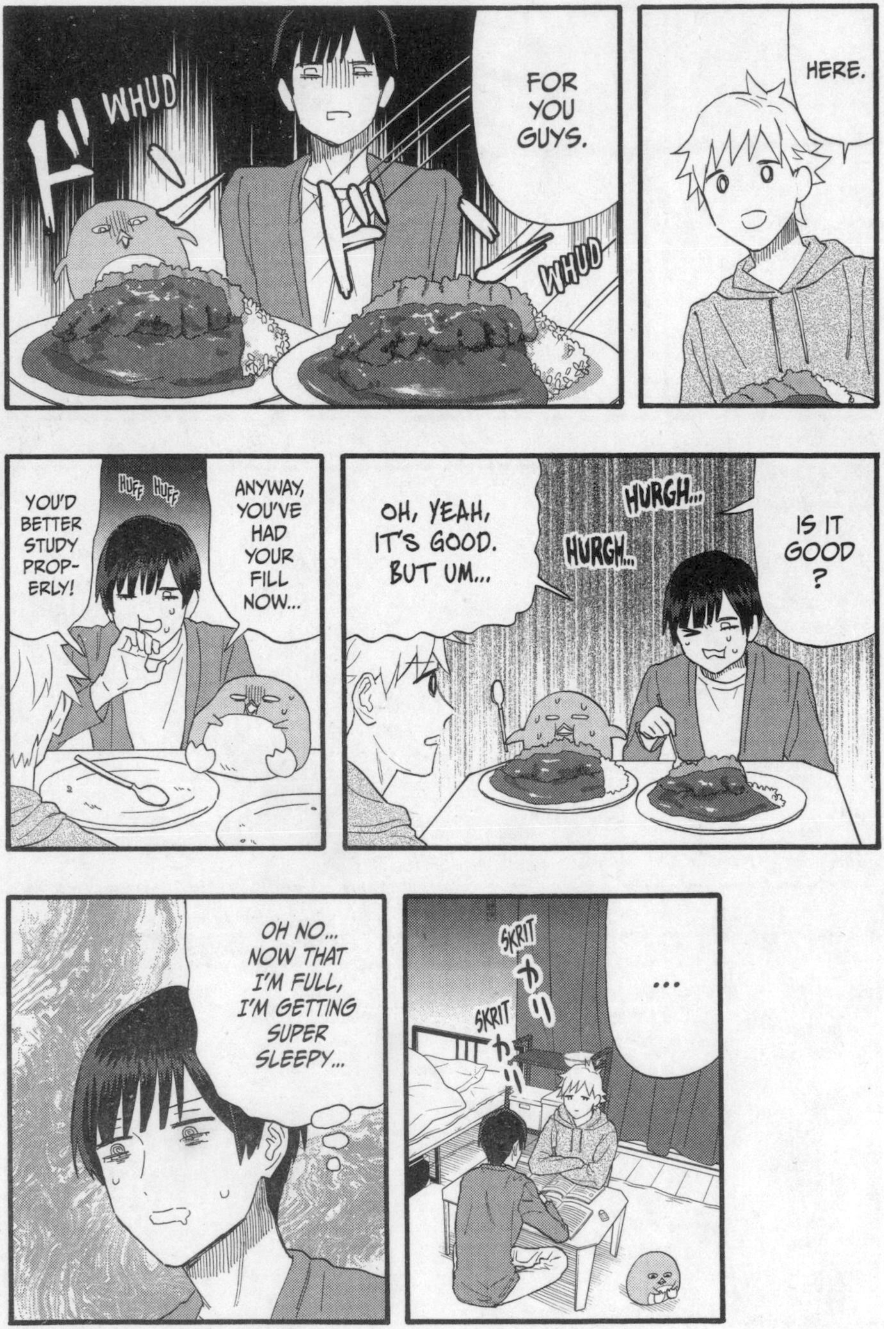
HERE.
FOR YOU GUYS.
WHUD
WHUD
IS IT GOOD?
HURGH...
HURGH...
OH, YEAH, IT'S GOOD. BUT UM...
ANYWAY, YOU'VE HAD YOUR FILL NOW...
HUFF HUFF
YOU'D BETTER STUDY PROPERLY!
...
SKRIT かり
SKRIT かり
OH NO... NOW THAT I'M FULL, I'M GETTING SUPER SLEEPY...

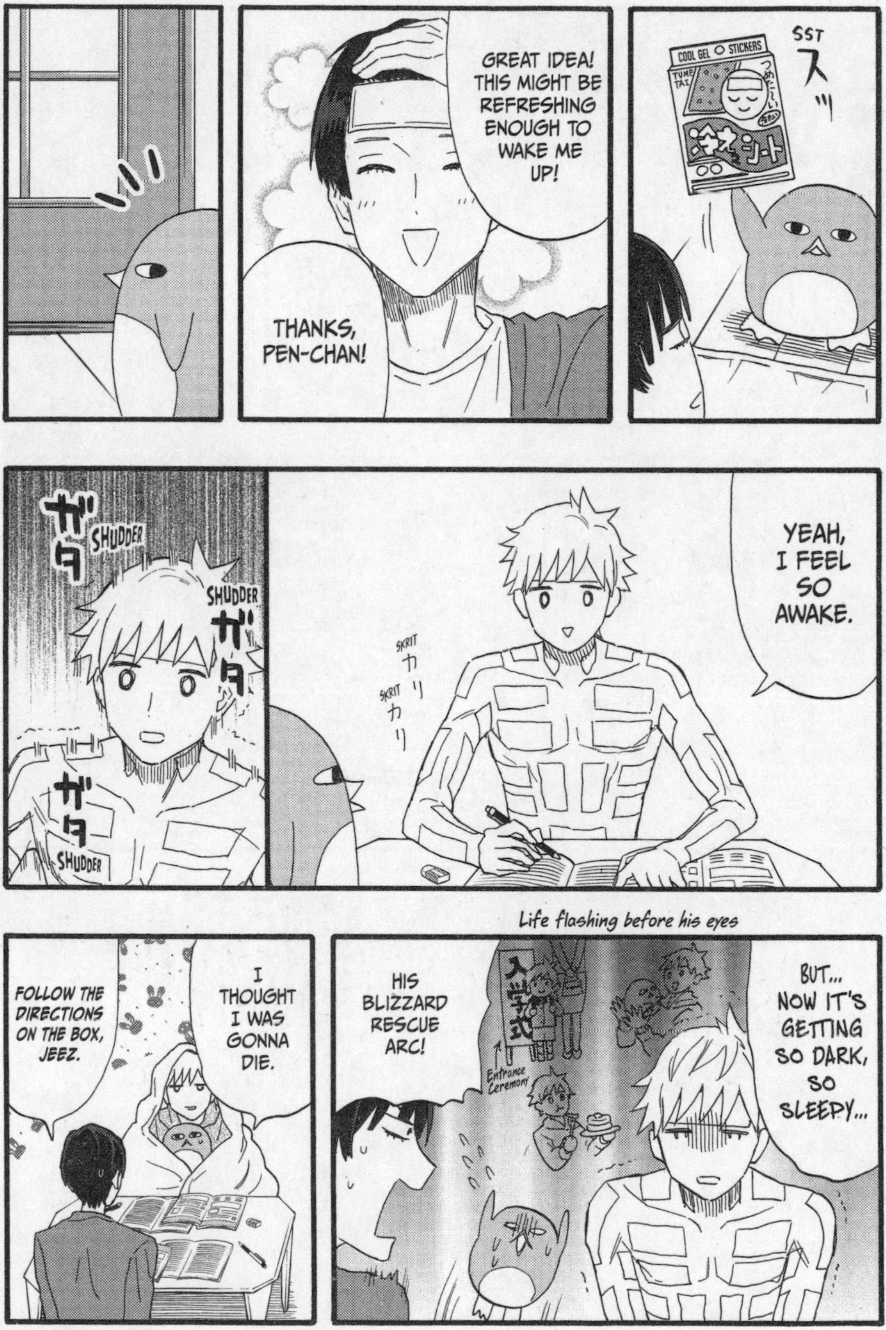
SST
スッ
COOL GEL STICKERS
GREAT IDEA! THIS MIGHT BE REFRESHING ENOUGH TO WAKE ME UP!
THANKS, PEN-CHAN!
YEAH, I FEEL SO AWAKE.
SKRIT カリ
SKRIT カリ
ガタ SHUDDER
SHUDDER ガタ
ガタ SHUDDER
Life flashing before his eyes
BUT... NOW IT'S GETTING SO DARK, SO SLEEPY...
HIS BLIZZARD RESCUE ARC!
入学式
Entrance Ceremony
I THOUGHT I WAS GONNA DIE.
FOLLOW THE DIRECTIONS ON THE BOX, JEEZ.

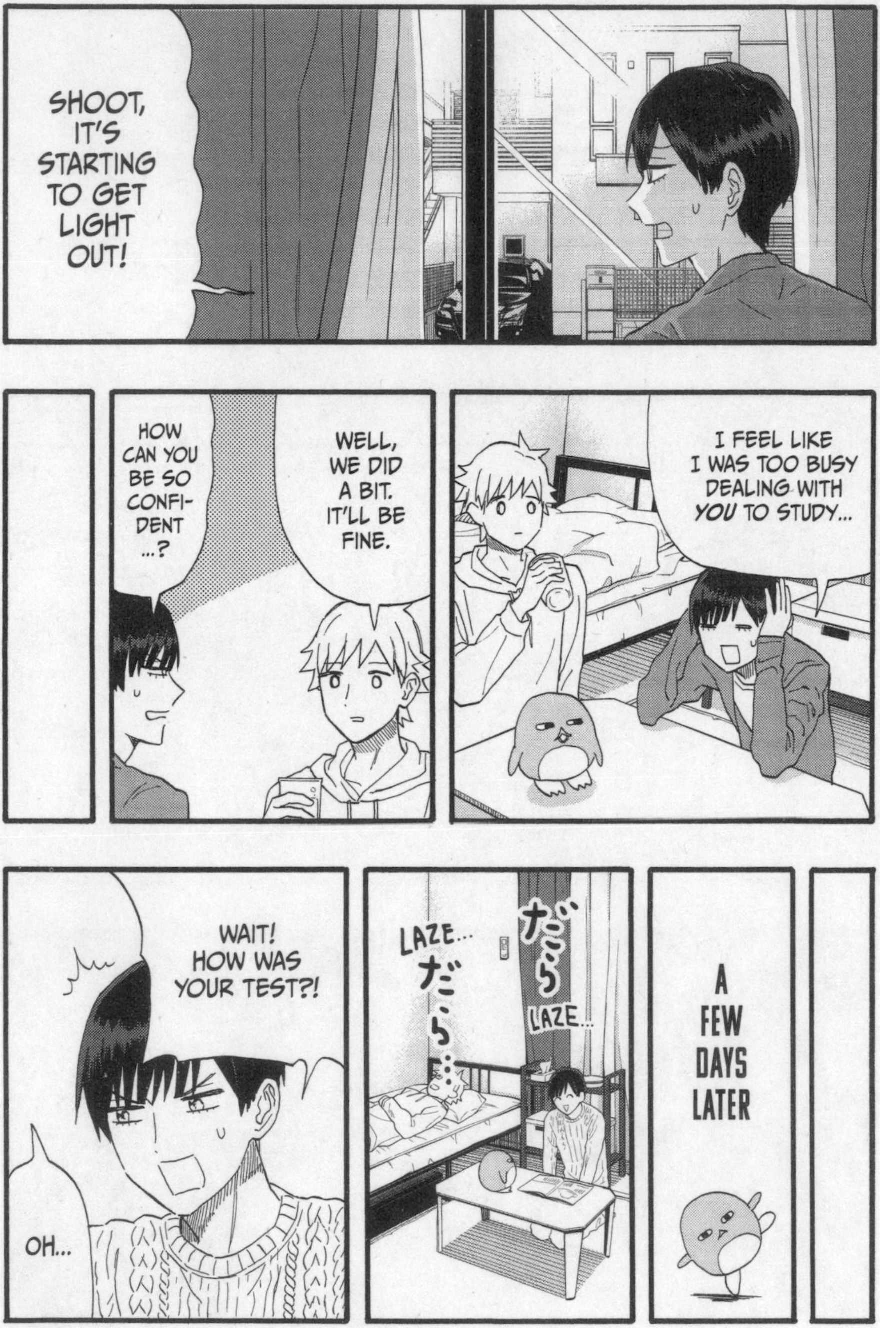
SHOOT, IT'S STARTING TO GET LIGHT OUT!
I FEEL LIKE I WAS TOO BUSY DEALING WITH *YOU* TO STUDY...
WELL, WE DID A BIT. IT'LL BE FINE.
HOW CAN YOU BE SO CONFI-DENT ...?
A FEW DAYS LATER
だら LAZE...
LAZE... だら...
WAIT! HOW WAS YOUR TEST?!
OH...

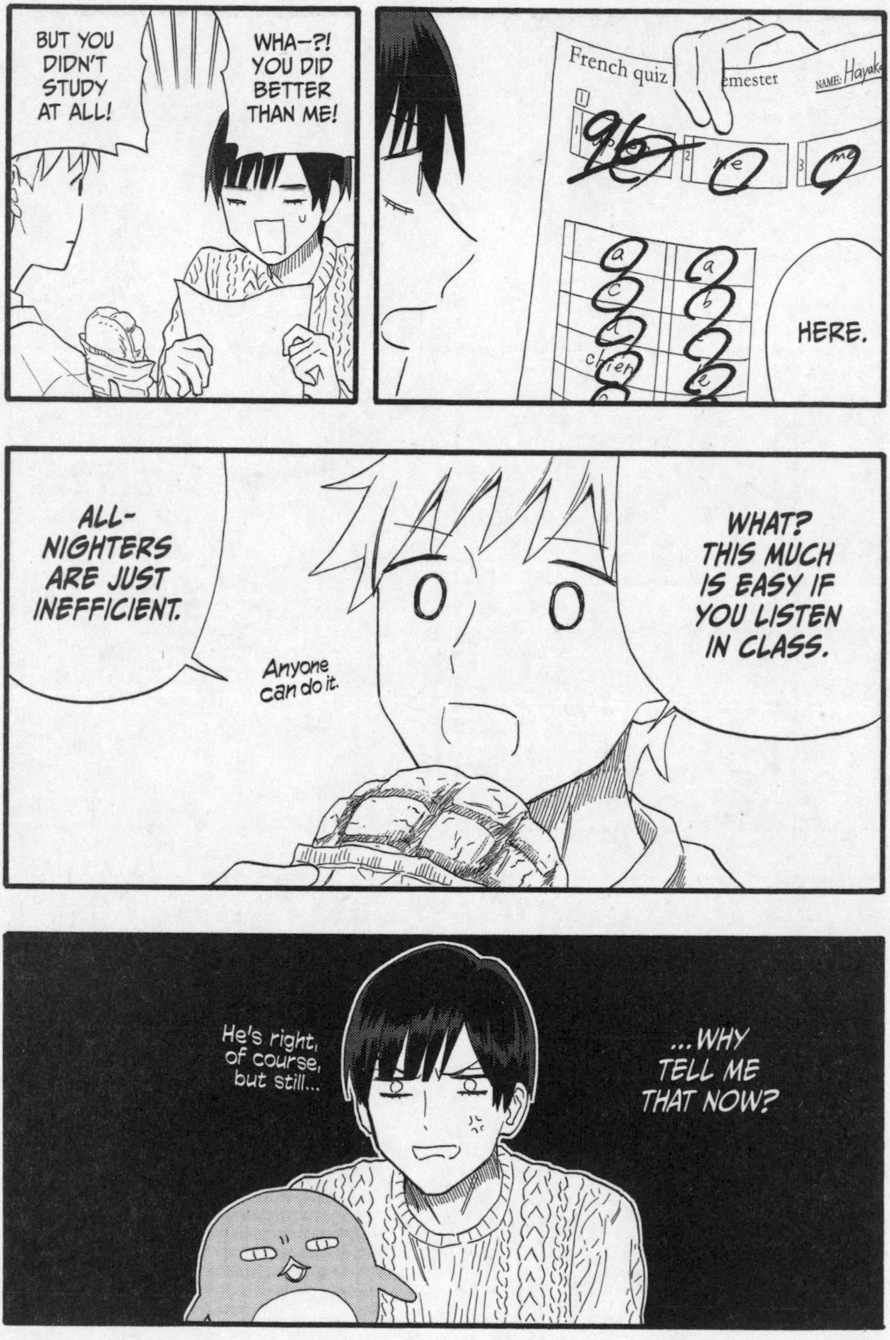
French quiz
HERE.
WHA—?! YOU DID BETTER THAN ME!
BUT YOU DIDN'T STUDY AT ALL!
WHAT? THIS MUCH IS EASY IF YOU LISTEN IN CLASS.
Anyone can do it.
ALL-NIGHTERS ARE JUST INEFFICIENT.
...WHY TELL ME THAT NOW?
He's right, of course, but still...

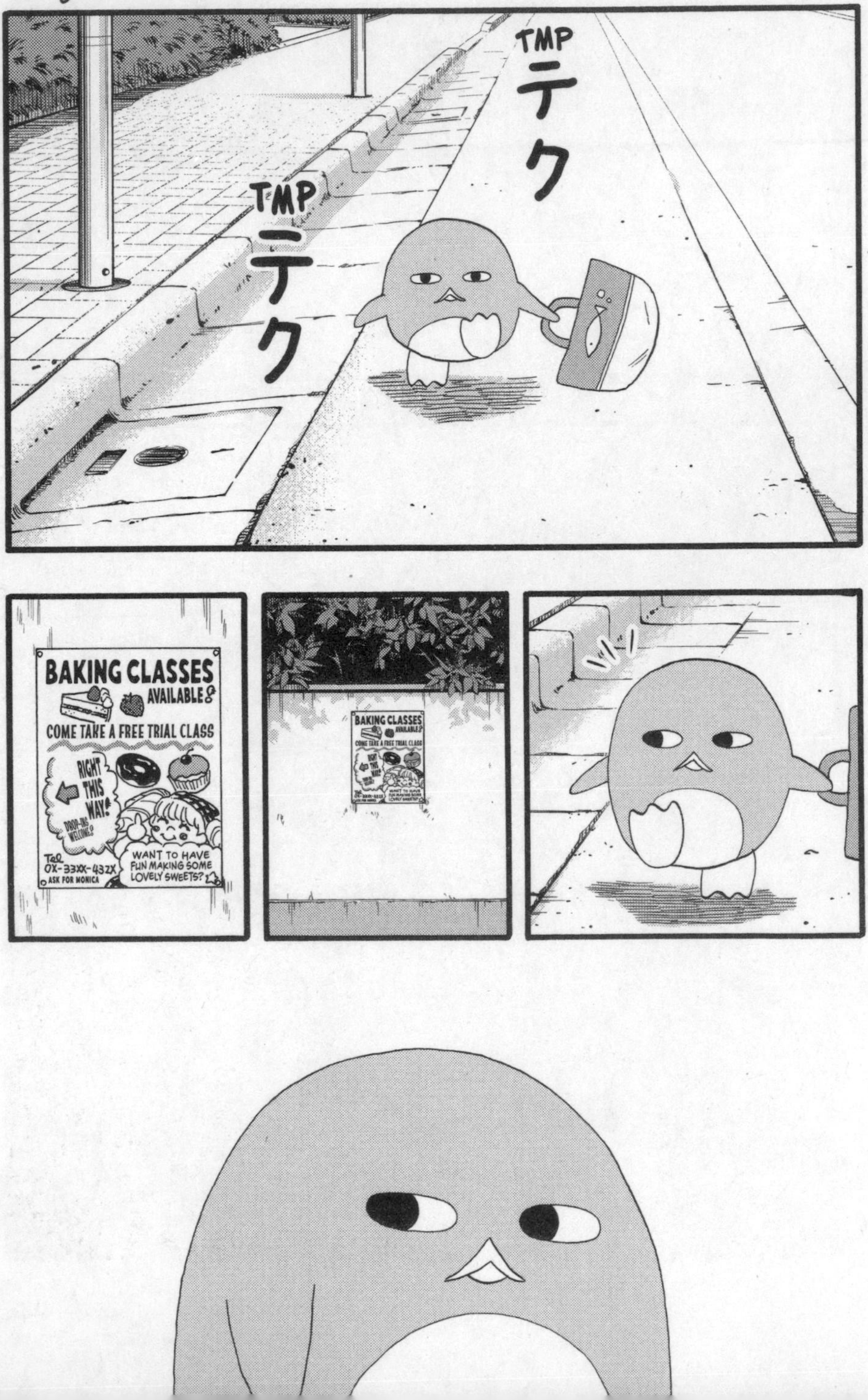
TMP
テク
TMP
テク
BAKING CLASSES
AVAILABLE
COME TAKE A FREE TRIAL CLASS
RIGHT THIS WAY!
DROP-INS WELCOME!
Tel
0X-33XX-43ZX
ASK FOR MONICA
WANT TO HAVE FUN MAKING SOME LOVELY SWEETS?

Pen 7 The Penguin Stops by a Baking Class

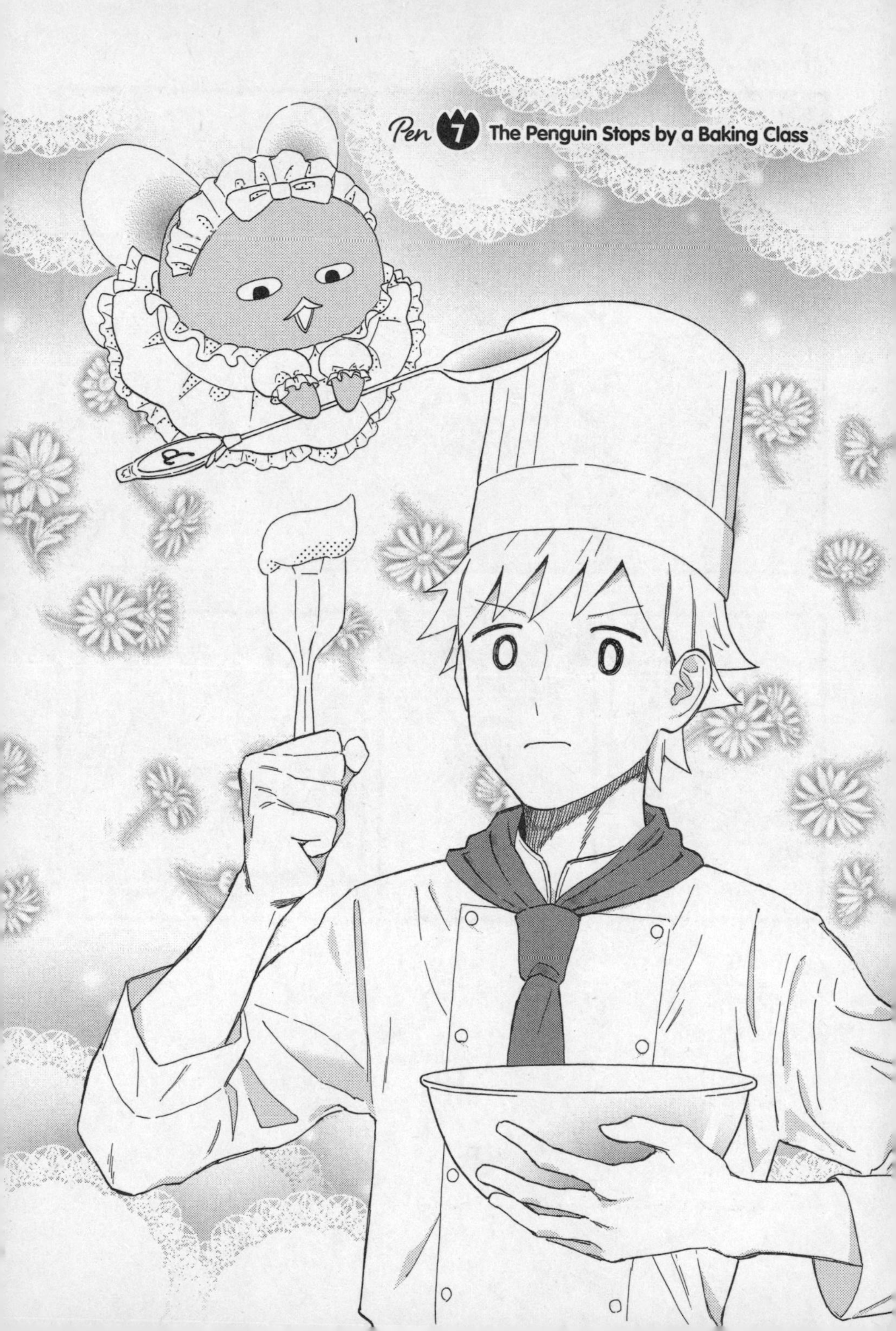

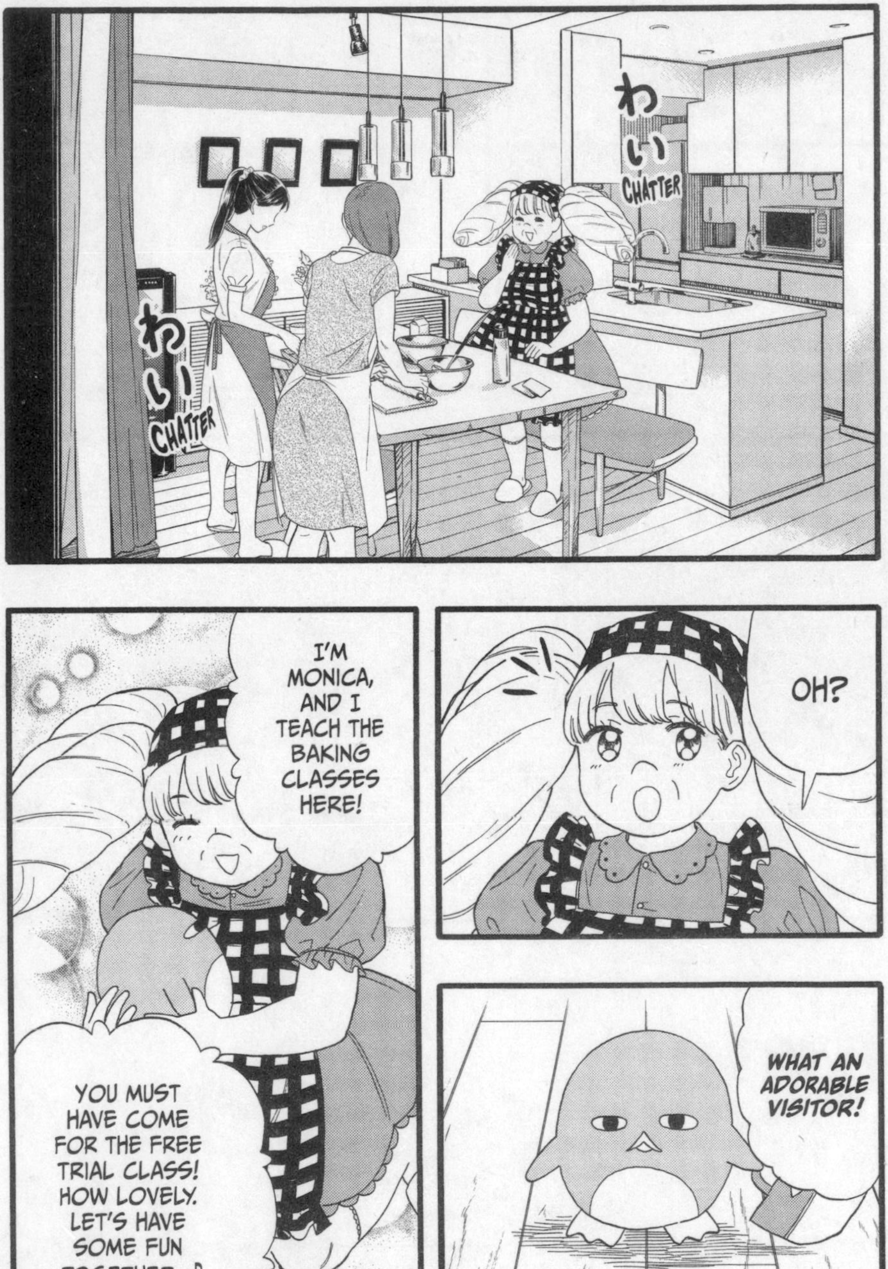
わい
CHATTER
わい
CHATTER
OH?
WHAT AN ADORABLE VISITOR!
I'M MONICA, AND I TEACH THE BAKING CLASSES HERE!
YOU MUST HAVE COME FOR THE FREE TRIAL CLASS! HOW LOVELY. LET'S HAVE SOME FUN TOGETHER. ♪

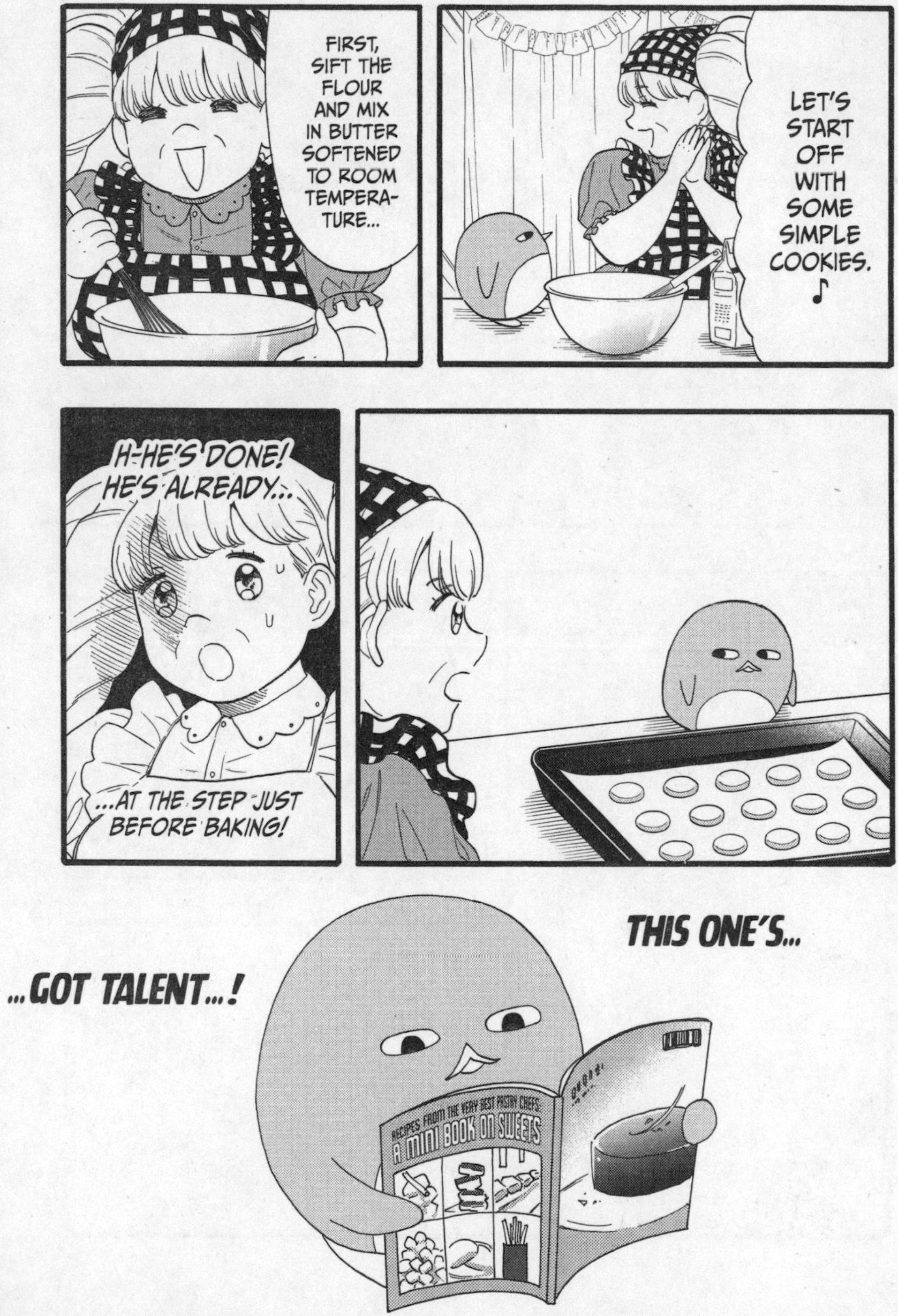
LET'S START OFF WITH SOME SIMPLE COOKIES. ♪
FIRST, SIFT THE FLOUR AND MIX IN BUTTER SOFTENED TO ROOM TEMPERA-TURE...
H-HE'S DONE! HE'S ALREADY...
...AT THE STEP JUST BEFORE BAKING!
THIS ONE'S...
...GOT TALENT...!
RECIPES FROM THE VERY BEST PASTRY CHEFS:
A MINI BOOK ON SWEETS

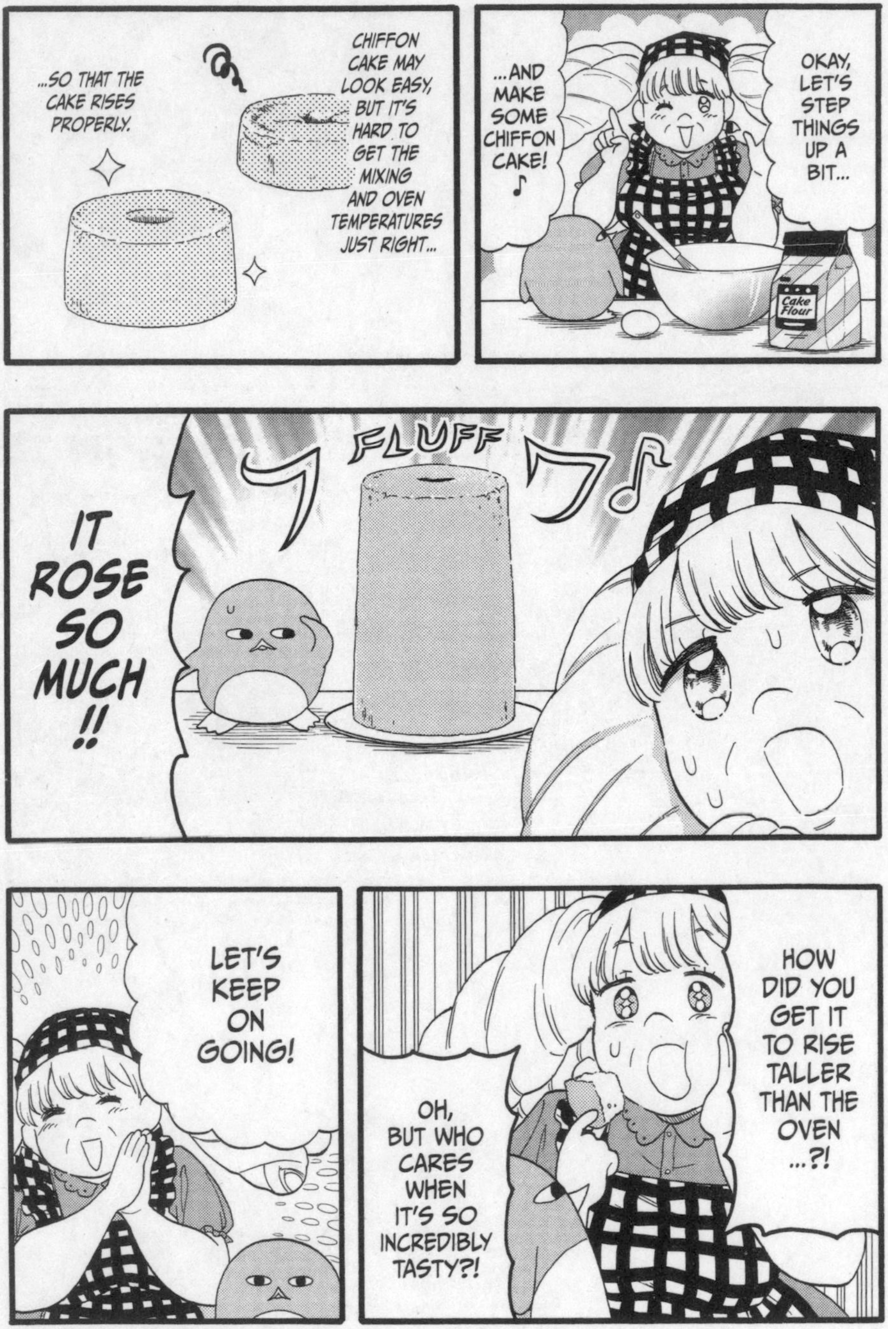
OKAY, LET'S STEP THINGS UP A BIT...
...AND MAKE SOME CHIFFON CAKE! ♪
Cake Flour
CHIFFON CAKE MAY LOOK EASY, BUT IT'S HARD TO GET THE MIXING AND OVEN TEMPERATURES JUST RIGHT...
...SO THAT THE CAKE RISES PROPERLY.
FLUFF
IT ROSE SO MUCH!!
HOW DID YOU GET IT TO RISE TALLER THAN THE OVEN ...?!
OH, BUT WHO CARES WHEN IT'S SO INCREDIBLY TASTY?!
LET'S KEEP ON GOING!

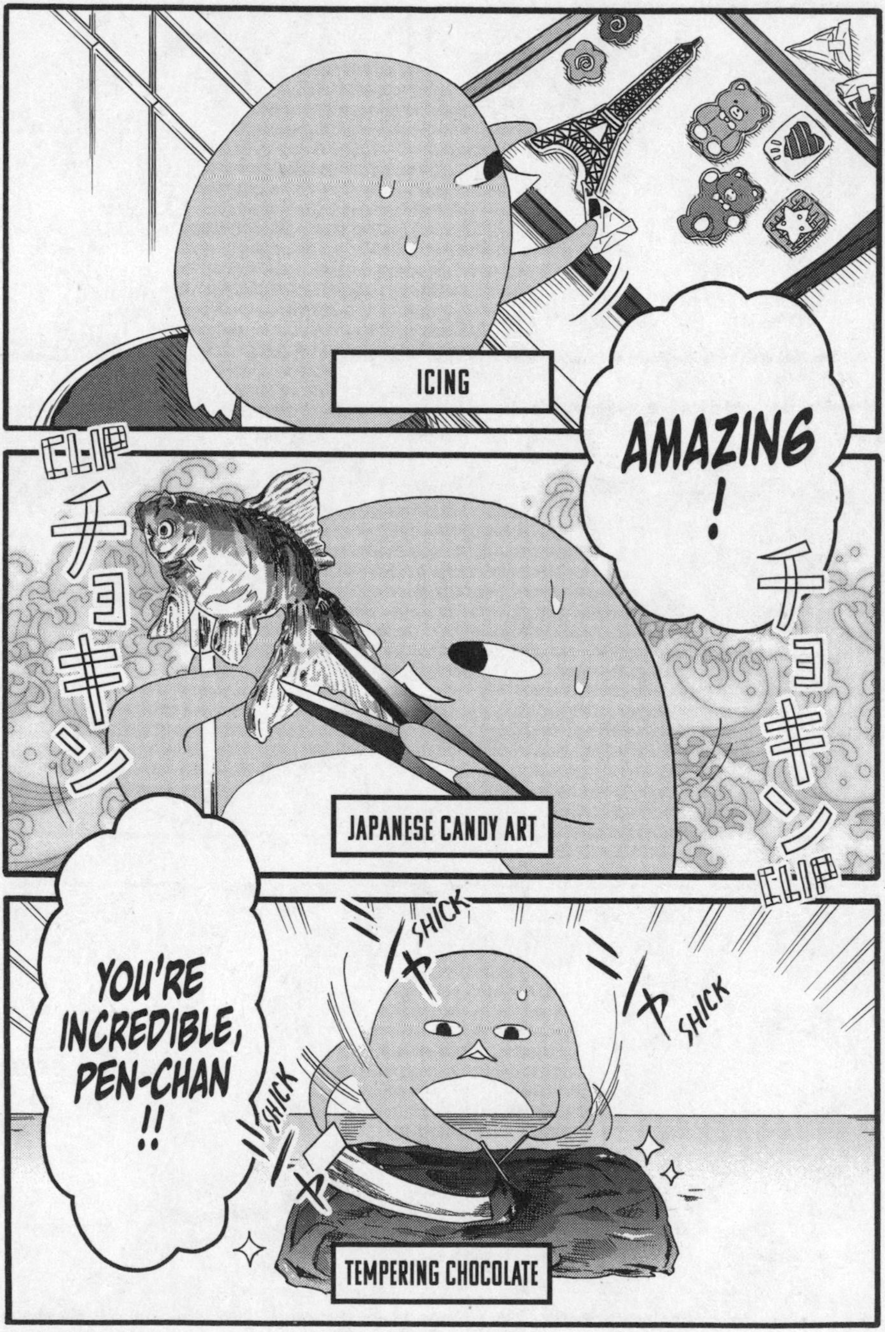
ICING
AMAZING!
チョキン CLIP
チョキン CLIP
JAPANESE CANDY ART
SHICK
SHICK
YOU'RE INCREDIBLE, PEN-CHAN!!
SHICK
TEMPERING CHOCOLATE

TEMPERING CHOCOLATE: A process that makes chocolate smooth and glossy.

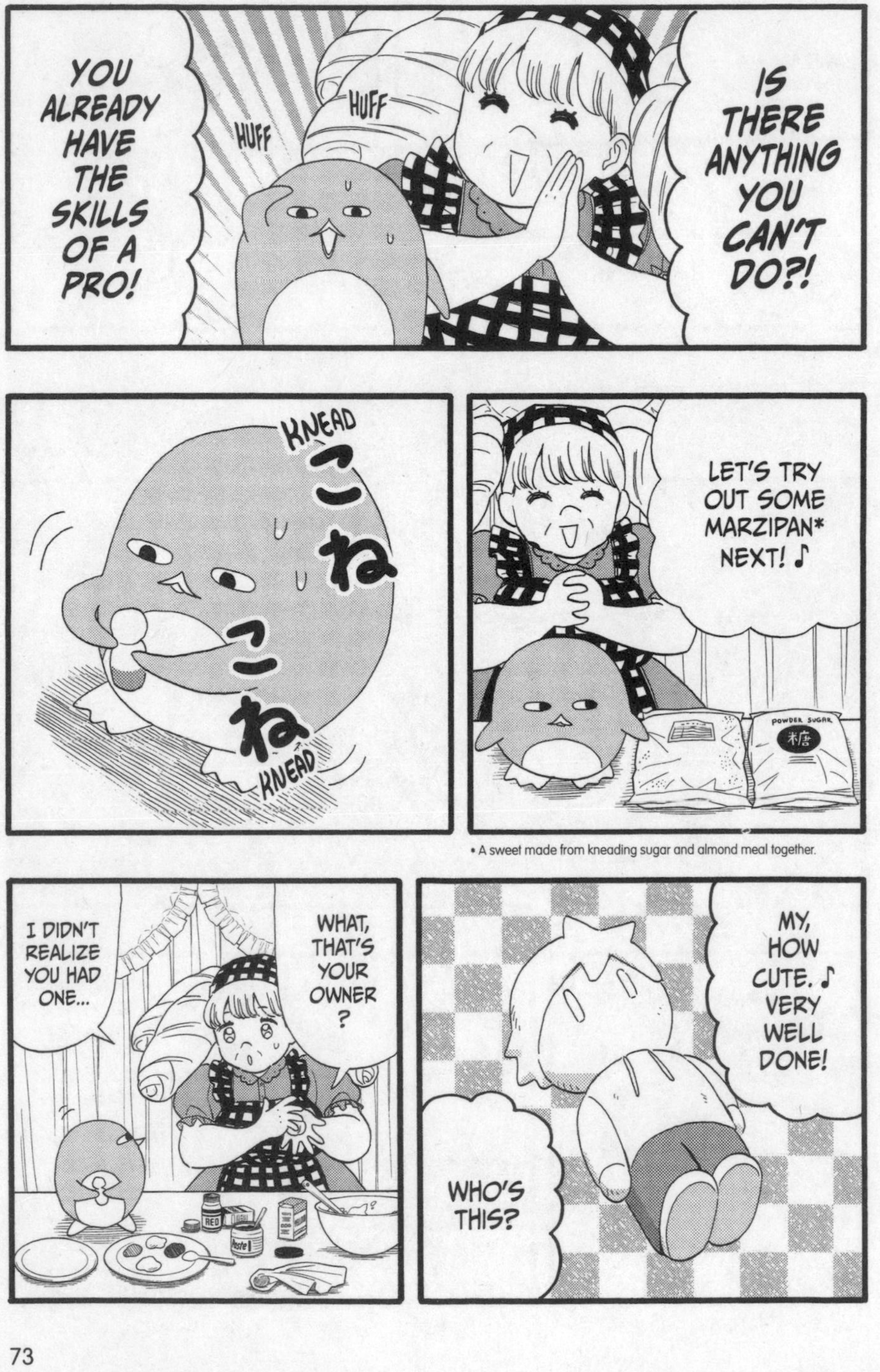
IS THERE ANYTHING YOU CAN'T DO?!
HUFF
HUFF
YOU ALREADY HAVE THE SKILLS OF A PRO!
LET'S TRY OUT SOME MARZIPAN* NEXT! ♪
POWDER SUGAR
糖
KNEAD
こね
こね
KNEAD
MY, HOW CUTE. ♪ VERY WELL DONE!
WHO'S THIS?
WHAT, THAT'S YOUR OWNER?
I DIDN'T REALIZE YOU HAD ONE...
RED

• A sweet made from kneading sugar and almond meal together.

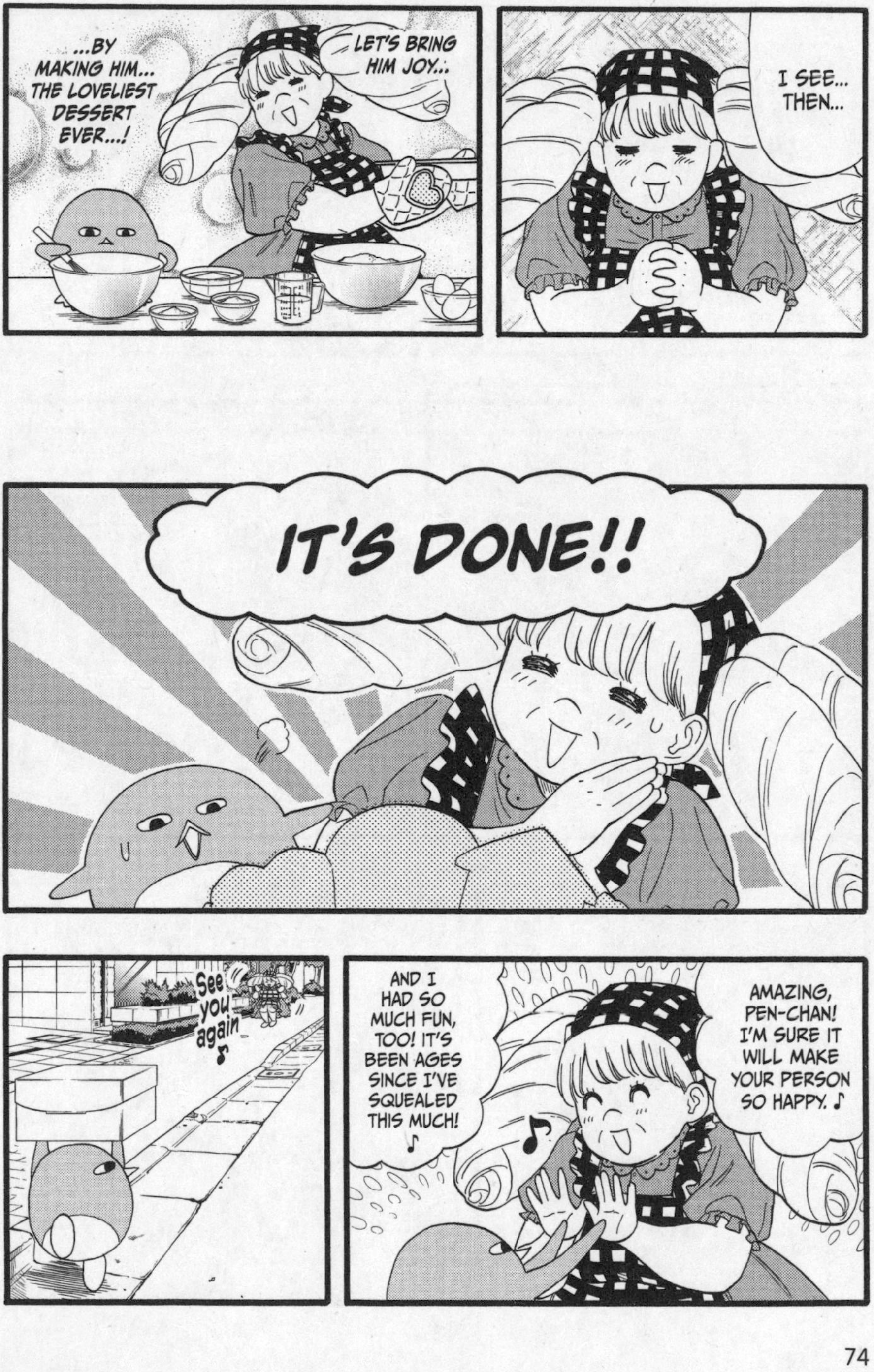
I SEE... THEN...
LET'S BRING HIM JOY...
...BY MAKING HIM... THE LOVELIEST DESSERT EVER...!
IT'S DONE!!
AMAZING, PEN-CHAN! I'M SURE IT WILL MAKE YOUR PERSON SO HAPPY. ♪
AND I HAD SO MUCH FUN, TOO! IT'S BEEN AGES SINCE I'VE SQUEALED THIS MUCH! ♪
See you again ♪

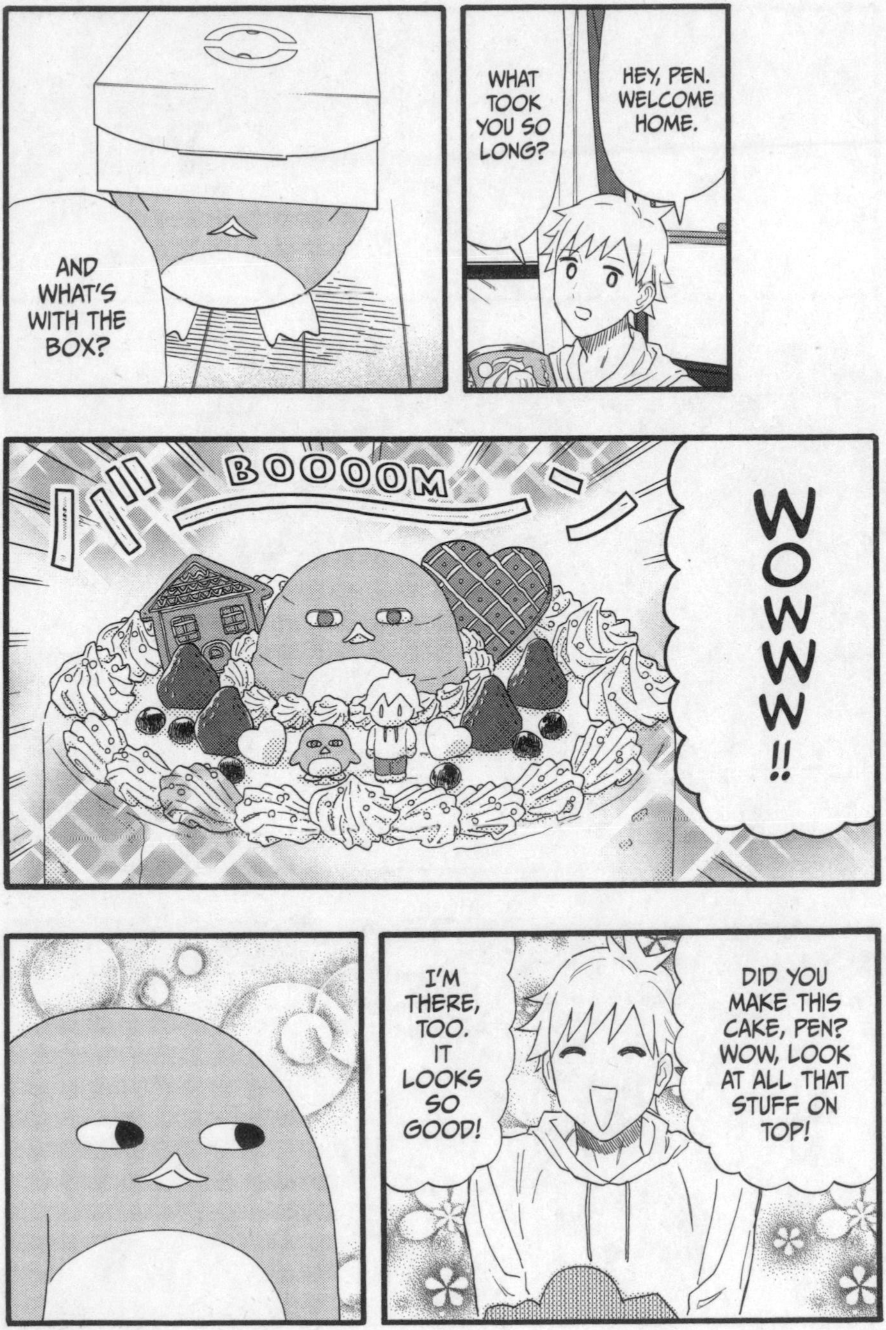
HEY, PEN. WELCOME HOME.
WHAT TOOK YOU SO LONG?
AND WHAT'S WITH THE BOX?
WOWWW!!
BOOOOM
DID YOU MAKE THIS CAKE, PEN? WOW, LOOK AT ALL THAT STUFF ON TOP!
I'M THERE, TOO. IT LOOKS SO GOOD!

I SHOULD EAT IT WHILE IT'S FRESH.
SHRIP
DON'T MIND IF I DO.
...
RUB...
SQUEAL SQUEAL
キャッキャッ
YUUUM!

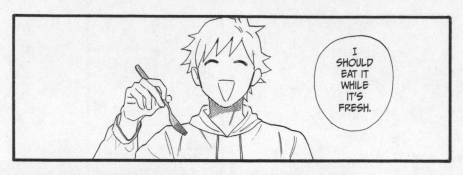

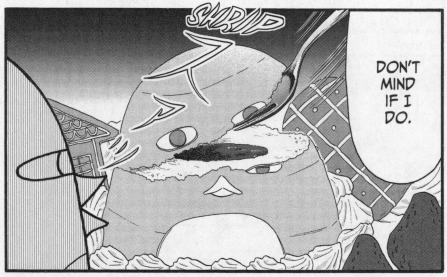

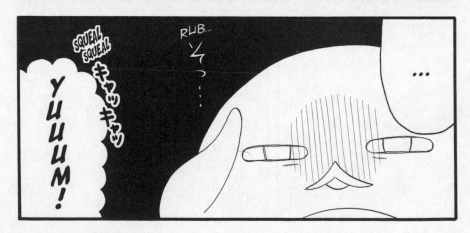

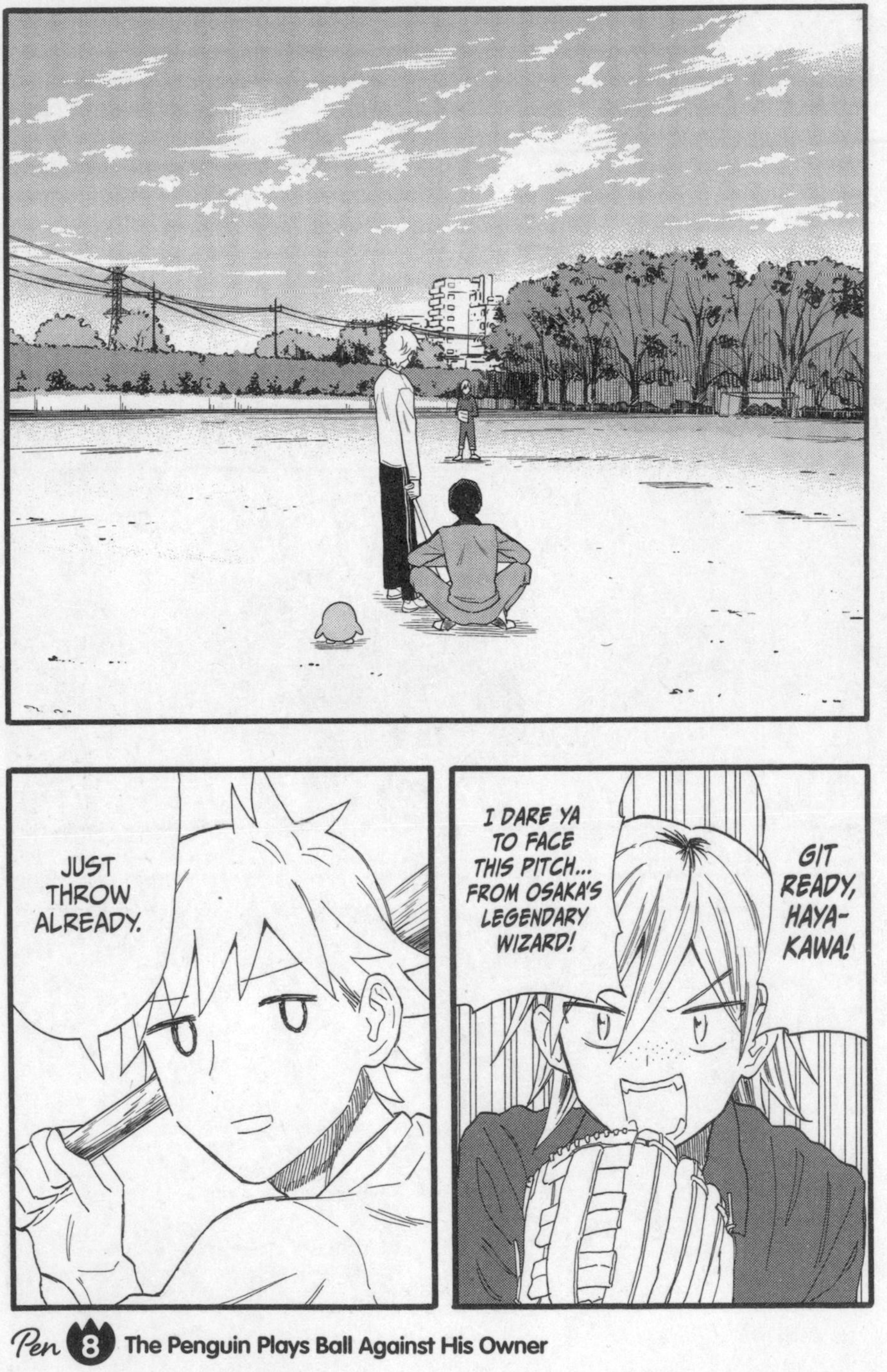
GIT READY, HAYA-KAWA!
I DARE YA TO FACE THIS PITCH... FROM OSAKA'S LEGENDARY WIZARD!
JUST THROW ALREADY.

Pen 8 The Penguin Plays Ball Against His Owner

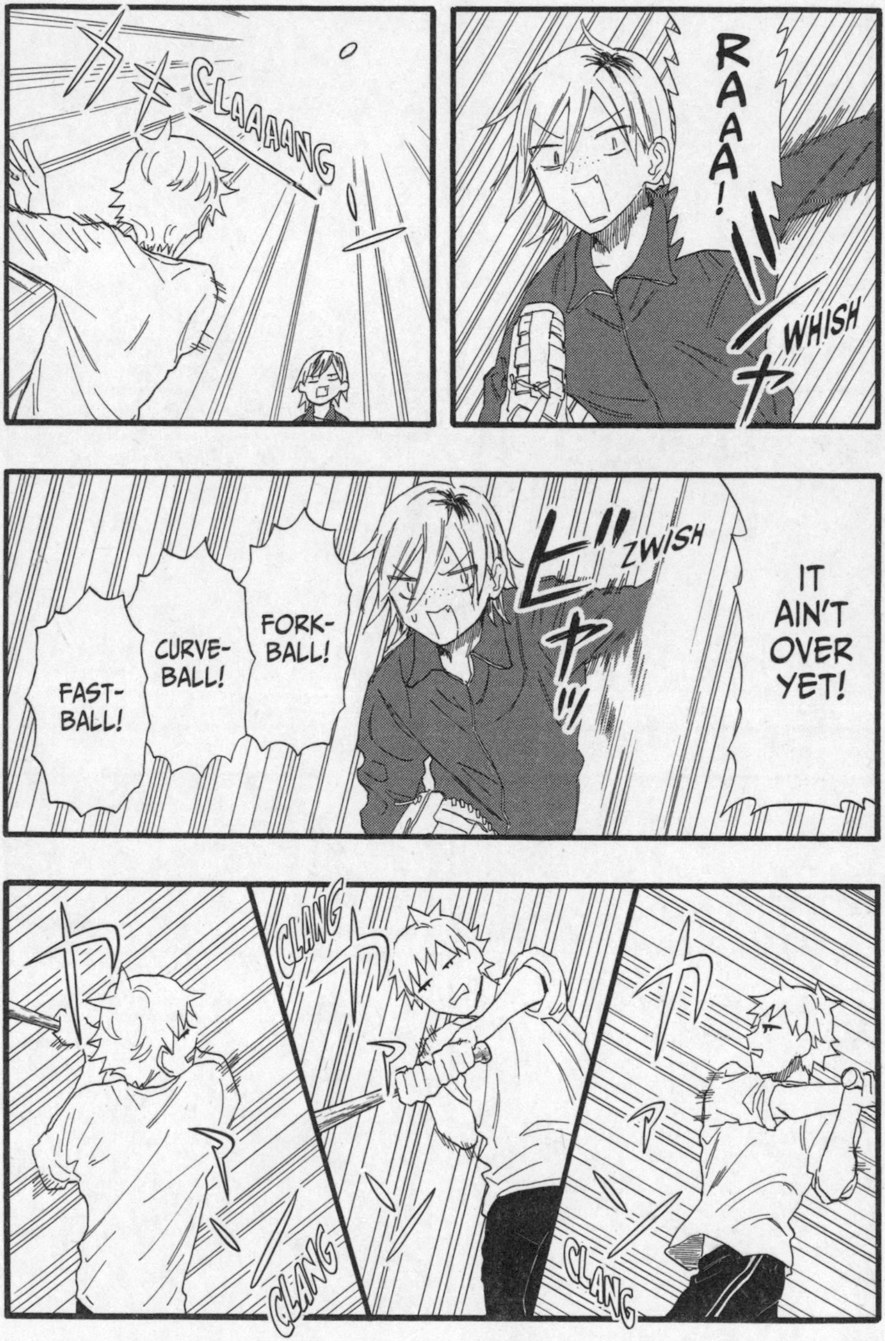
RAAA!
WHISH
CLAAAANG
IT AIN'T OVER YET!
ZWISH
FORK-BALL!
CURVE-BALL!
FAST-BALL!
CLANG
CLANG
CLANG

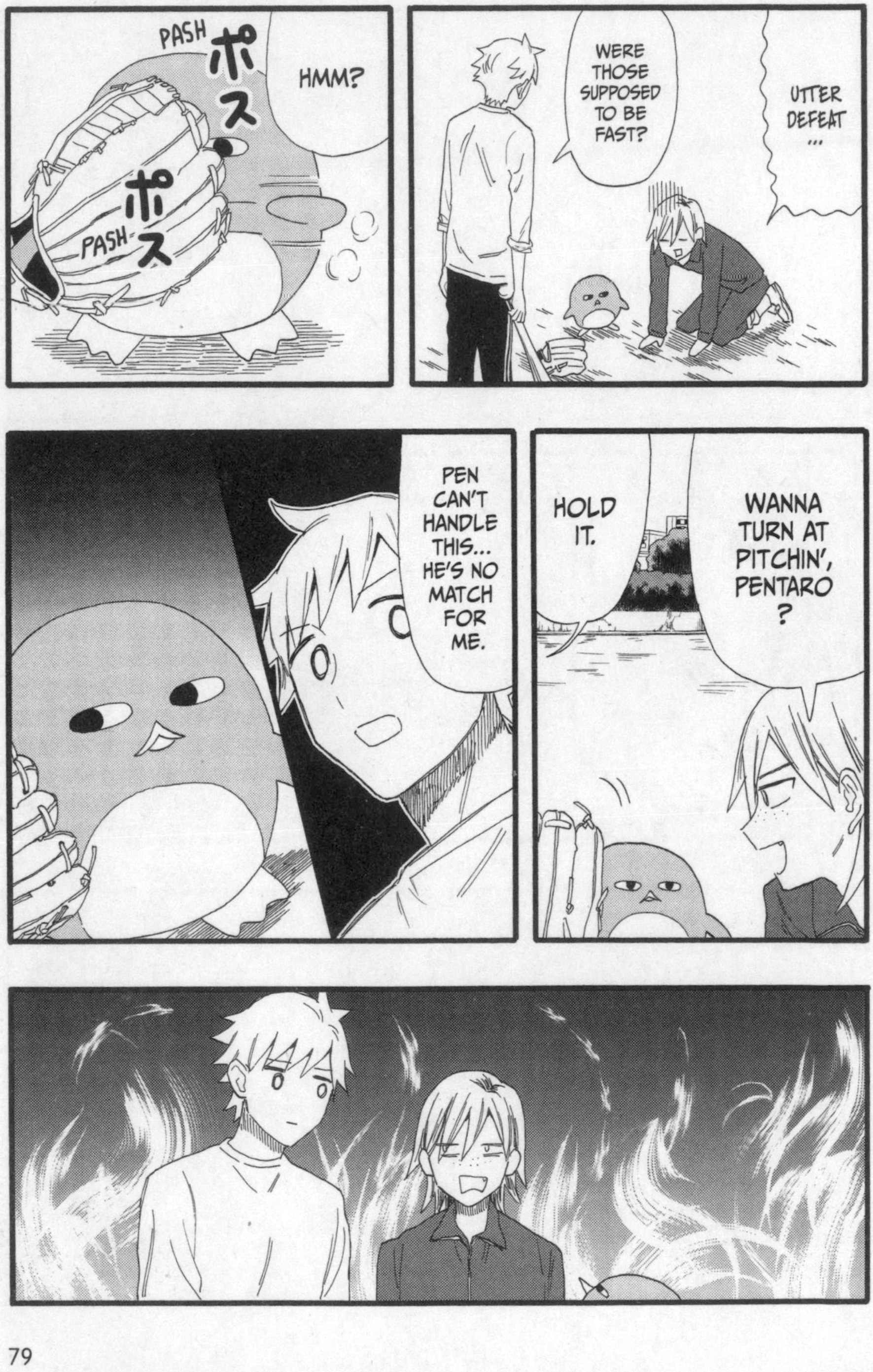
UTTER DEFEAT ...
WERE THOSE SUPPOSED TO BE FAST?
HMM?
PASH
ポス
PASH
ポス
WANNA TURN AT PITCHIN', PENTARO?
HOLD IT.
PEN CAN'T HANDLE THIS... HE'S NO MATCH FOR ME.

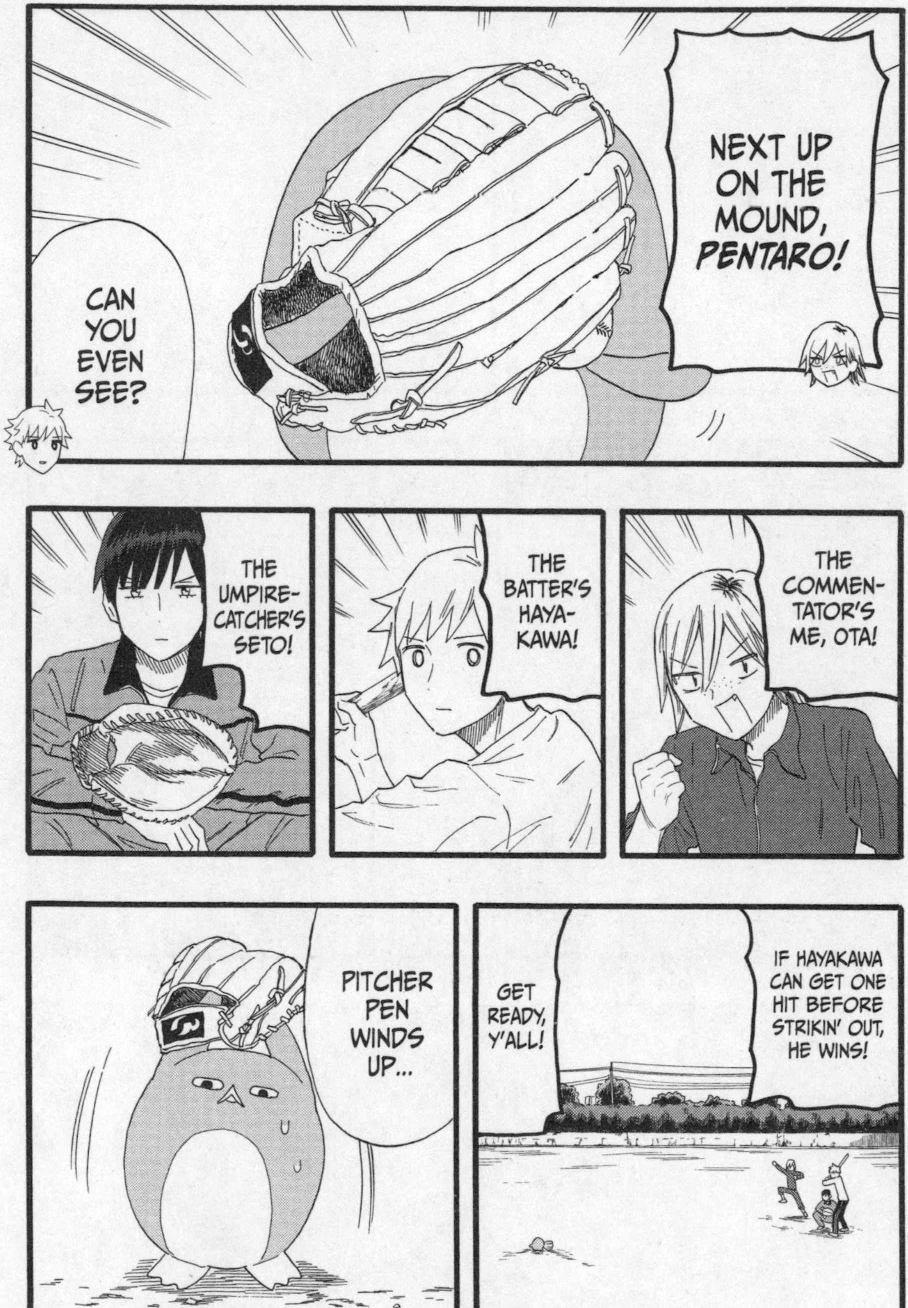
NEXT UP ON THE MOUND, PENTARO!
CAN YOU EVEN SEE?
THE COMMENTATOR'S ME, OTA!
THE BATTER'S HAYAKAWA!
THE UMPIRE-CATCHER'S SETO!
IF HAYAKAWA CAN GET ONE HIT BEFORE STRIKIN' OUT, HE WINS!
GET READY, Y'ALL!
PITCHER PEN WINDS UP...

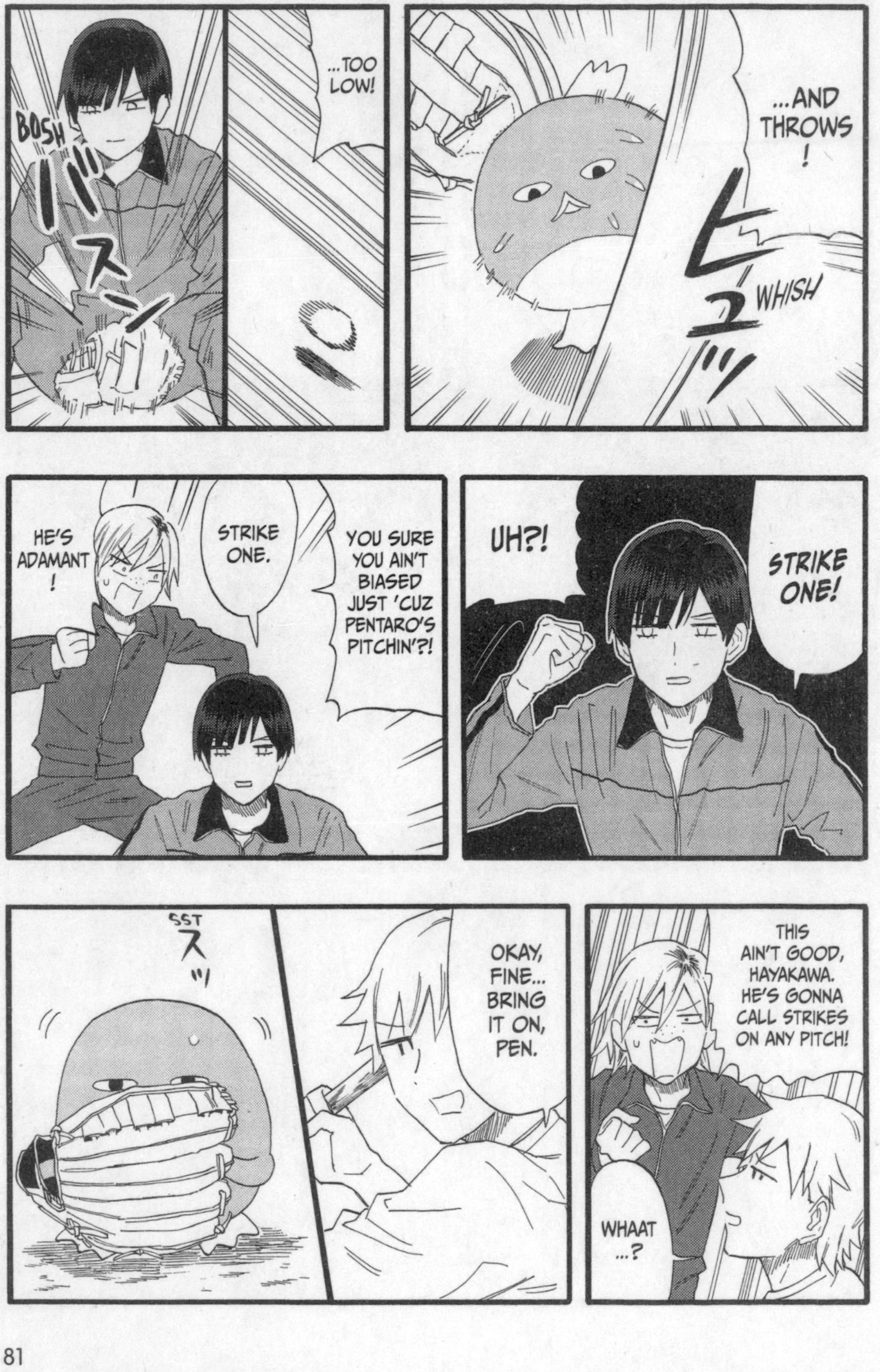
...AND THROWS!
WHISH
...TOO LOW!
BOSH
STRIKE ONE!
UH?!
YOU SURE YOU AIN'T BIASED JUST 'CUZ PENTARO'S PITCHIN'?!
STRIKE ONE.
HE'S ADAMANT!
THIS AIN'T GOOD, HAYAKAWA. HE'S GONNA CALL STRIKES ON ANY PITCH!
WHAAT ...?
OKAY, FINE... BRING IT ON, PEN.
SST

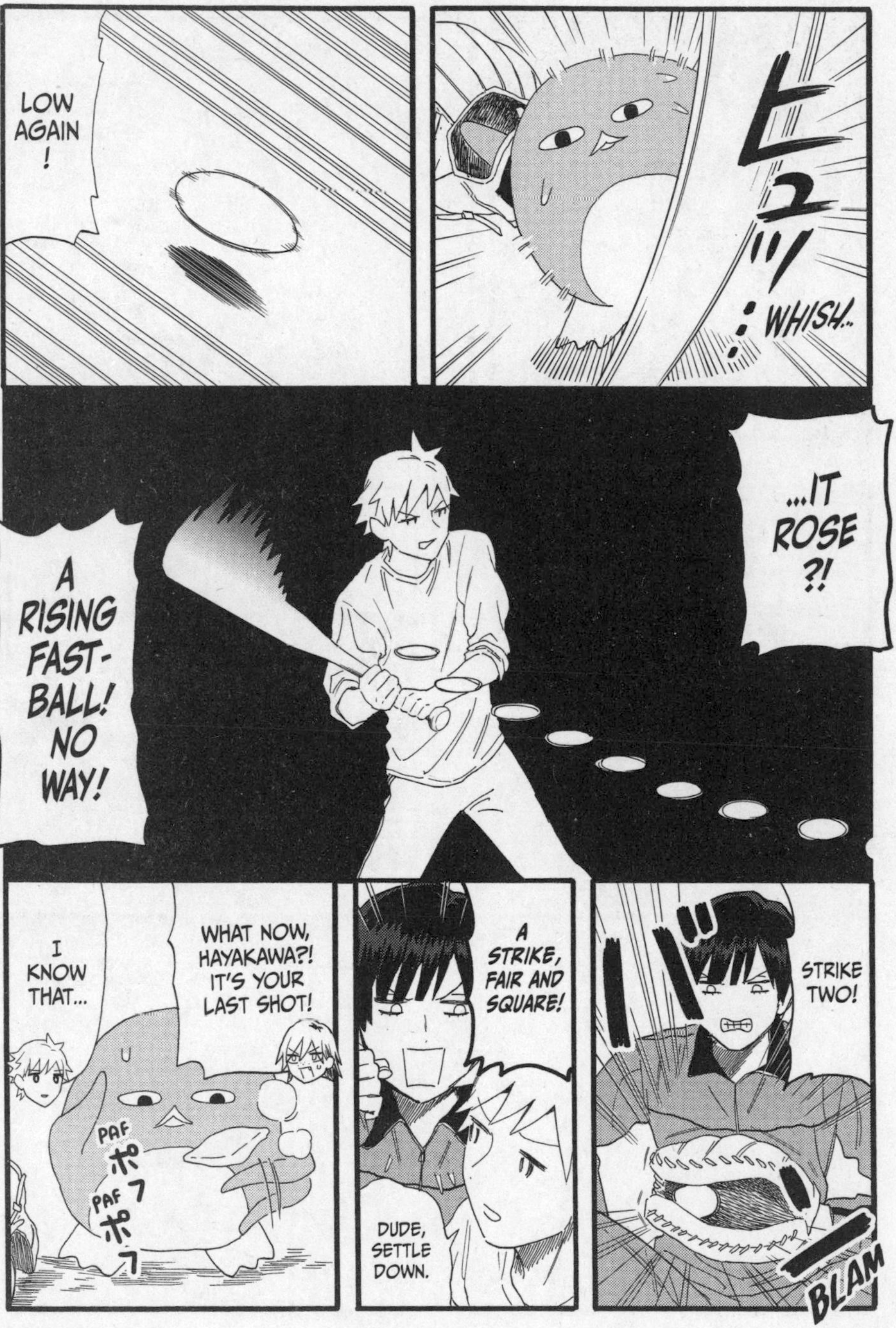
ヒュッ…
WHISH..
LOW AGAIN!
...IT ROSE?!
A RISING FAST-BALL! NO WAY!
バ
BLAM
STRIKE TWO!
A STRIKE, FAIR AND SQUARE!
DUDE, SETTLE DOWN.
WHAT NOW, HAYAKAWA?! IT'S YOUR LAST SHOT!
I KNOW THAT...
PAF
ポフ
PAF
ポフ

PEN, I'VE FIGURED OUT YOUR PITCHES.
I'M HITTING THE NEXT ONE FOR SURE!
FWOO
SST.
ZWISH

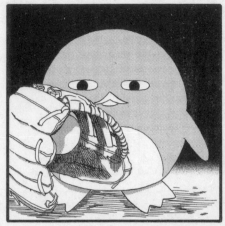

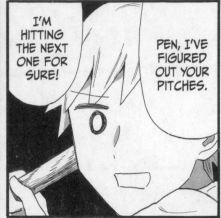

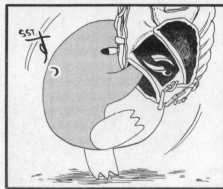

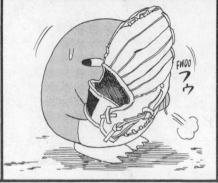

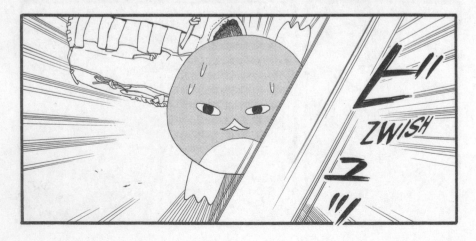

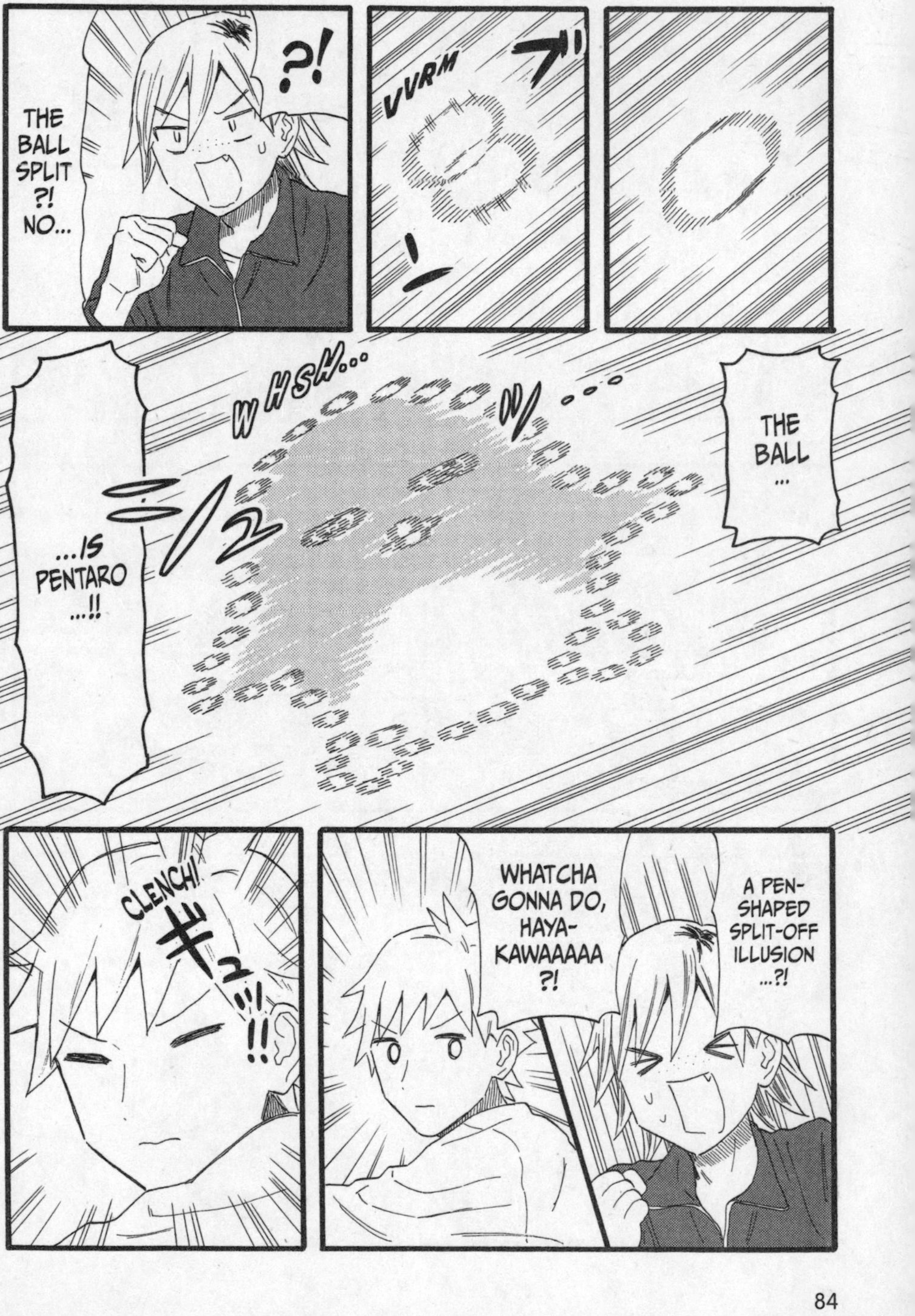
VVRM
?!
THE BALL SPLIT ?! NO...
THE BALL ...
WHSH...
...IS PENTARO ...!!
A PEN-SHAPED SPLIT-OFF ILLUSION ...?!
WHATCHA GONNA DO, HAYA-KAWAAAAAA ?!
CLENCH!

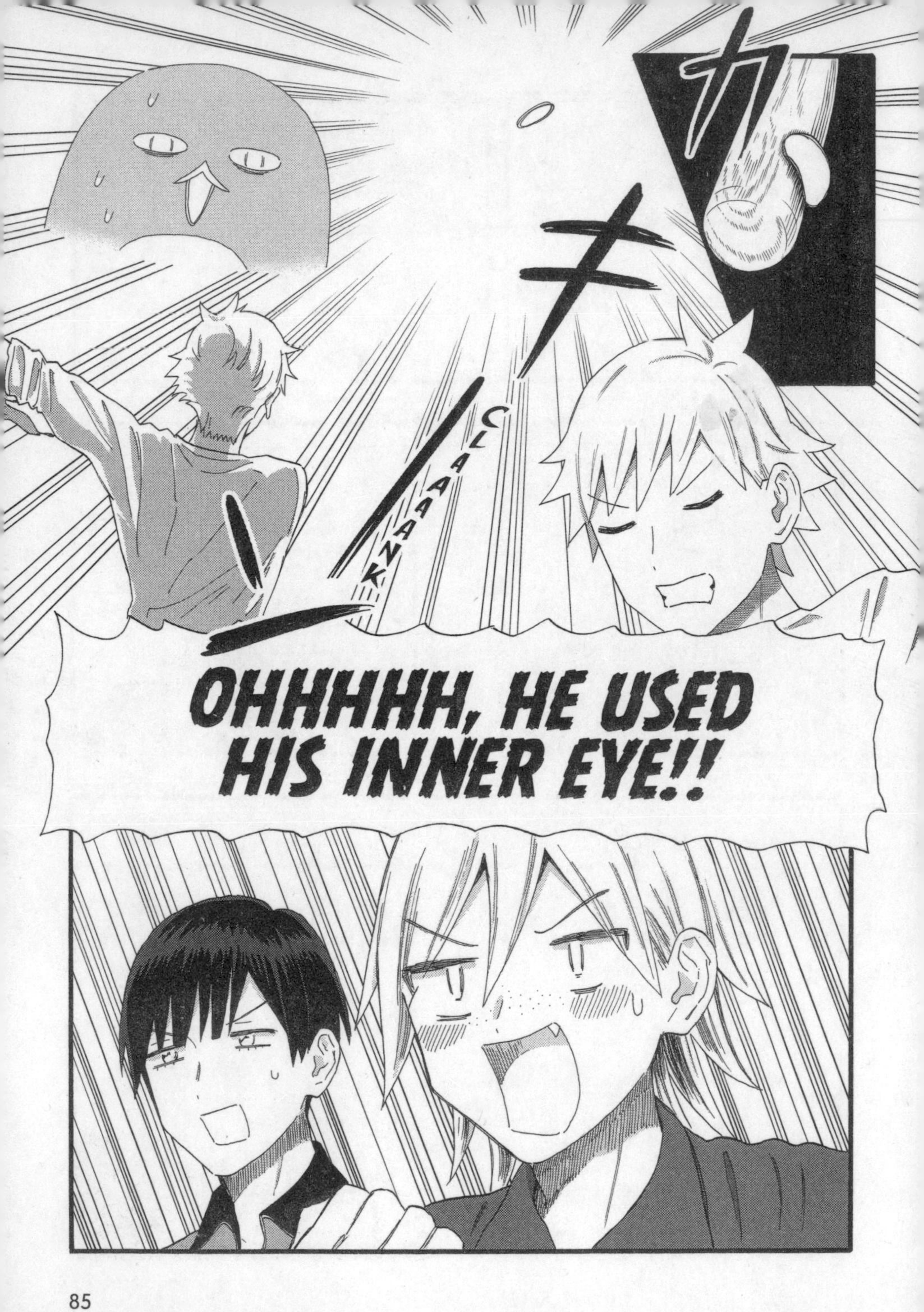
カ
キ
CLAAAANK
OHHHHH, HE USED HIS INNER EYE!!

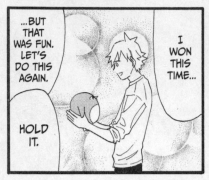

PEN.
I WON THIS TIME...
...BUT THAT WAS FUN. LET'S DO THIS AGAIN.
HOLD IT.
HAYA-KAWA... DIDN'T YA NOTICE?
HUH?
THIS WHOLE TIME...
PENTARO WAS PITCHIN' WITH MY LEFT-HANDED GLOVE...
I'M POOPED.
LET'S GET FOOD. PEN-CHAN'S PORTION'S ON ME, OF COURSE.
...WHEN HE'S ACTUALLY RIGHT-FLIPPERED ...!!
IS A LEFTY ONLY WHEN IT COMES TO...PITCHING!

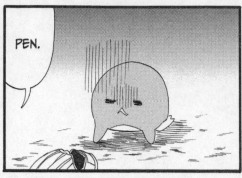

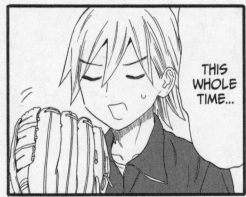

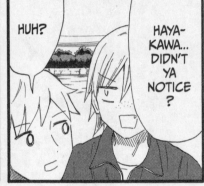

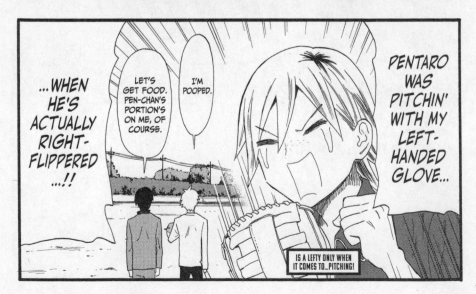

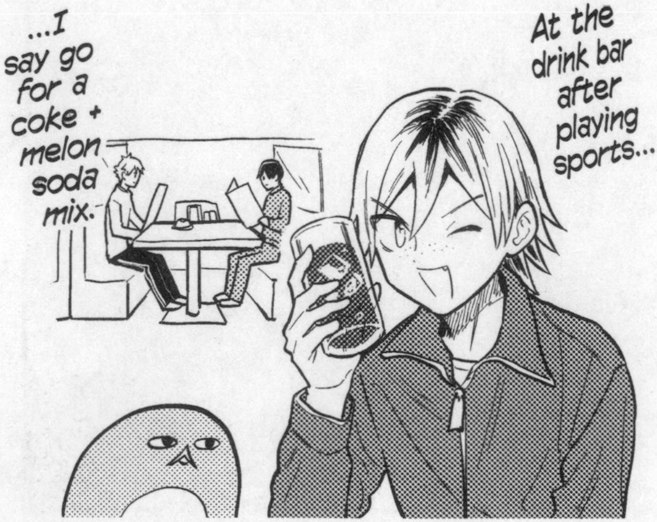
At the drink bar after playing sports...
...I say go for a coke + melon soda mix.

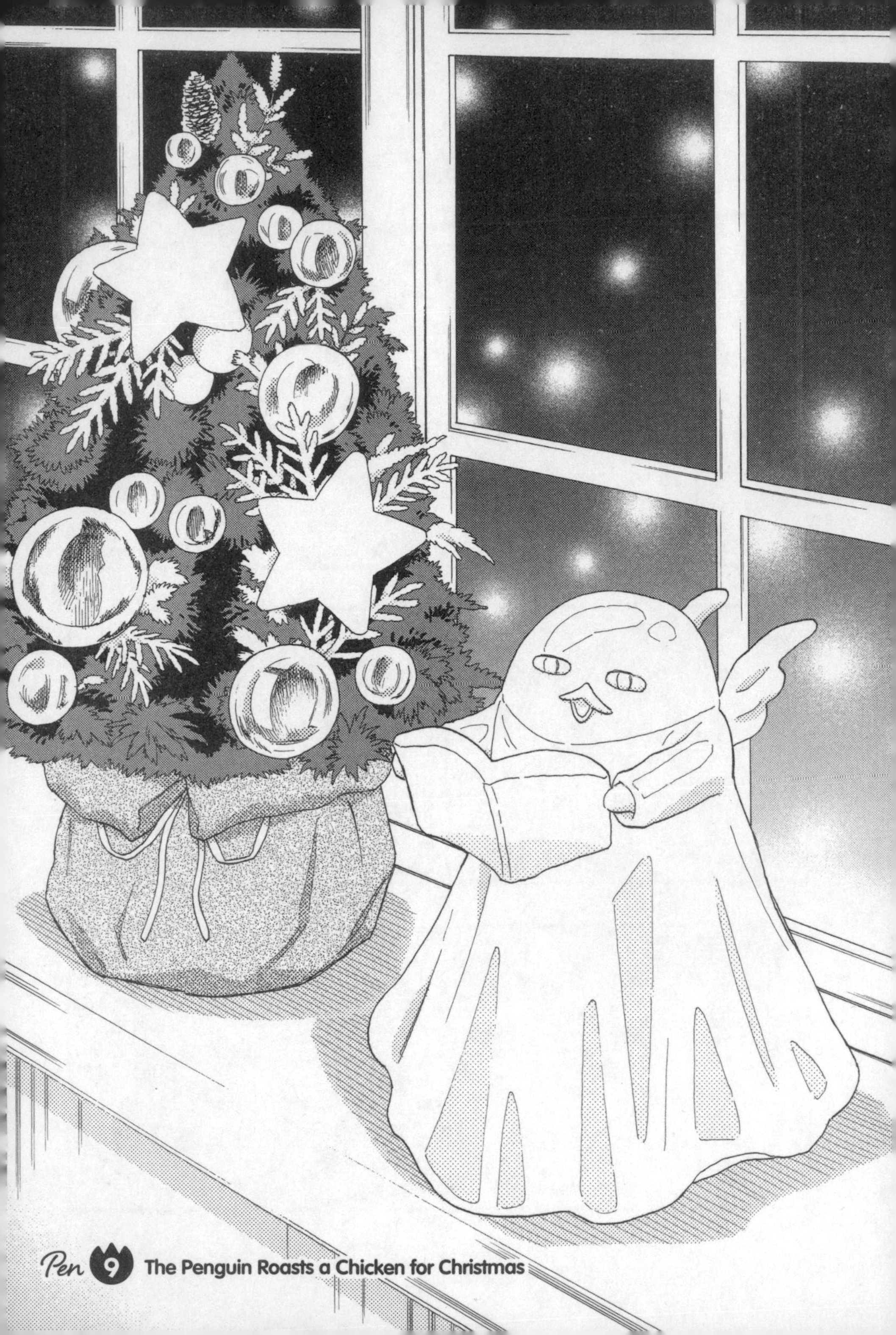

Pen 9 The Penguin Roasts a Chicken for Christmas

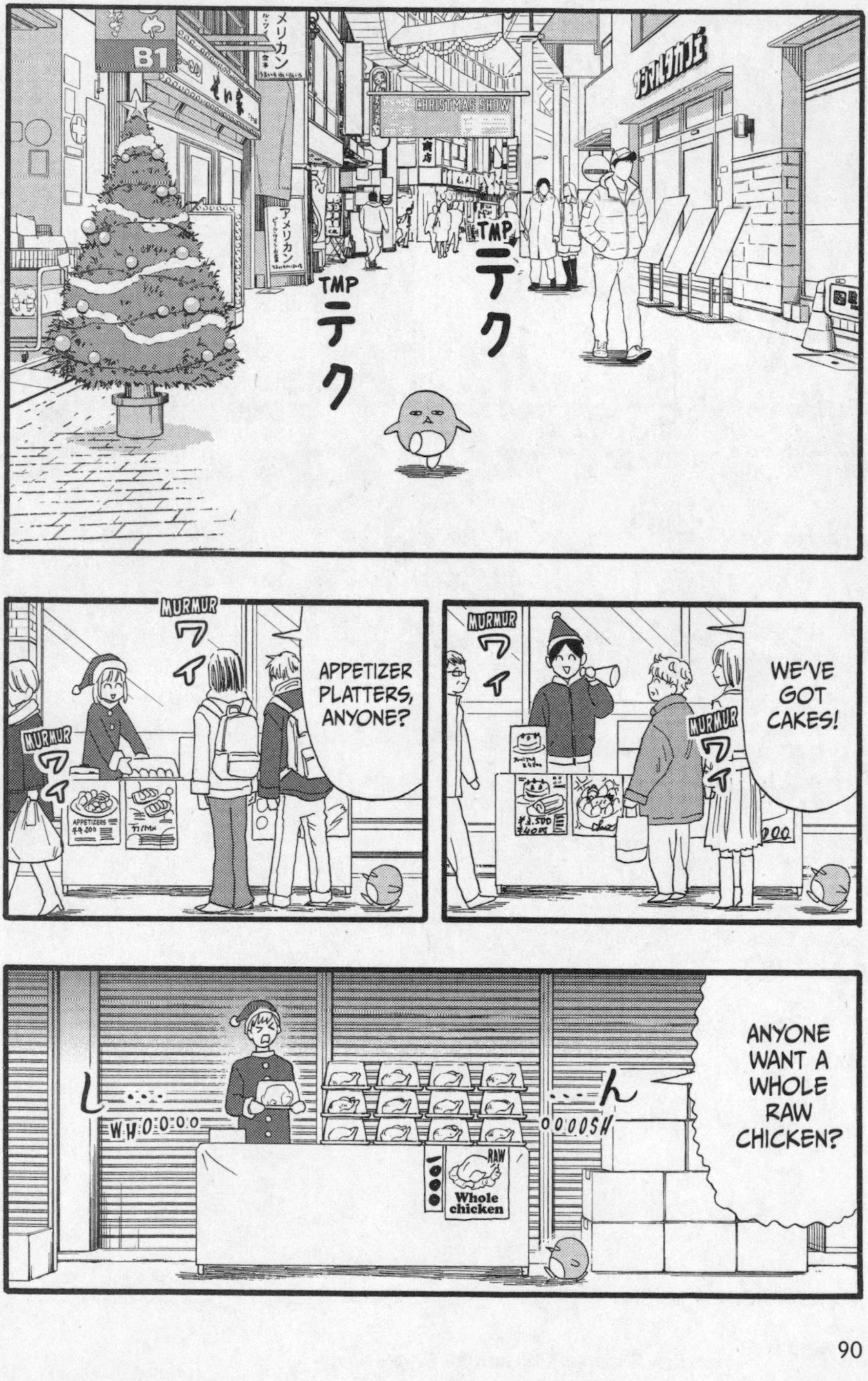

B1
CHRISTMAS SHOW
メリカン
アメリカン
TMP
テク
TMP
テク
MURMUR
ワイ
WE'VE GOT CAKES!
MURMUR
ワイ
MURMUR
ワイ
APPETIZER PLATTERS, ANYONE?
MURMUR
ワイ
APPETIZERS
ANYONE WANT A WHOLE RAW CHICKEN?
…ん
OOOOSH
RAW
Whole chicken
し…
WHOOOO

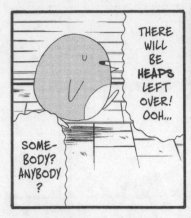

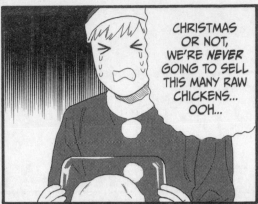

CHRISTMAS OR NOT, WE'RE NEVER GOING TO SELL THIS MANY RAW CHICKENS... OOH...
THERE WILL BE HEAPS LEFT OVER! OOH...
SOME-BODY? ANYBODY?
IT'S CHRISTMAS TODAY, SO EVERYONE'S COMING OVER TONIGHT.
"Everyone" (two people)
DOES ANYONE WANT A WHOLE CHICKEN ...?

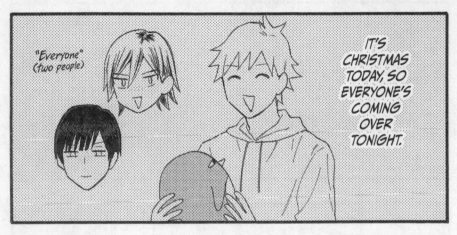

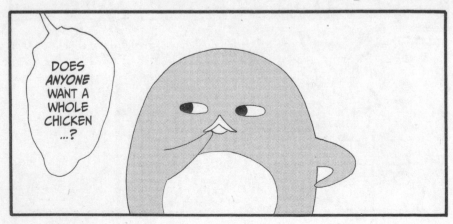

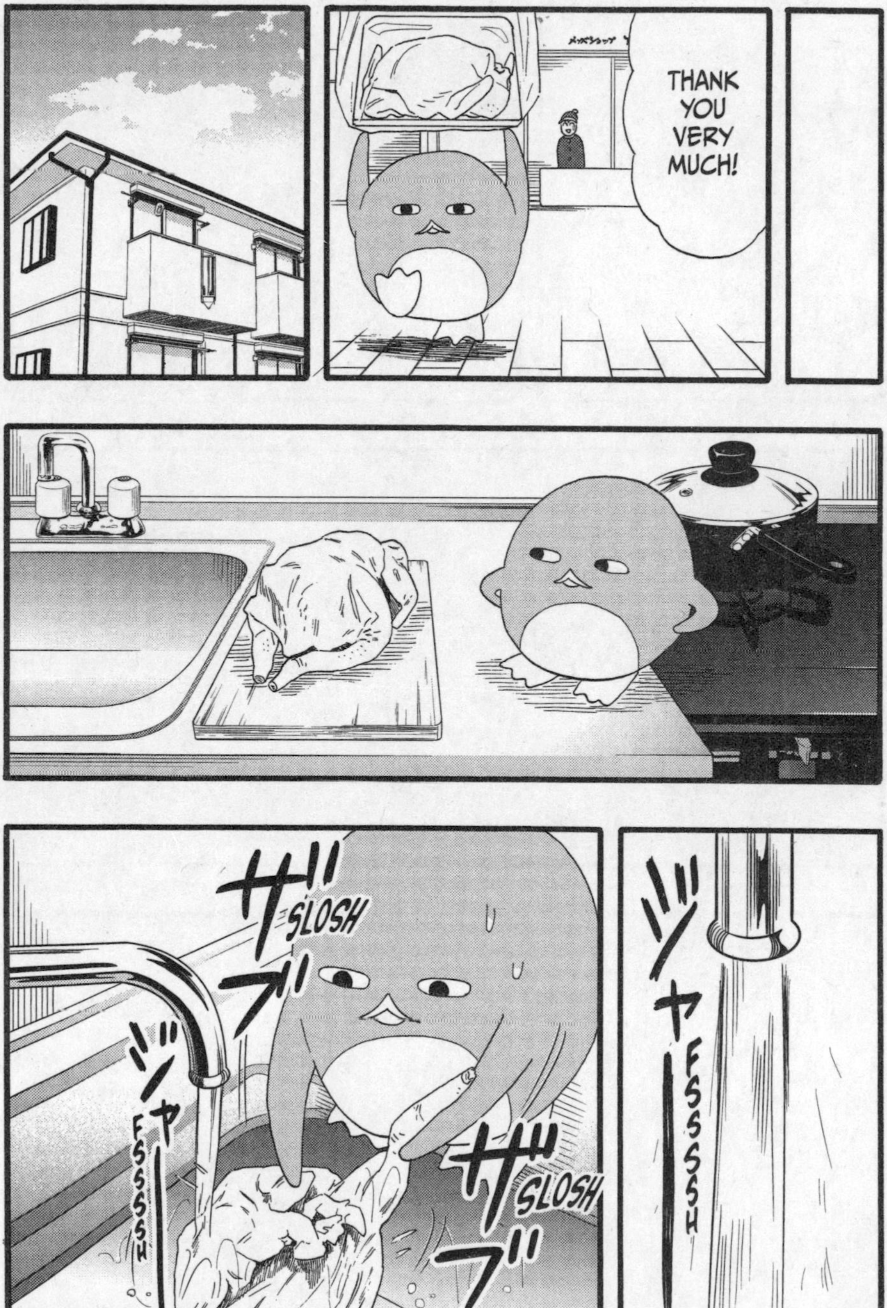
THANK YOU VERY MUCH!
ジャー
FSSSSH
ザブ
SLOSH
ジャー
FSSSSH
ザブ
SLOSH

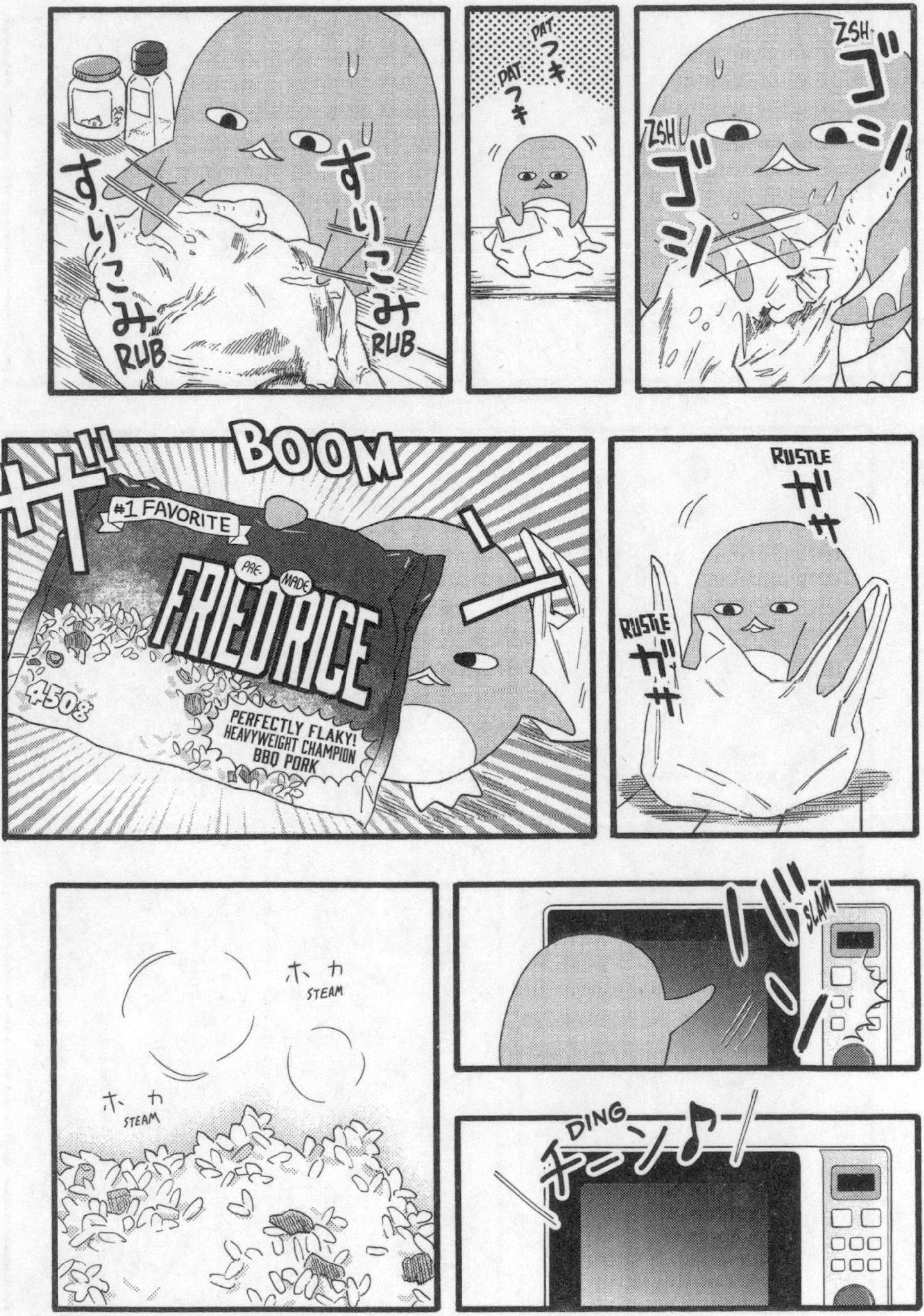
ZSH
ゴシ
ZSH
ゴシ
PAT
フキ
PAT
フキ
すりこみ
RUB
すりこみ
RUB
RUSTLE
ガサ
RUSTLE
ガサ
BOOM
ザー
#1 FAVORITE
PRE-MADE
FRIED RICE
450g
PERFECTLY FLAKY!
HEAVYWEIGHT CHAMPION
BBQ PORK
SLAM
バン
DING
チーン♪
ホカ
STEAM
ホカ
STEAM

SST
スッ
STUFF
つめ
つめ
STUFF
SST
スッ
JAB
ブッ
HEAP
のせ
HEAP
のせ
PLAP
ペタ
ペタ
PLAP
Olive Oil
SST
すっ
Aluminum Foil
Aluminum Foil

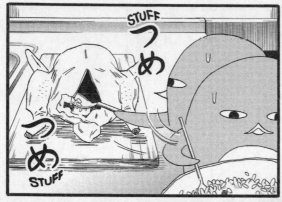

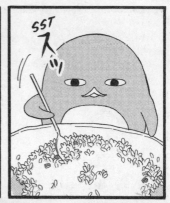

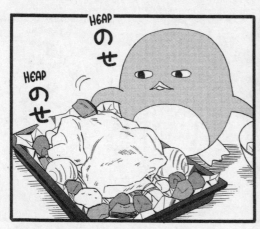

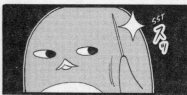

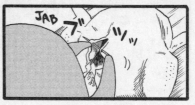

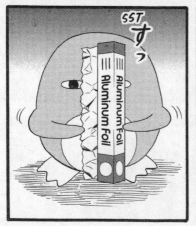

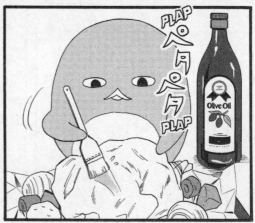

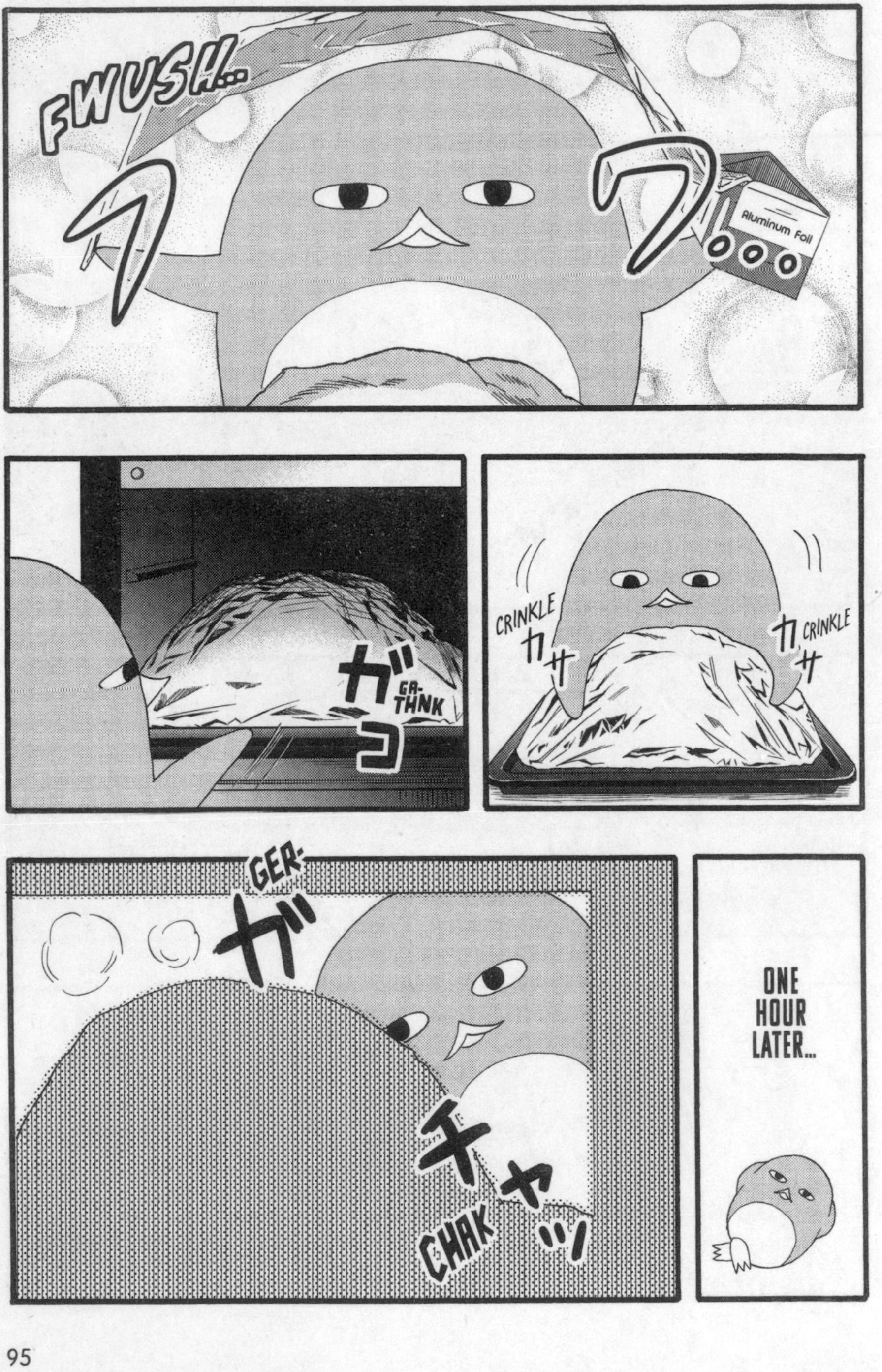
FWUSH...
フワ...
Aluminum Foil
CRINKLE
カサ
カサ
CRINKLE
ガコ
GA-THNK
ONE HOUR LATER...
ガ
GER-
チャッ
CHAK

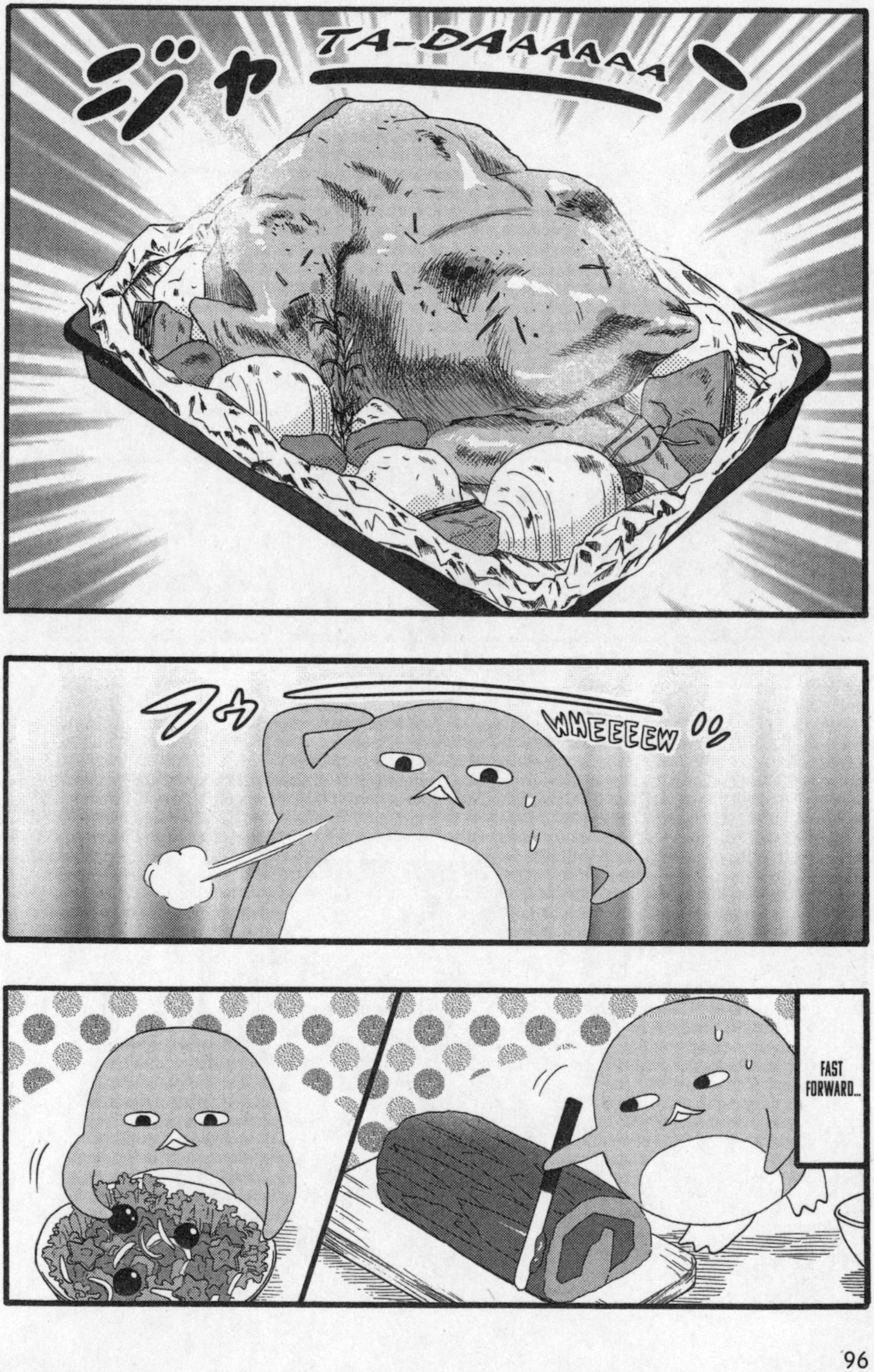
ジャーー
TA-DAAAAAA
フゥ
WHEEEEW
FAST FORWARD...

SPARKLE

SPARKLE

YOU MADE US DINNER, PEN?!

HUH ?!

CHATTER

CHATTER

I'M HOOOME!

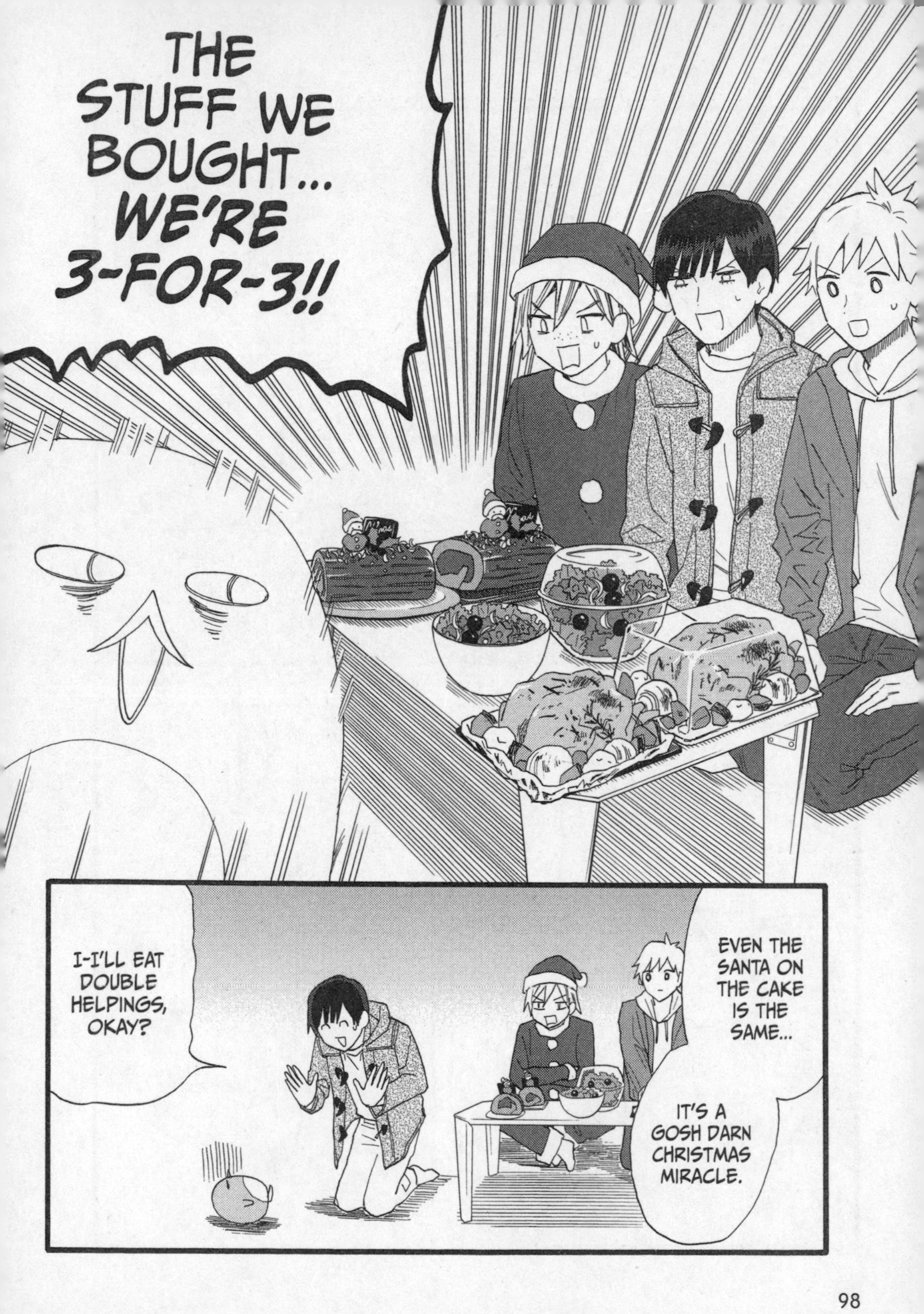
THE STUFF WE BOUGHT... WE'RE 3-FOR-3!!
EVEN THE SANTA ON THE CAKE IS THE SAME...
IT'S A GOSH DARN CHRISTMAS MIRACLE.
I-I'LL EAT DOUBLE HELPINGS, OKAY?

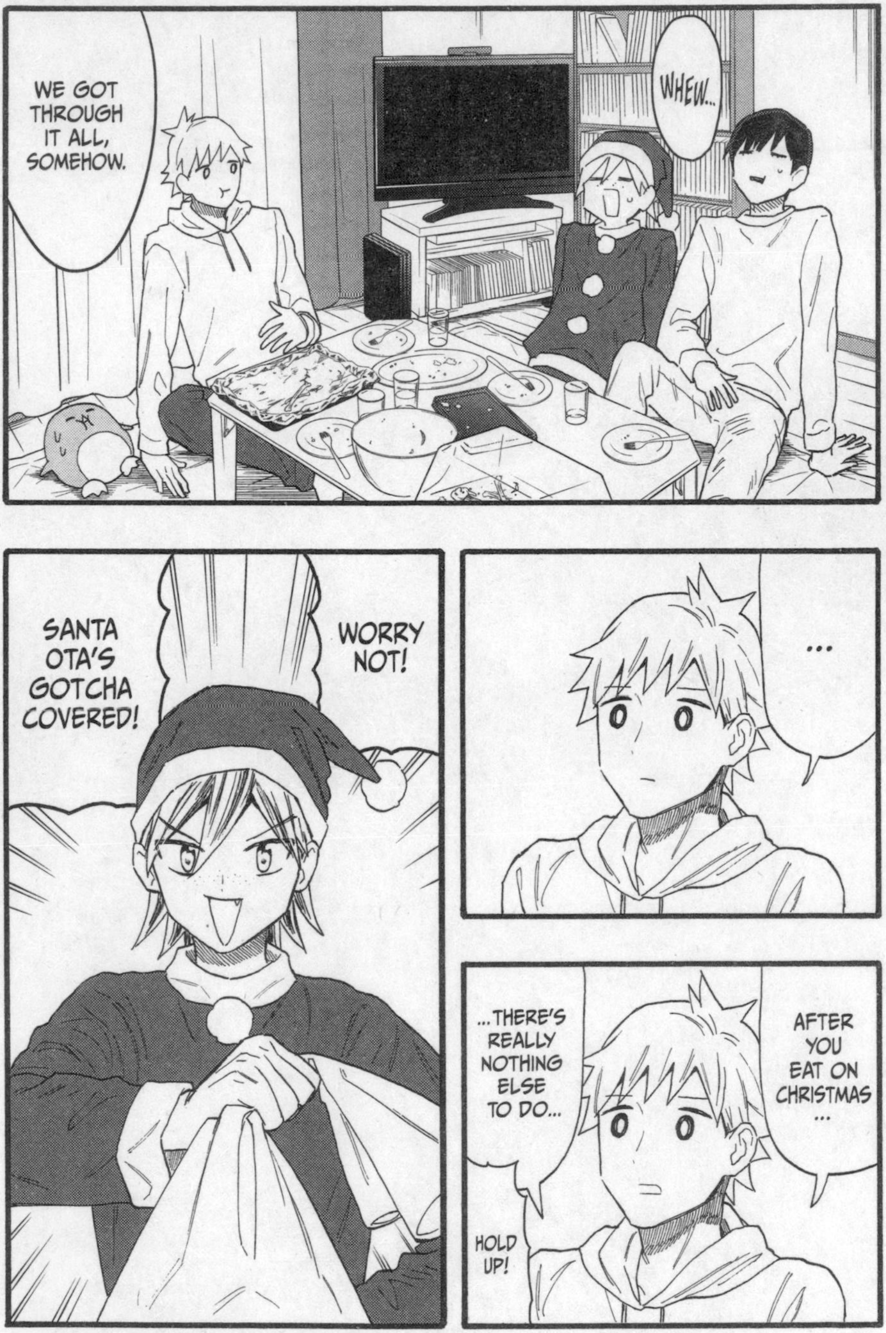
WHEW...
WE GOT THROUGH IT ALL, SOMEHOW.
...
AFTER YOU EAT ON CHRISTMAS ...
...THERE'S REALLY NOTHING ELSE TO DO...
HOLD UP!
WORRY NOT!
SANTA OTA'S GOTCHA COVERED!

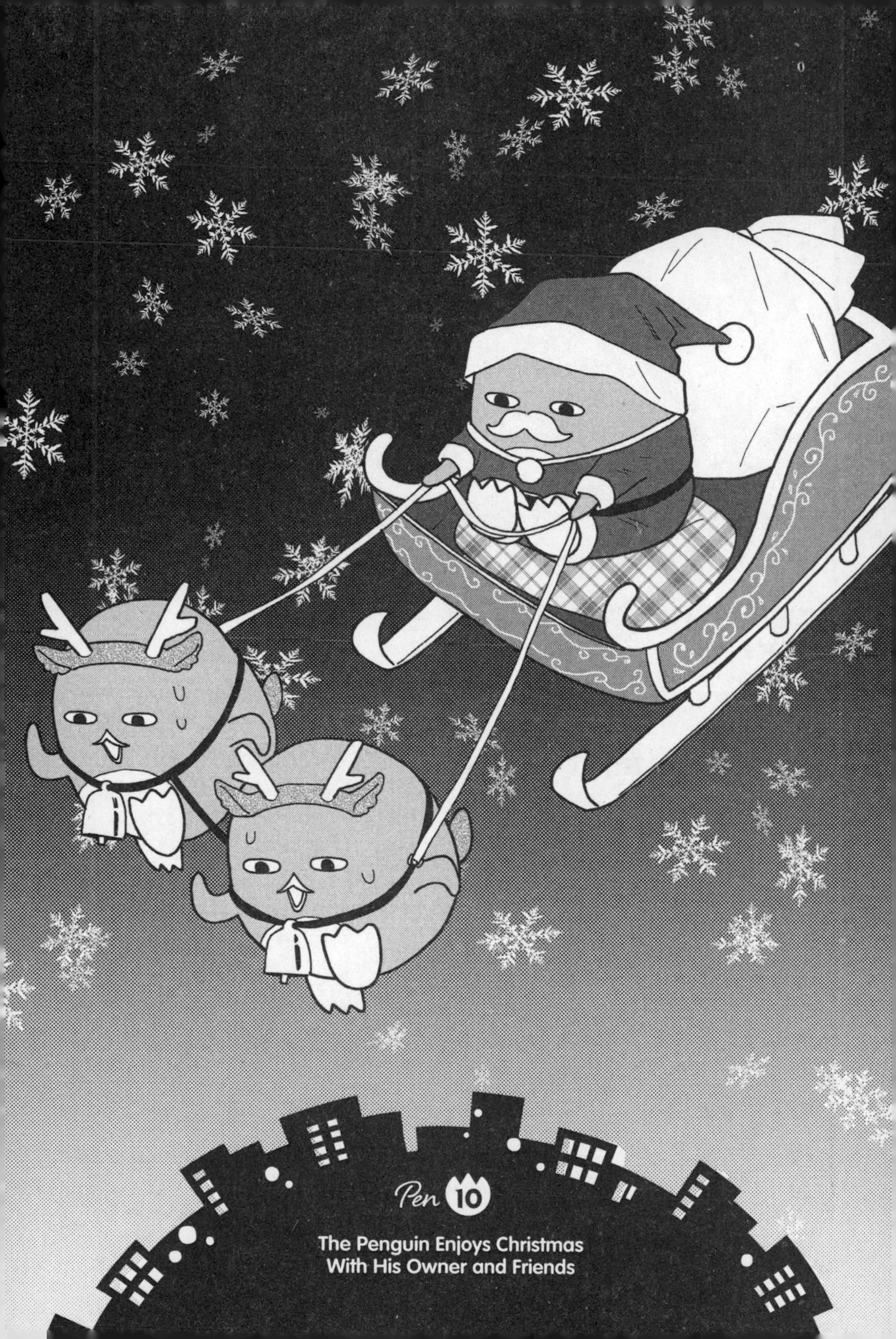
Pen 10
The Penguin Enjoys Christmas
With His Owner and Friends

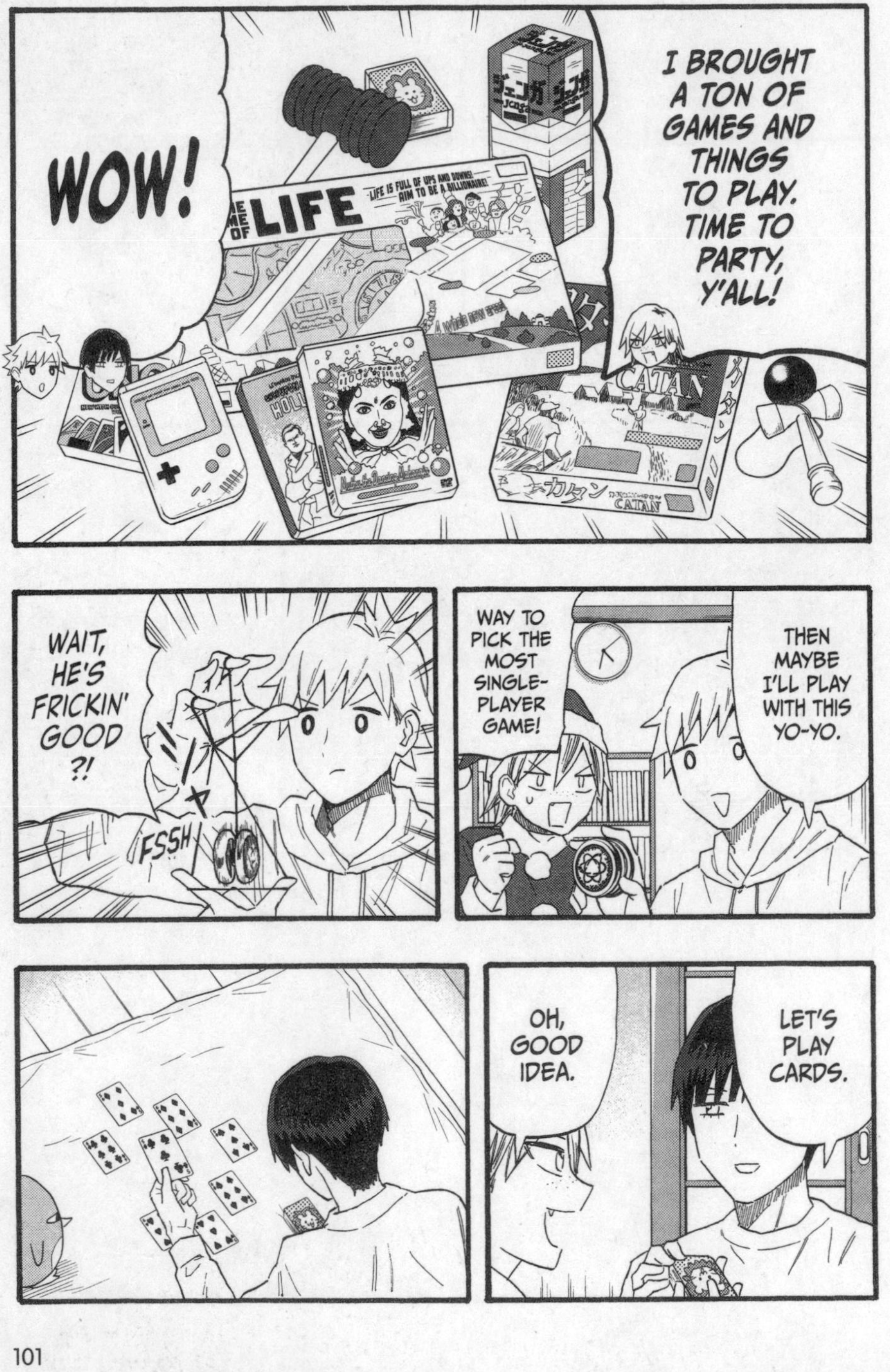
I BROUGHT A TON OF GAMES AND THINGS TO PLAY. TIME TO PARTY, Y'ALL!
WOW!
LIFE IS FULL OF UPS AND DOWNS! AIM TO BE A BILLIONAIRE!
CATAN
THEN MAYBE I'LL PLAY WITH THIS YO-YO.
WAY TO PICK THE MOST SINGLE-PLAYER GAME!
WAIT, HE'S FRICKIN' GOOD ?!
FSSH
LET'S PLAY CARDS.
OH, GOOD IDEA.

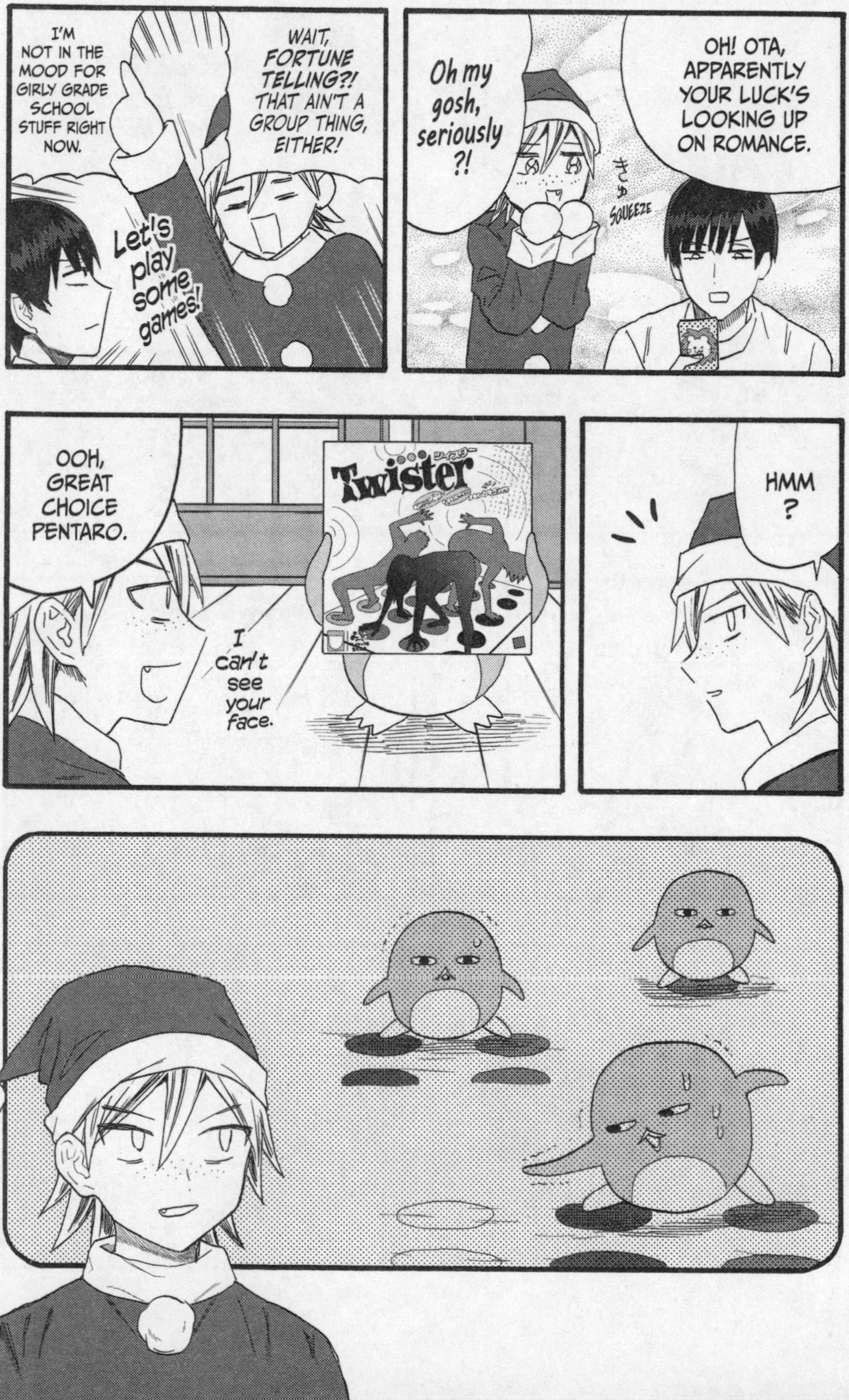
OH! OTA, APPARENTLY YOUR LUCK'S LOOKING UP ON ROMANCE.
きゅ
SQUEEZE
Oh my gosh, seriously?!
WAIT, FORTUNE TELLING?! THAT AIN'T A GROUP THING, EITHER!
I'M NOT IN THE MOOD FOR GIRLY GRADE SCHOOL STUFF RIGHT NOW.
Let's play some games!
HMM?
OOH, GREAT CHOICE PENTARO.
ツイスター
Twister
I can't see your face.

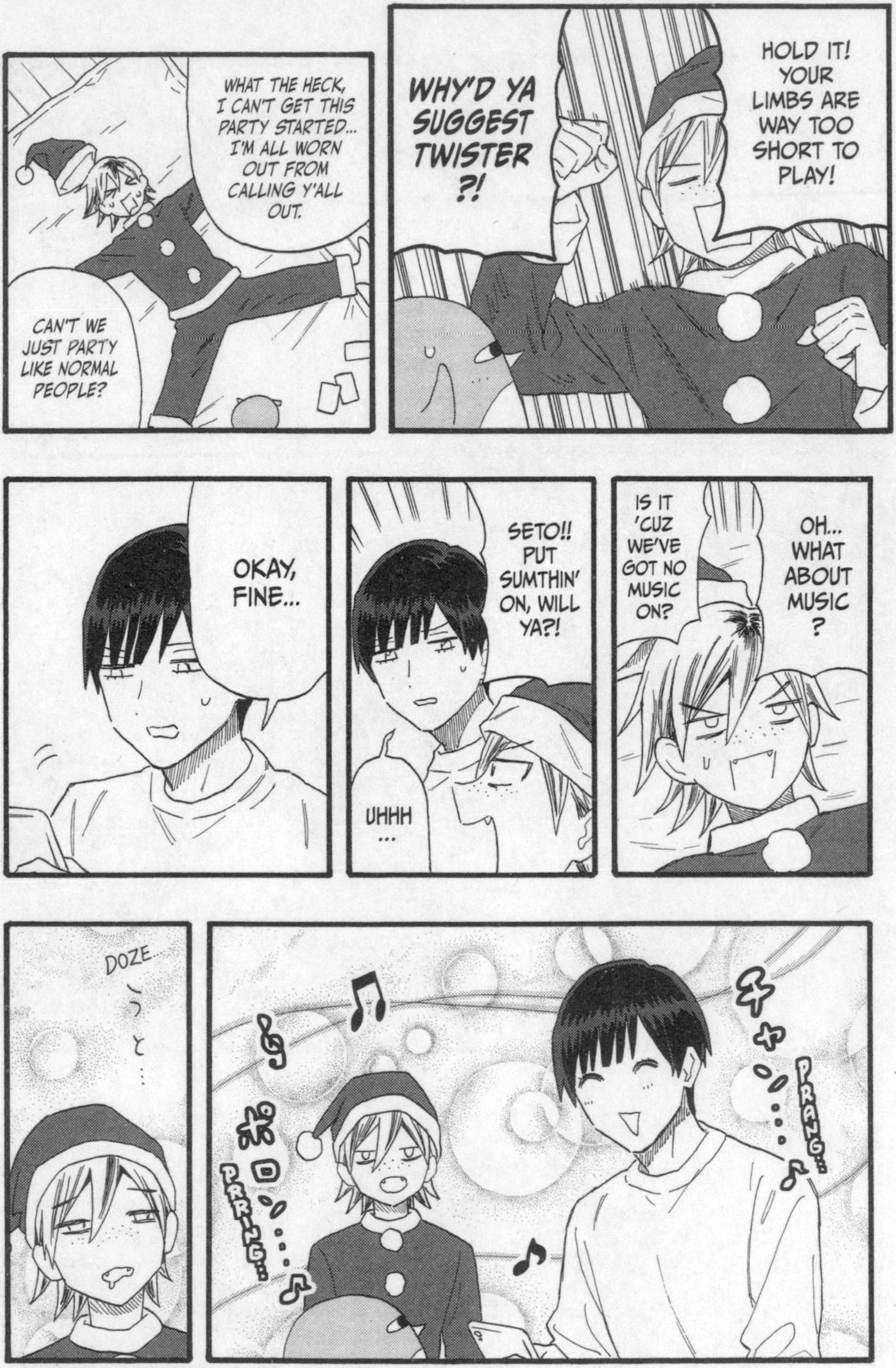
HOLD IT! YOUR LIMBS ARE WAY TOO SHORT TO PLAY!
WHY'D YA SUGGEST TWISTER ?!
WHAT THE HECK, I CAN'T GET THIS PARTY STARTED... I'M ALL WORN OUT FROM CALLING Y'ALL OUT.
CAN'T WE JUST PARTY LIKE NORMAL PEOPLE?
OH... WHAT ABOUT MUSIC ?
IS IT 'CUZ WE'VE GOT NO MUSIC ON?
SETO!! PUT SUMTHIN' ON, WILL YA?!
UHHH ...
OKAY, FINE...
PRANG...
PRRING...
DOZE...
うと…

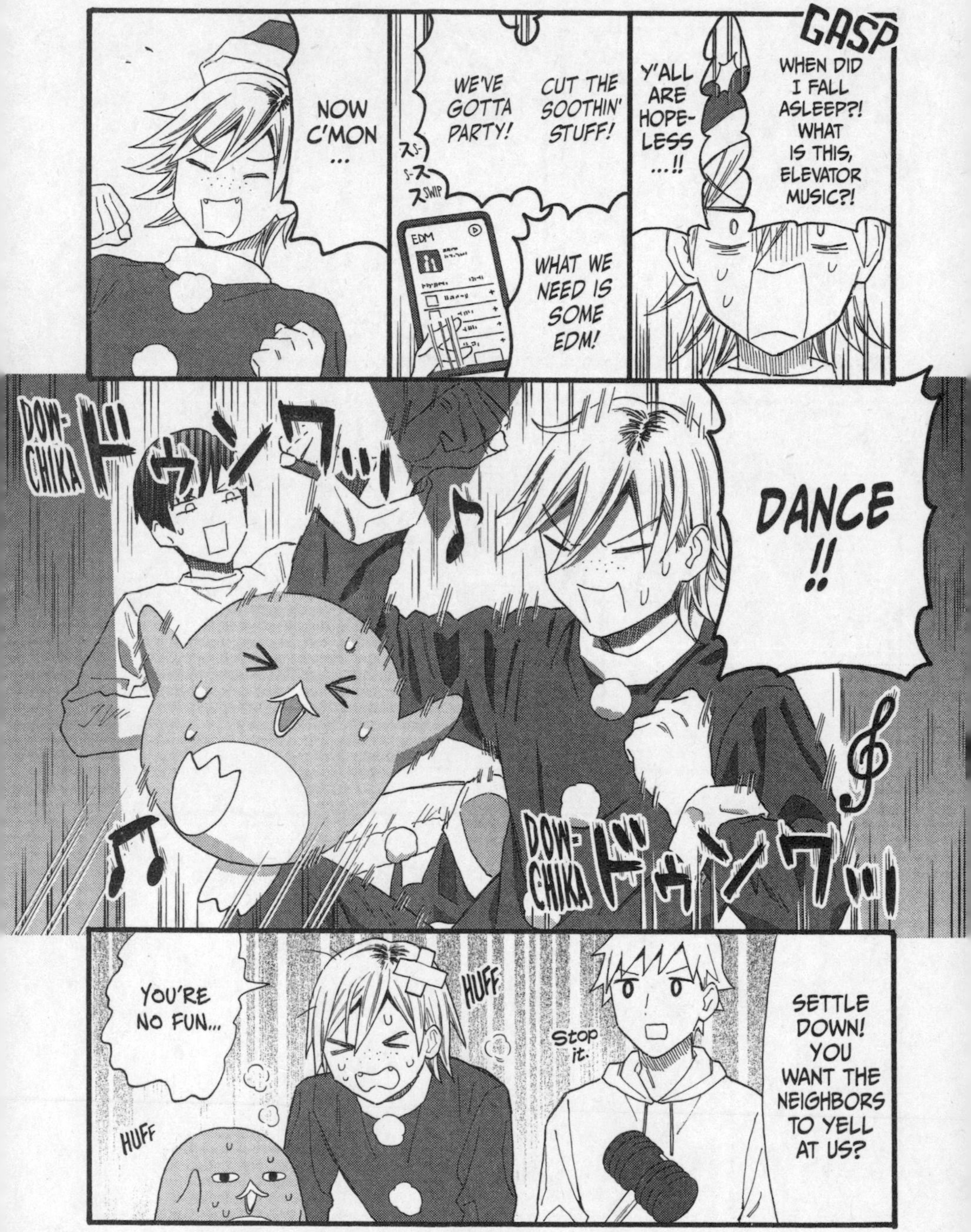
GASP
WHEN DID I FALL ASLEEP?! WHAT IS THIS, ELEVATOR MUSIC?!
Y'ALL ARE HOPE-LESS ...!!
CUT THE SOOTHIN' STUFF!
WE'VE GOTTA PARTY!
ス-ス-ス SWIP
EDM
WHAT WE NEED IS SOME EDM!
NOW C'MON ...
DANCE !!
DOW-CHIKA ドゥンワッ…
DOW-CHIKA ドゥンワッ…
SETTLE DOWN! YOU WANT THE NEIGHBORS TO YELL AT US?
Stop it.
HUFF
YOU'RE NO FUN...
HUFF

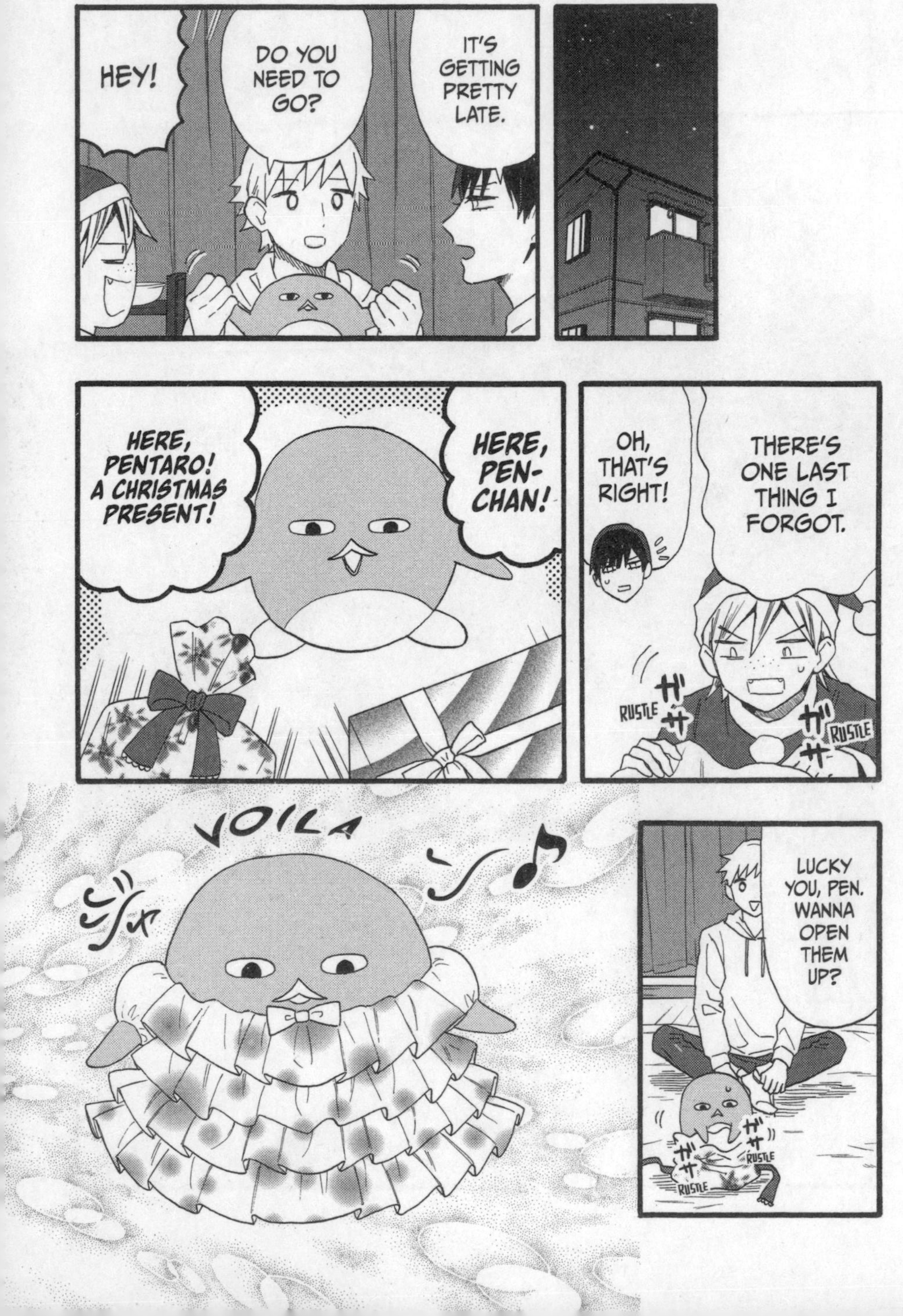
IT'S GETTING PRETTY LATE.
DO YOU NEED TO GO?
HEY!
THERE'S ONE LAST THING I FORGOT.
OH, THAT'S RIGHT!
RUSTLE
RUSTLE
HERE, PEN-CHAN!
HERE, PENTARO! A CHRISTMAS PRESENT!
LUCKY YOU, PEN. WANNA OPEN THEM UP?
RUSTLE
RUSTLE
VOILA

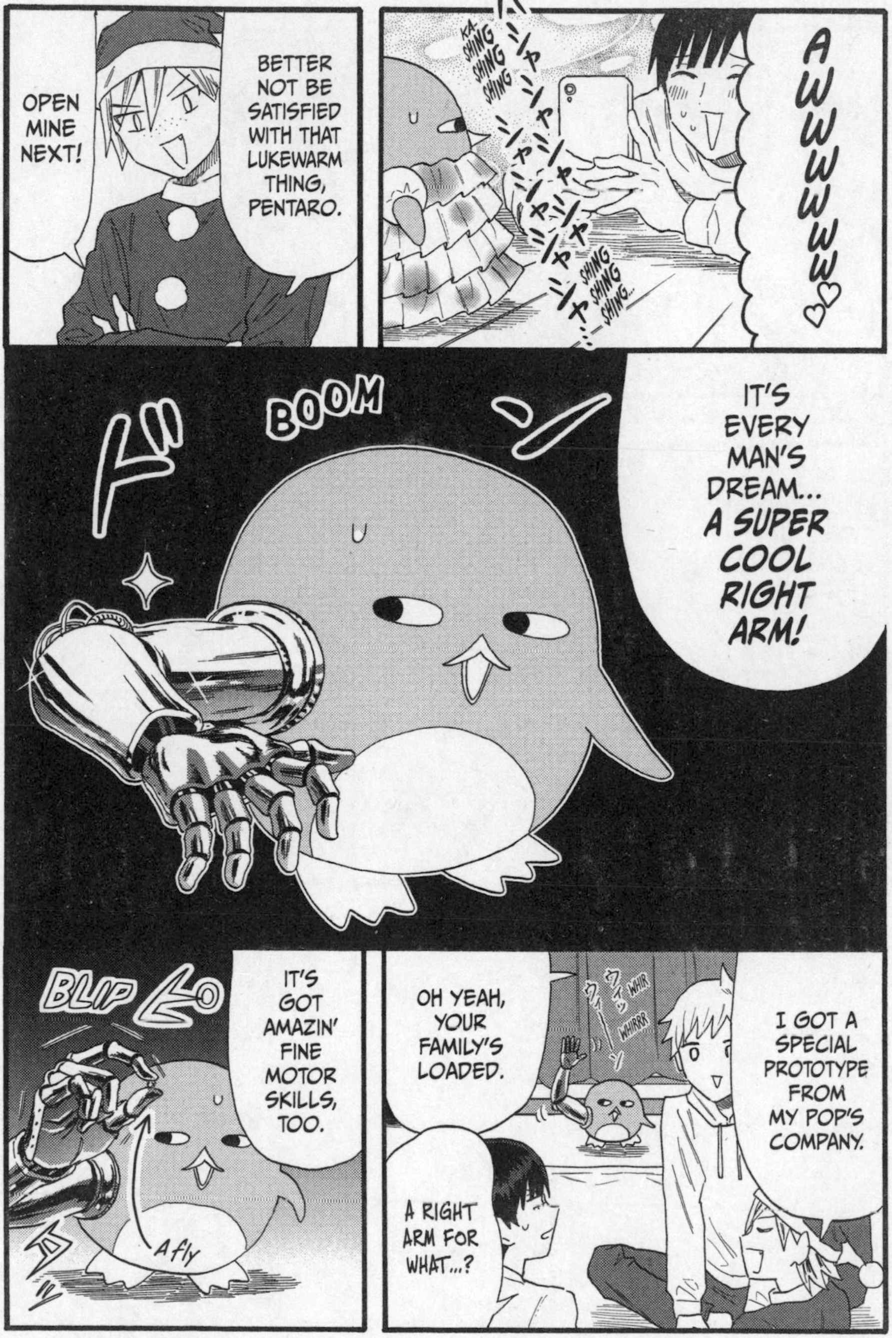
AWWWWWWW♡♡
KA SHING SHING SHING
SHING SHING SHING...
BETTER NOT BE SATISFIED WITH THAT LUKEWARM THING, PENTARO.
OPEN MINE NEXT!
IT'S EVERY MAN'S DREAM... A SUPER COOL RIGHT ARM!
BOOM
I GOT A SPECIAL PROTOTYPE FROM MY POP'S COMPANY.
WHIR WHIRRR
OH YEAH, YOUR FAMILY'S LOADED.
A RIGHT ARM FOR WHAT...?
IT'S GOT AMAZIN' FINE MOTOR SKILLS, TOO.
BLIP
A fly

WHAT NICE PRESENTS, HUH?
WELL, WE'RE OFF, THEN.
SEE YOU NEXT YEAR, PEN-CHAN!
Bye!
GUESS WE SHOULD SLEEP, TOO!
GOOD NIGHT.
グ
ZZZZZ
グ
ZZZZZ
GASP!!

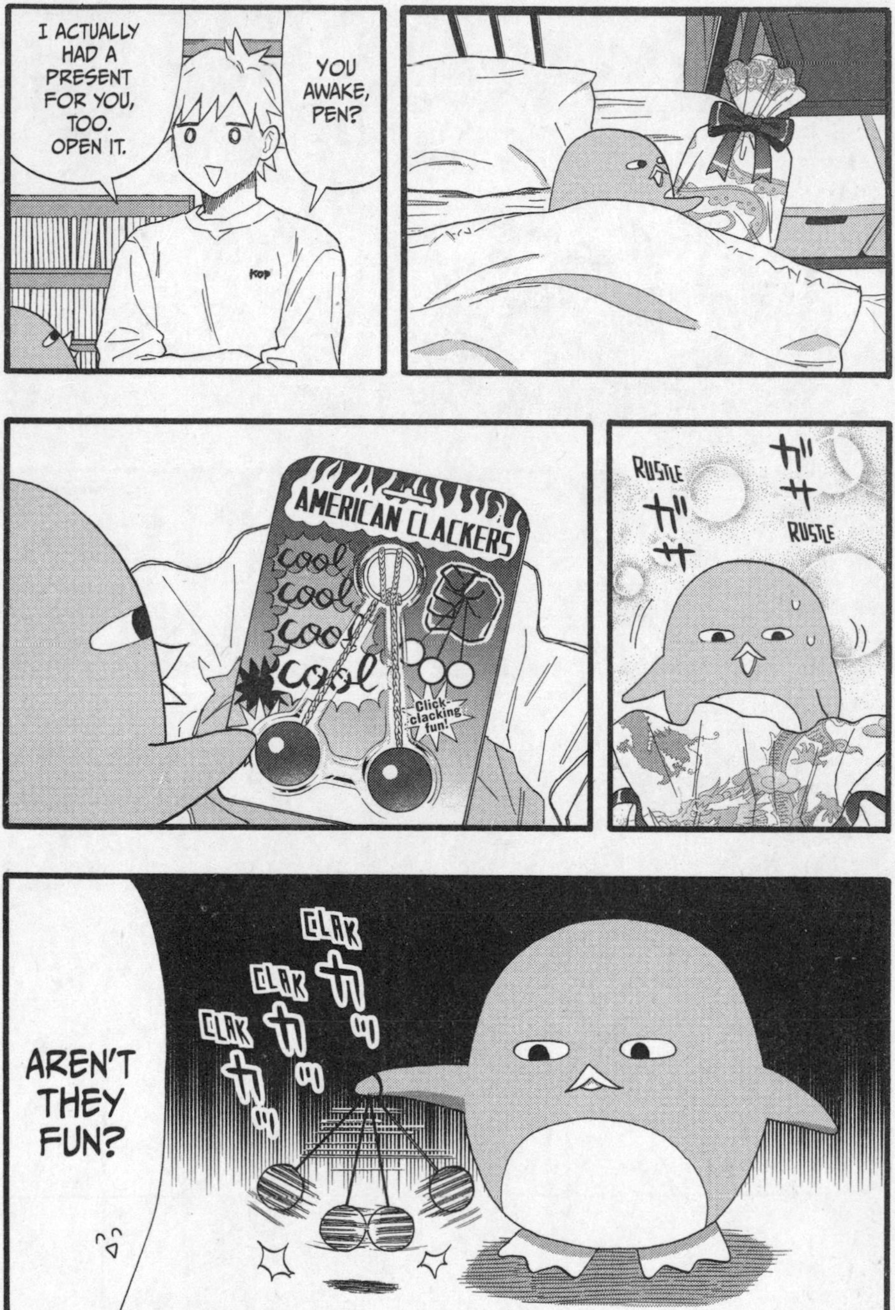
YOU AWAKE, PEN?
I ACTUALLY HAD A PRESENT FOR YOU, TOO. OPEN IT.
ガサ
RUSTLE
ガサ
RUSTLE
AMERICAN CLACKERS
cool
cool
cool
cool
Click-clacking fun!
CLAK カッ
CLAK カッ
CLAK カッ
AREN'T THEY FUN?

GLAK
GLAK
GLAK
GLAK
GLAK
GLAK
Pen after mastering the clackers.

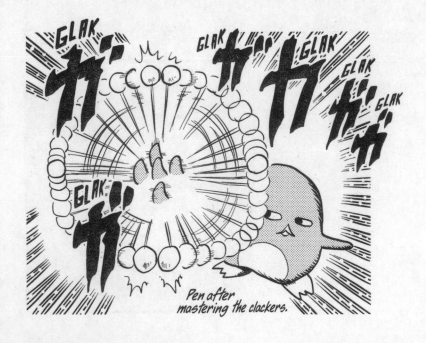

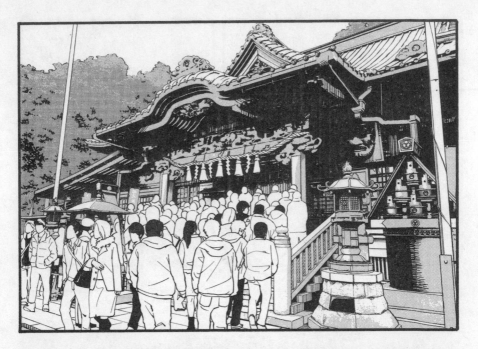

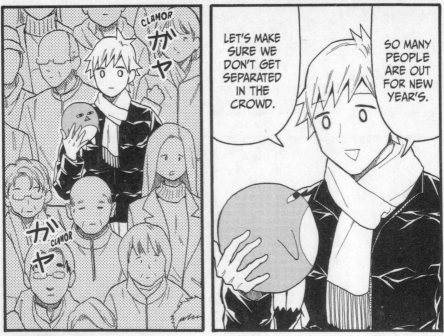

SO MANY PEOPLE ARE OUT FOR NEW YEAR'S.
LET'S MAKE SURE WE DON'T GET SEPARATED IN THE CROWD.
CLAMOR
ガヤ
ガヤ
CLAMOR

Pen 11 The Penguin Does a New Year's Shrine Visit With His Owner

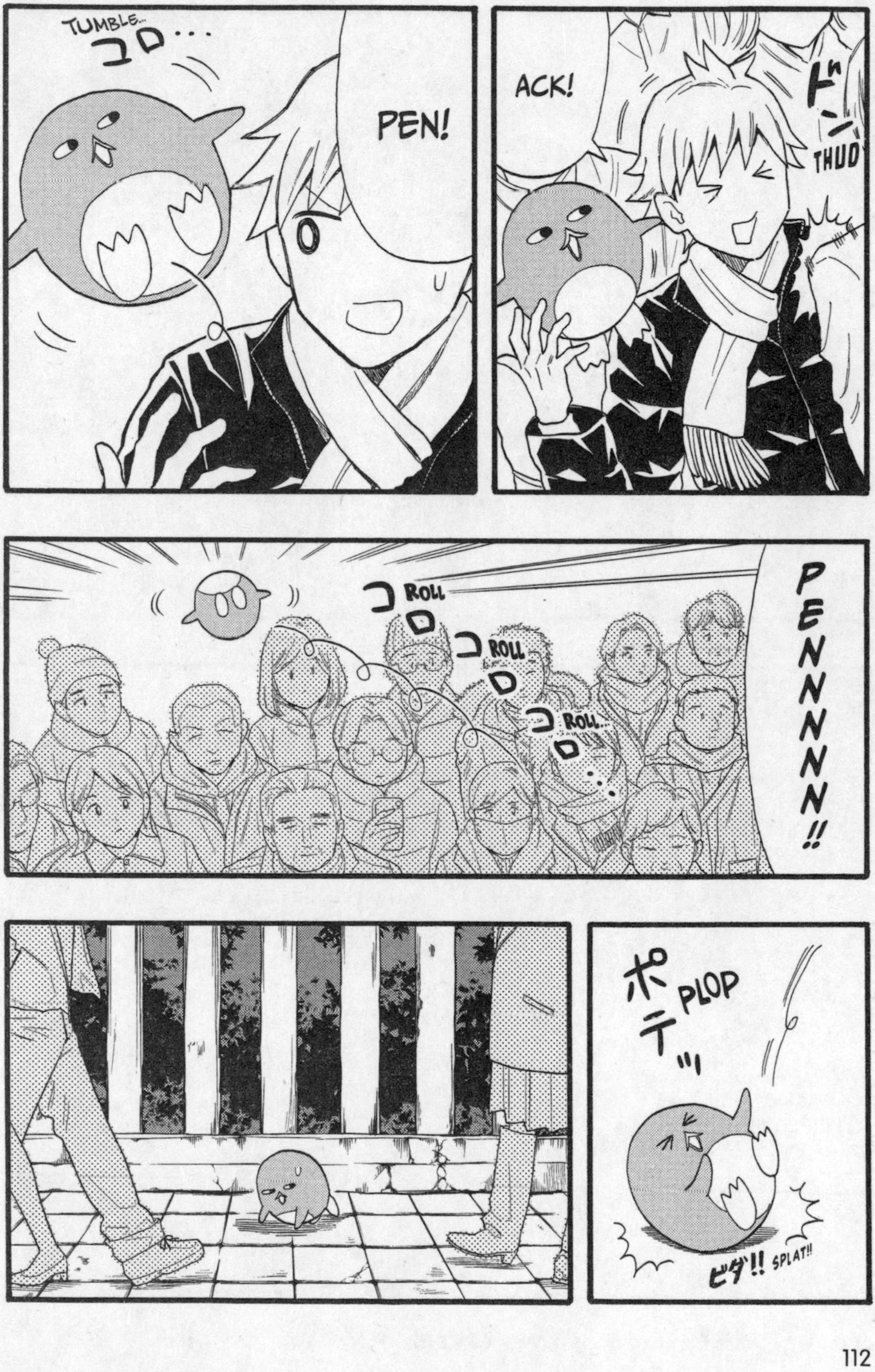
ACK!
ドン THUD
TUMBLE.. コロ...
PEN!
PENNNNNN!!
コロ ROLL
コロ ROLL
コロ ROLL...
ポテッ PLOP
ビタ!! SPLAT!!

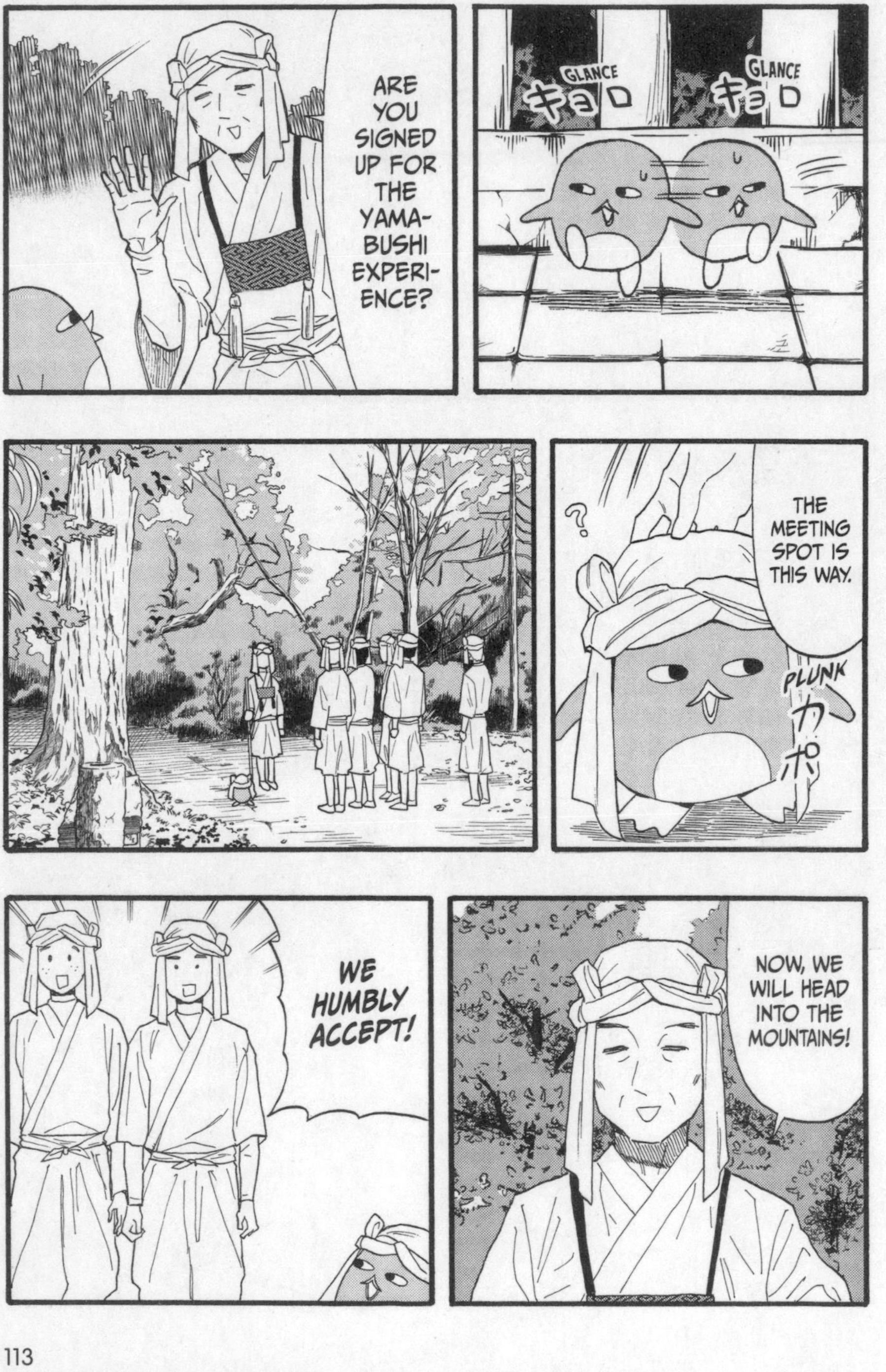
GLANCE
キョロ
GLANCE
キョロ
ARE YOU SIGNED UP FOR THE YAMA-BUSHI EXPERI-ENCE?
?
THE MEETING SPOT IS THIS WAY.
PLUNK
カポ
NOW, WE WILL HEAD INTO THE MOUNTAINS!
WE HUMBLY ACCEPT!

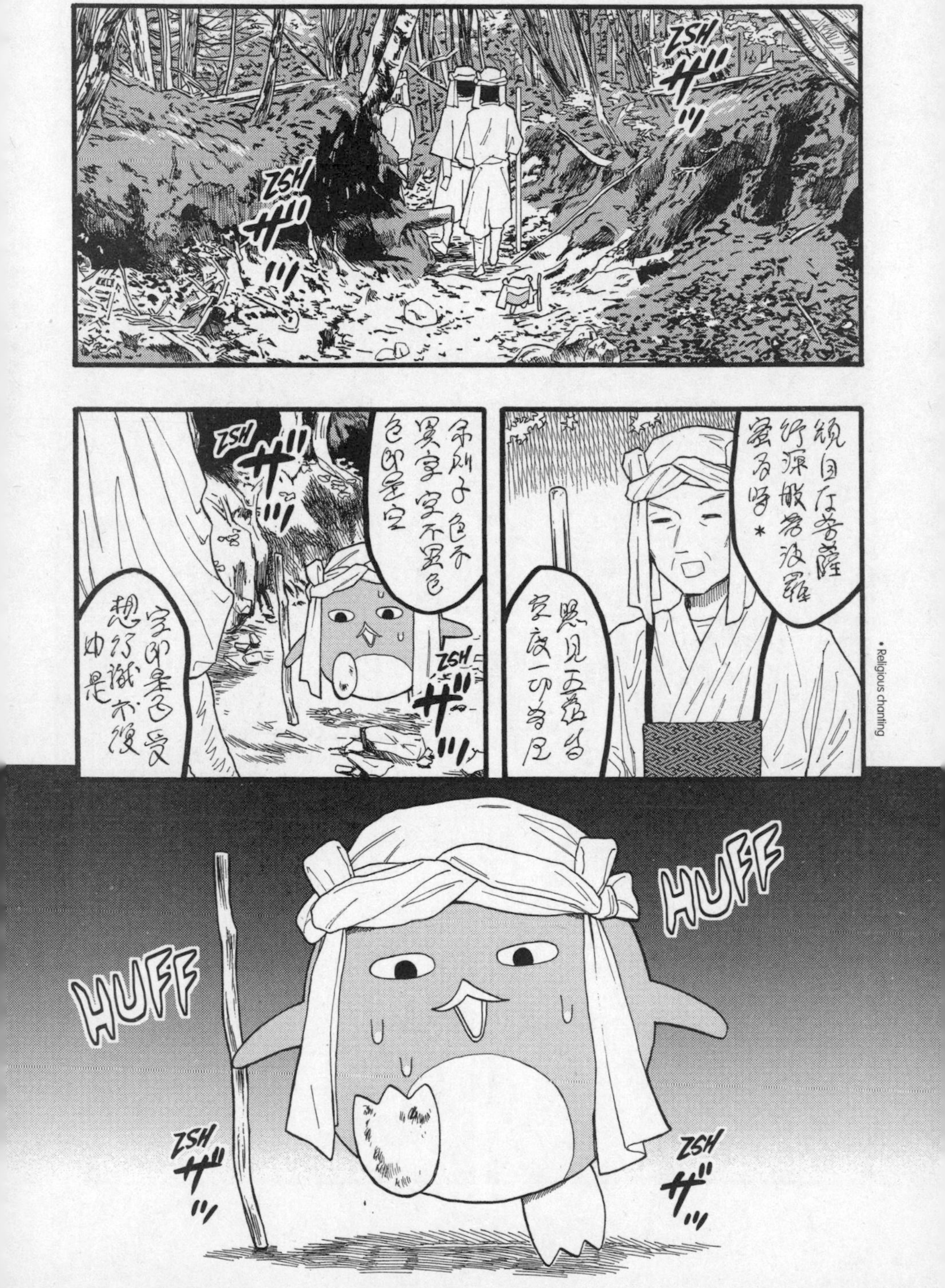
ZSH
ザッ
ZSH
ザッ
観自在菩薩
行深般若波羅
蜜多時*
照見五蘊皆
空度一切苦厄
ZSH
ザッ
舎利子色不
異空空不異色
色即是空
ZSH
ザッ
空即是色受
想行識亦復
如是
HUFF
HUFF
ZSH
ザッ
ZSH
ザッ

* Religious chanting

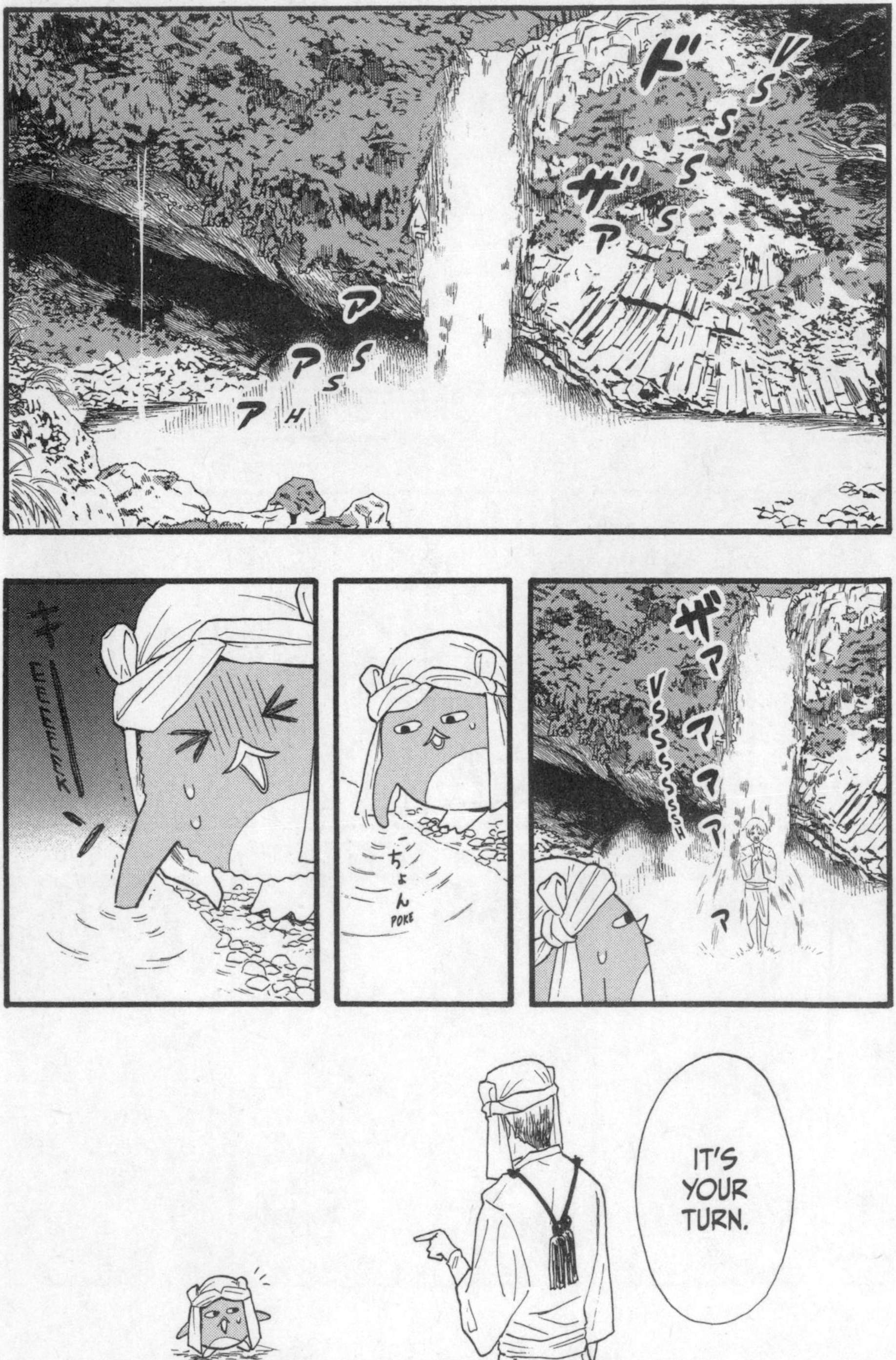
ド
VSSSS
ザア
アアア
SSH
ザアアアア
VSSSSSSH
ちょん
POKE
キ
EEEEEEK
IT'S YOUR TURN.

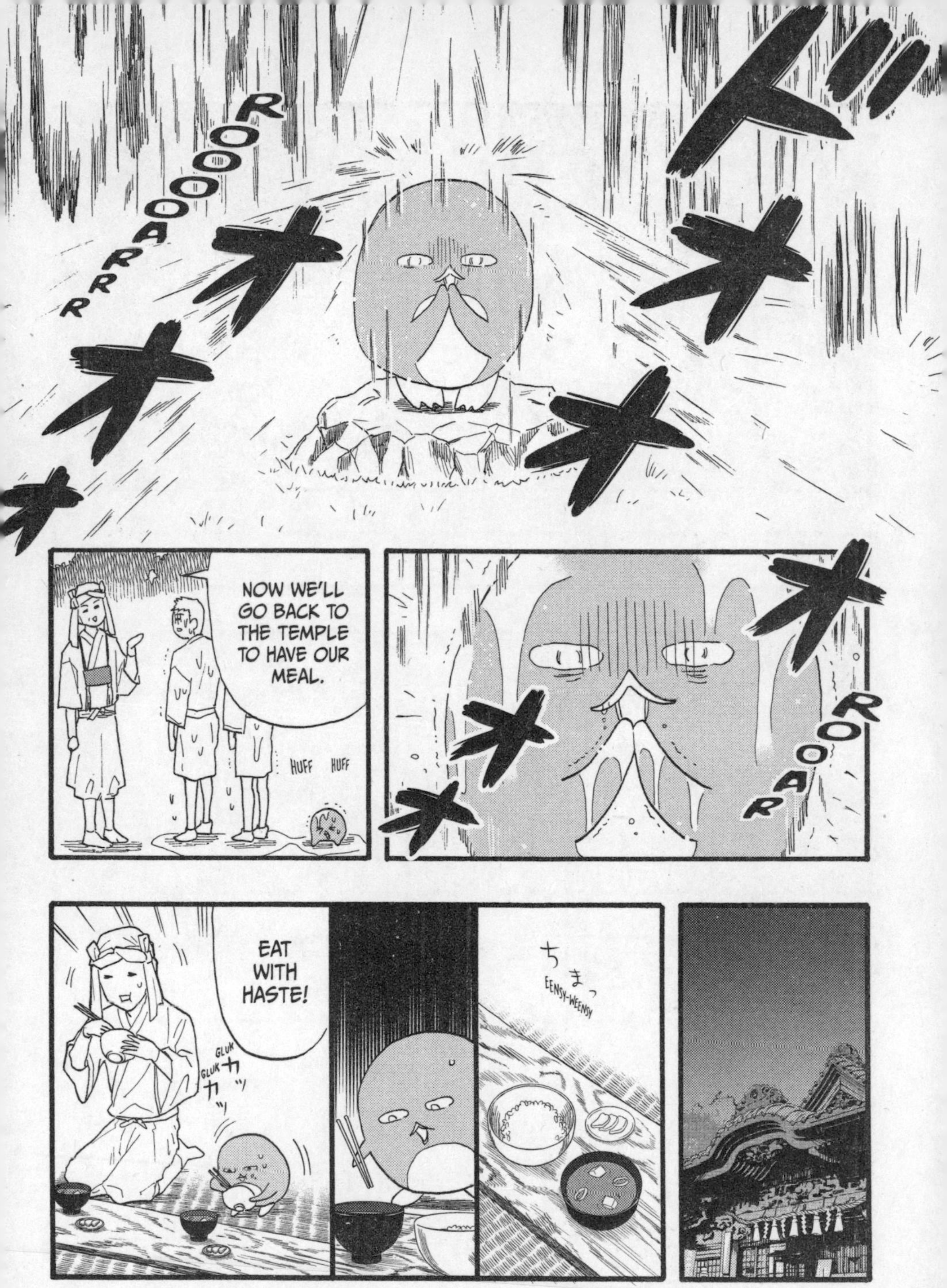

ドッ
ROOOOOARRRR
ROOAR
NOW WE'LL GO BACK TO THE TEMPLE TO HAVE OUR MEAL.
HUFF HUFF
ちまっ
EENSY-WEENSY
EAT WITH HASTE!
GLUK GLUK
カッ カッ

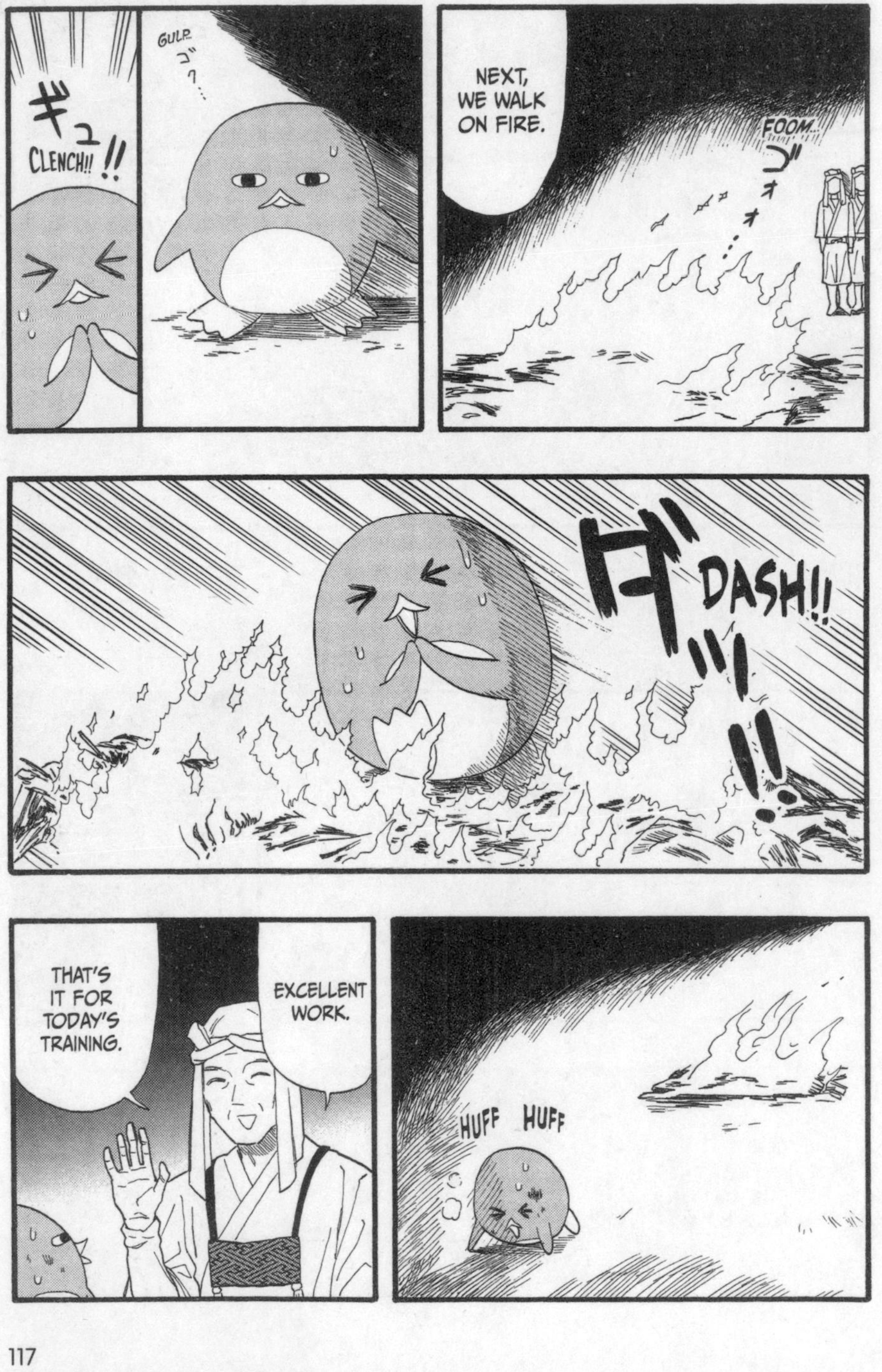
NEXT, WE WALK ON FIRE.
FOOM...
ゴォォ…
GULP...
ゴク…
ギュ
CLENCH!! !!
ダッ!!
DASH!!
HUFF HUFF
EXCELLENT WORK.
THAT'S IT FOR TODAY'S TRAINING.

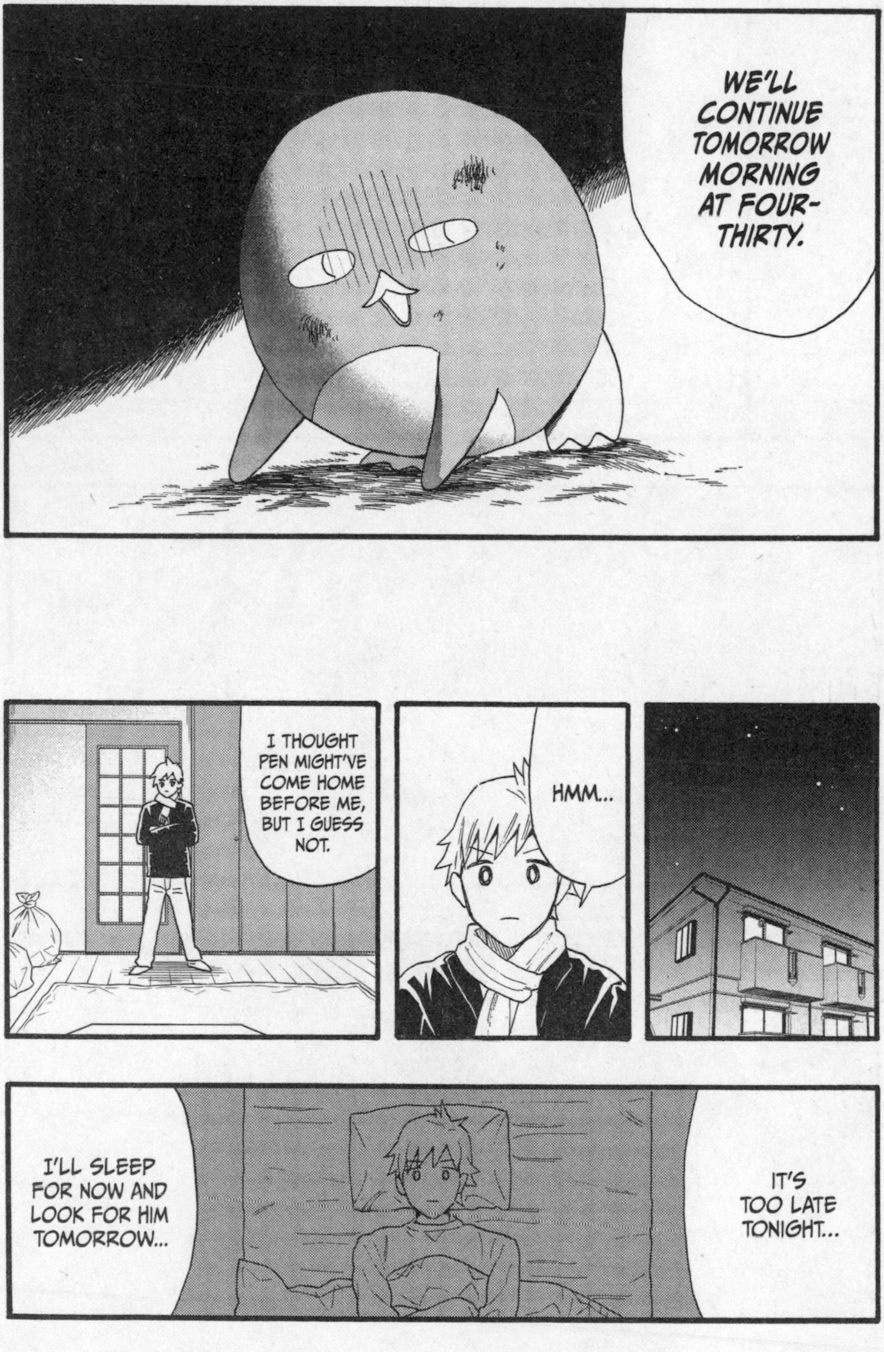
WE'LL CONTINUE TOMORROW MORNING AT FOUR-THIRTY.
HMM...
I THOUGHT PEN MIGHT'VE COME HOME BEFORE ME, BUT I GUESS NOT.
IT'S TOO LATE TONIGHT...
I'LL SLEEP FOR NOW AND LOOK FOR HIM TOMORROW...

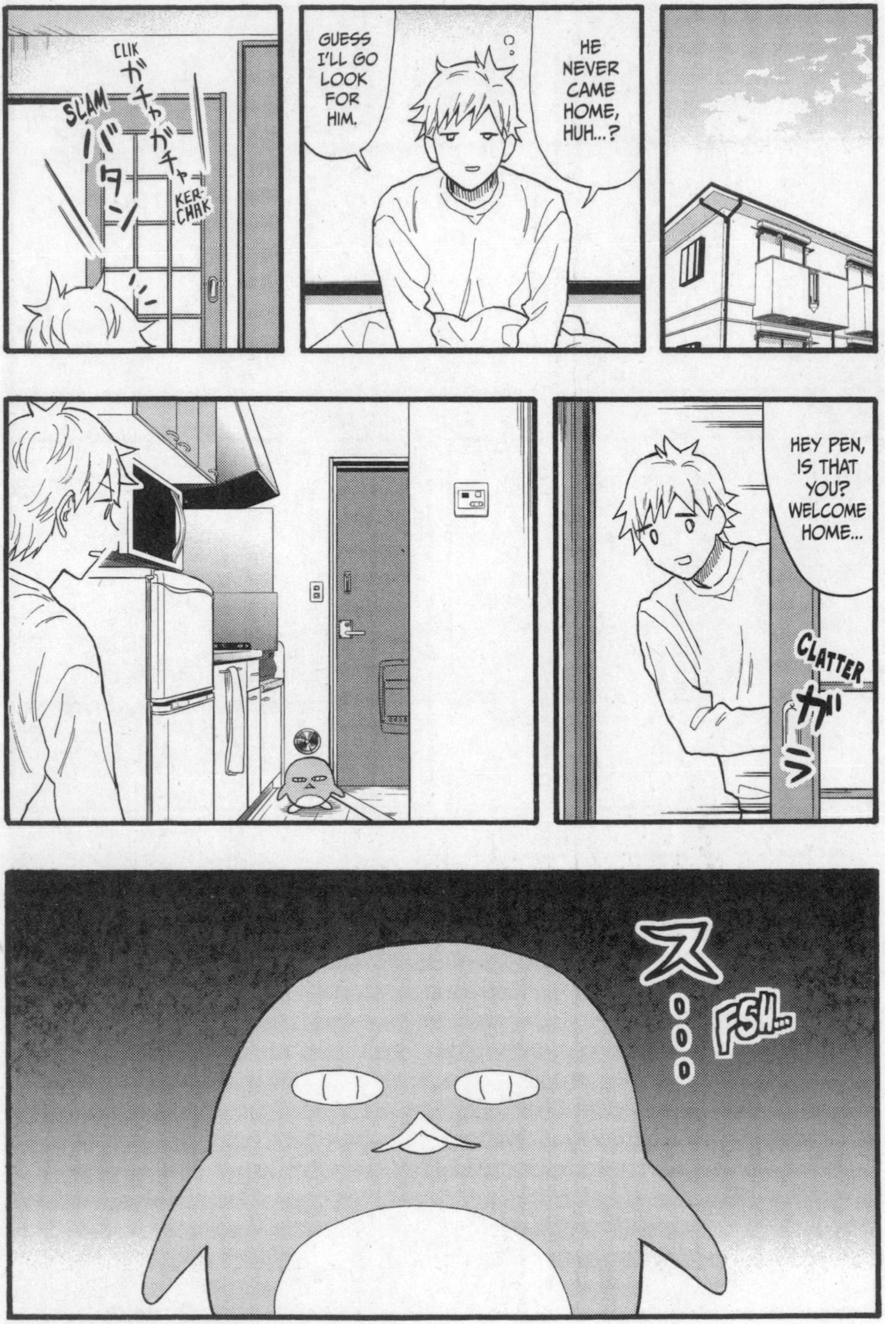
HE NEVER CAME HOME, HUH...?
GUESS I'LL GO LOOK FOR HIM.
ガチャガチャ
CLIK
KER-CHAK
バタン
SLAM
HEY PEN, IS THAT YOU? WELCOME HOME...
ガラ
CLATTER
ス...
FSH...

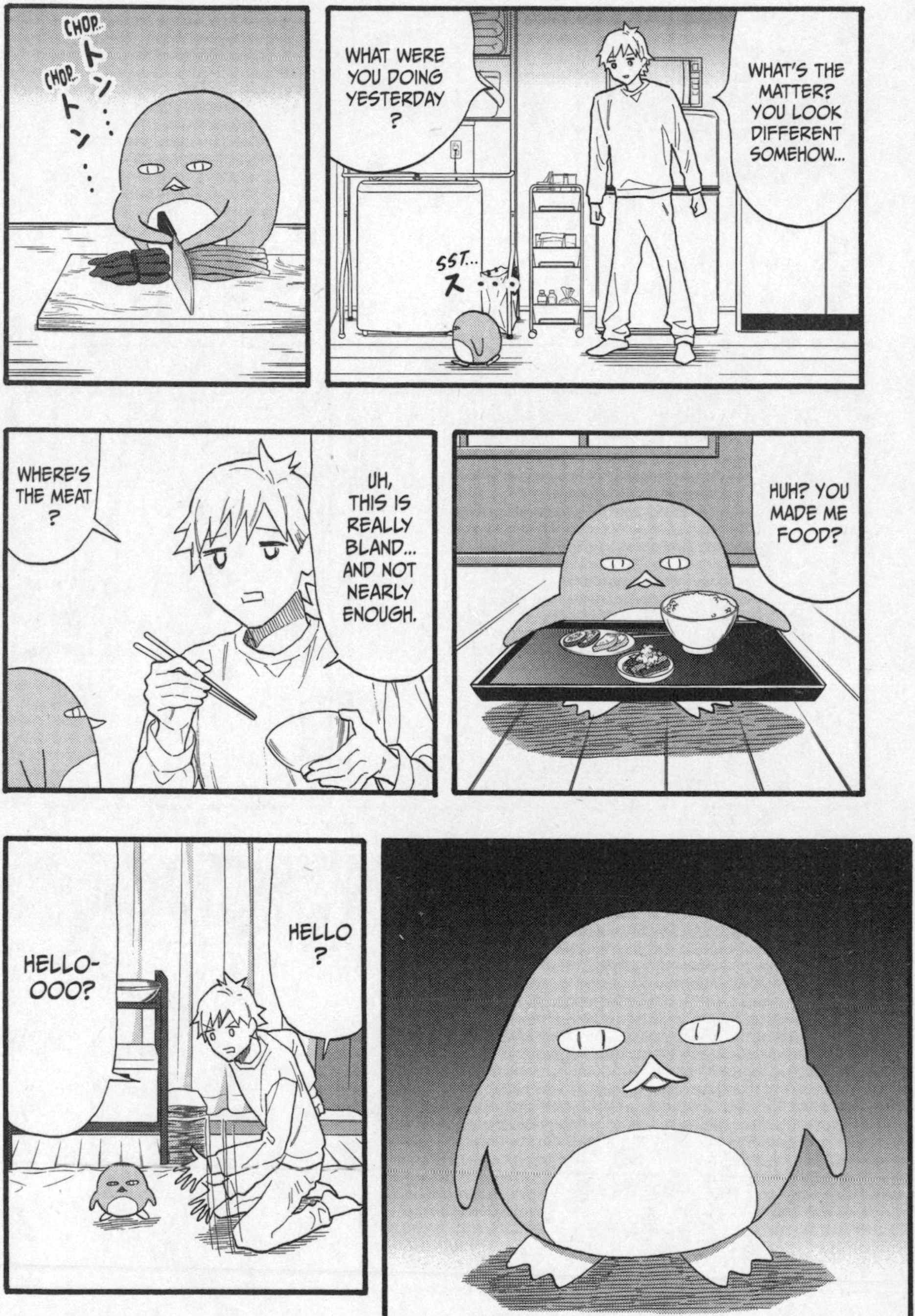
WHAT'S THE MATTER? YOU LOOK DIFFERENT SOMEHOW...
WHAT WERE YOU DOING YESTERDAY ?
SST... ス…
CHOP... トン…
CHOP... トン…
HUH? YOU MADE ME FOOD?
UH, THIS IS REALLY BLAND... AND NOT NEARLY ENOUGH.
WHERE'S THE MEAT ?
HELLO ?
HELLO-OOO?

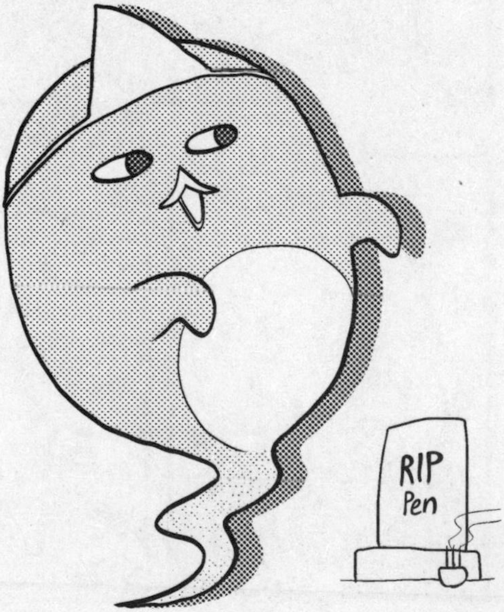
RIP
Pen

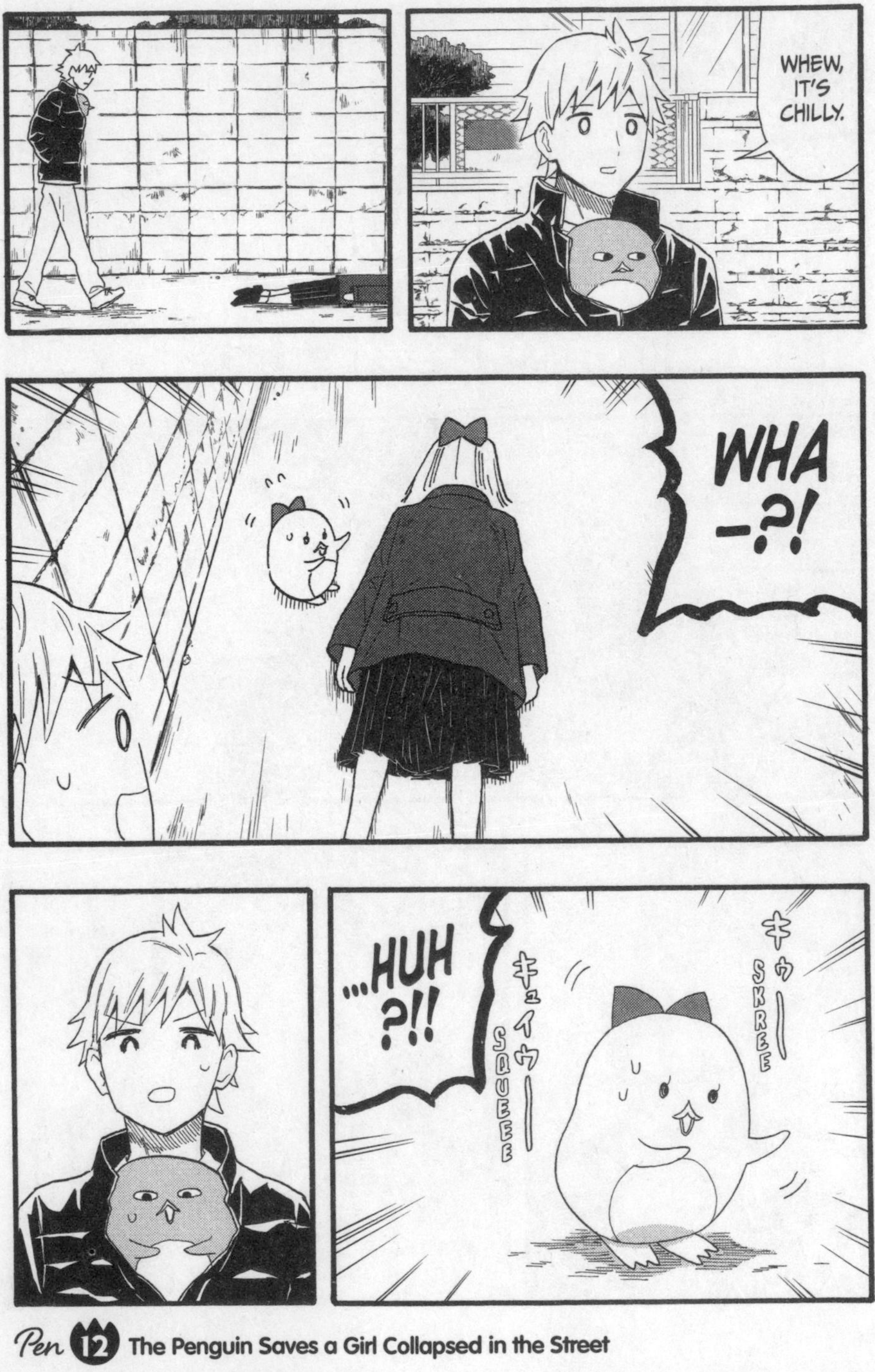
WHEW, IT'S CHILLY.
WHA-?!
キュー
SKREE
キュイウー
SQUEEE
...HUH?!!

Pen 12 The Penguin Saves a Girl Collapsed in the Street

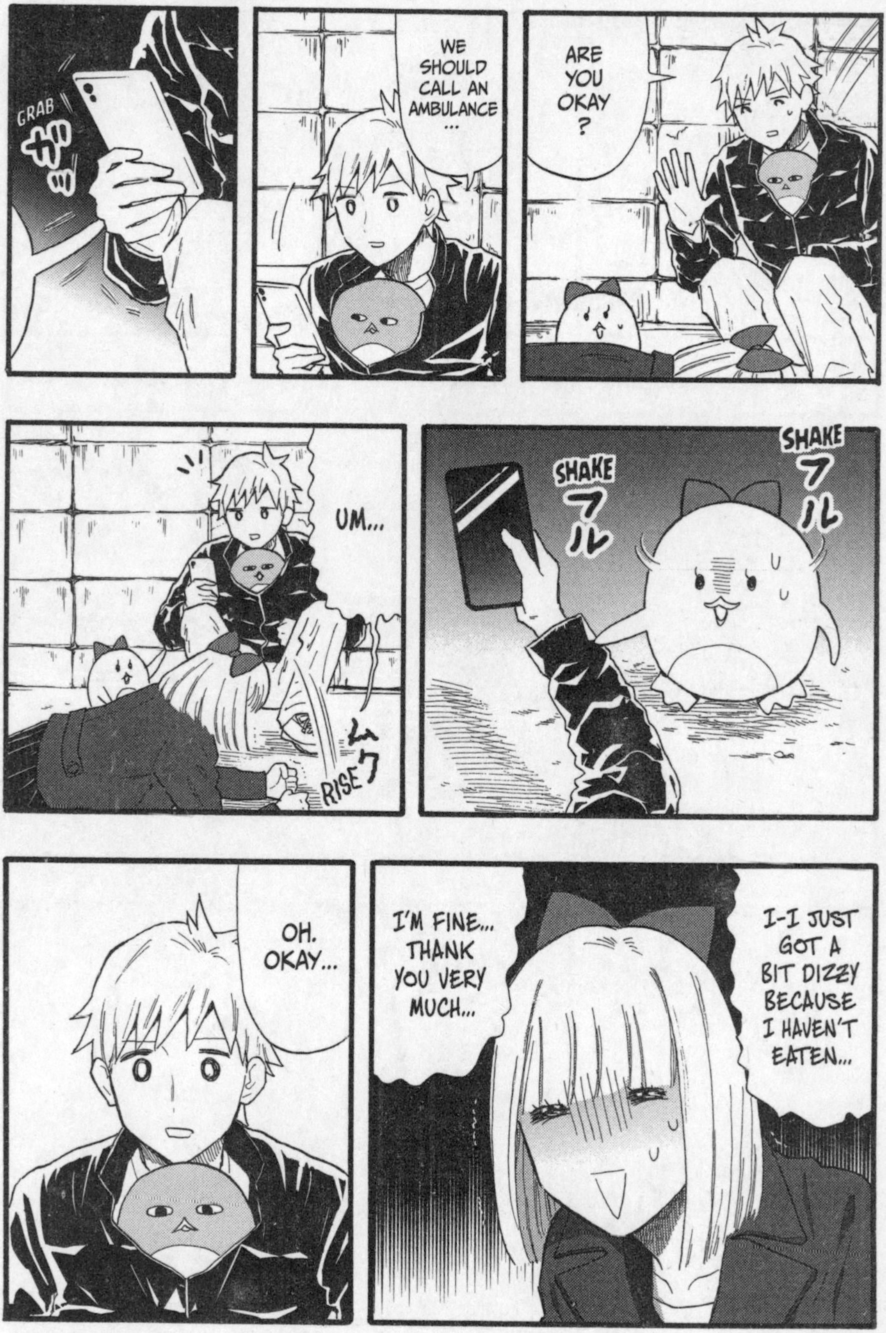
ARE YOU OKAY?
WE SHOULD CALL AN AMBULANCE...
GRAB
ガッ
SHAKE
フル
SHAKE
フル
UM...
RISE
ムク
I-I JUST GOT A BIT DIZZY BECAUSE I HAVEN'T EATEN...
I'M FINE... THANK YOU VERY MUCH...
OH. OKAY...

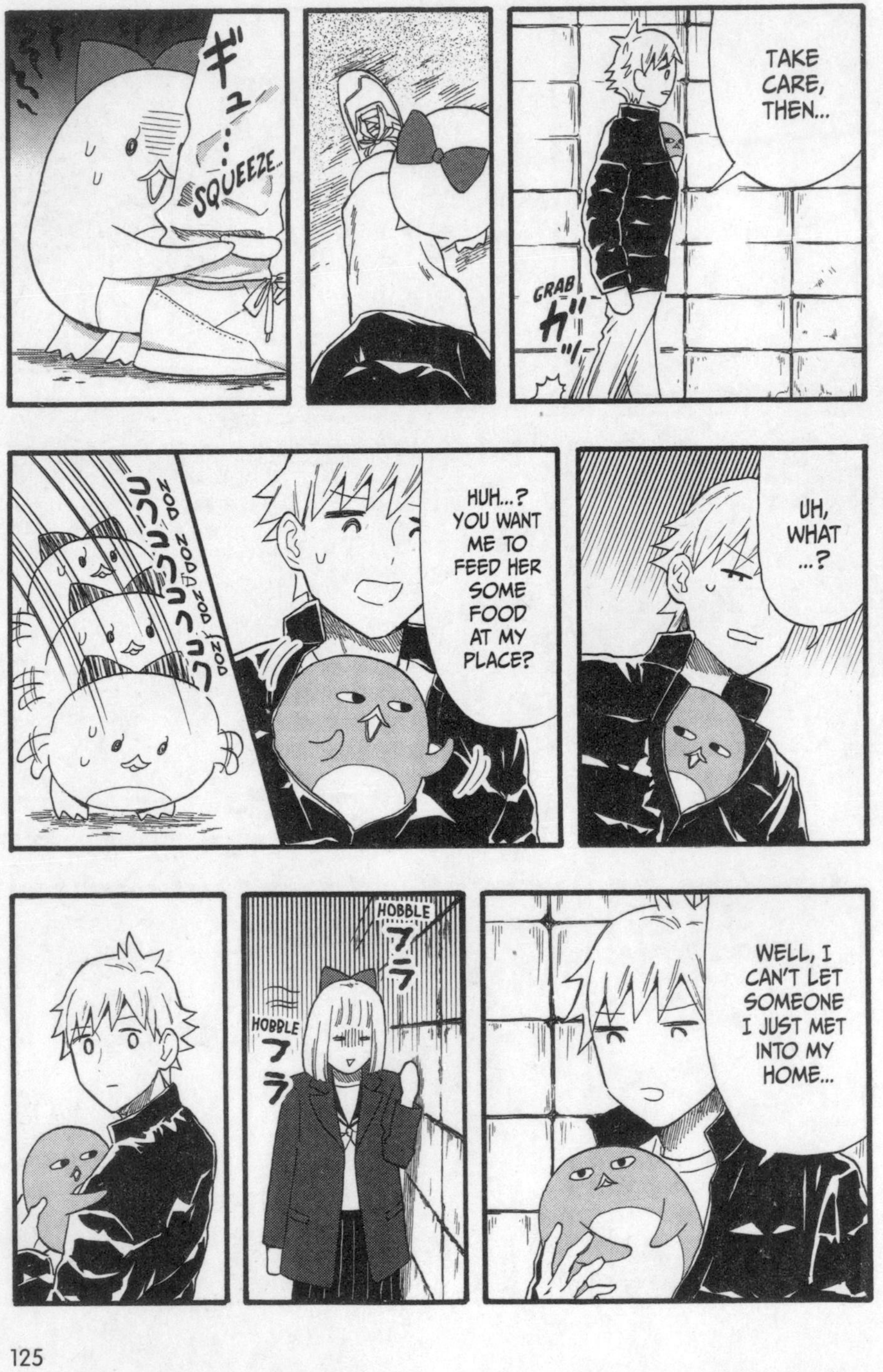
TAKE CARE, THEN...
GRAB
ガッ
ギュ...
SQUEEZE...
UH, WHAT ...?
HUH...? YOU WANT ME TO FEED HER SOME FOOD AT MY PLACE?
NOD NOD NOD NOD
WELL, I CAN'T LET SOMEONE I JUST MET INTO MY HOME...
HOBBLE
フラ
HOBBLE
フラ

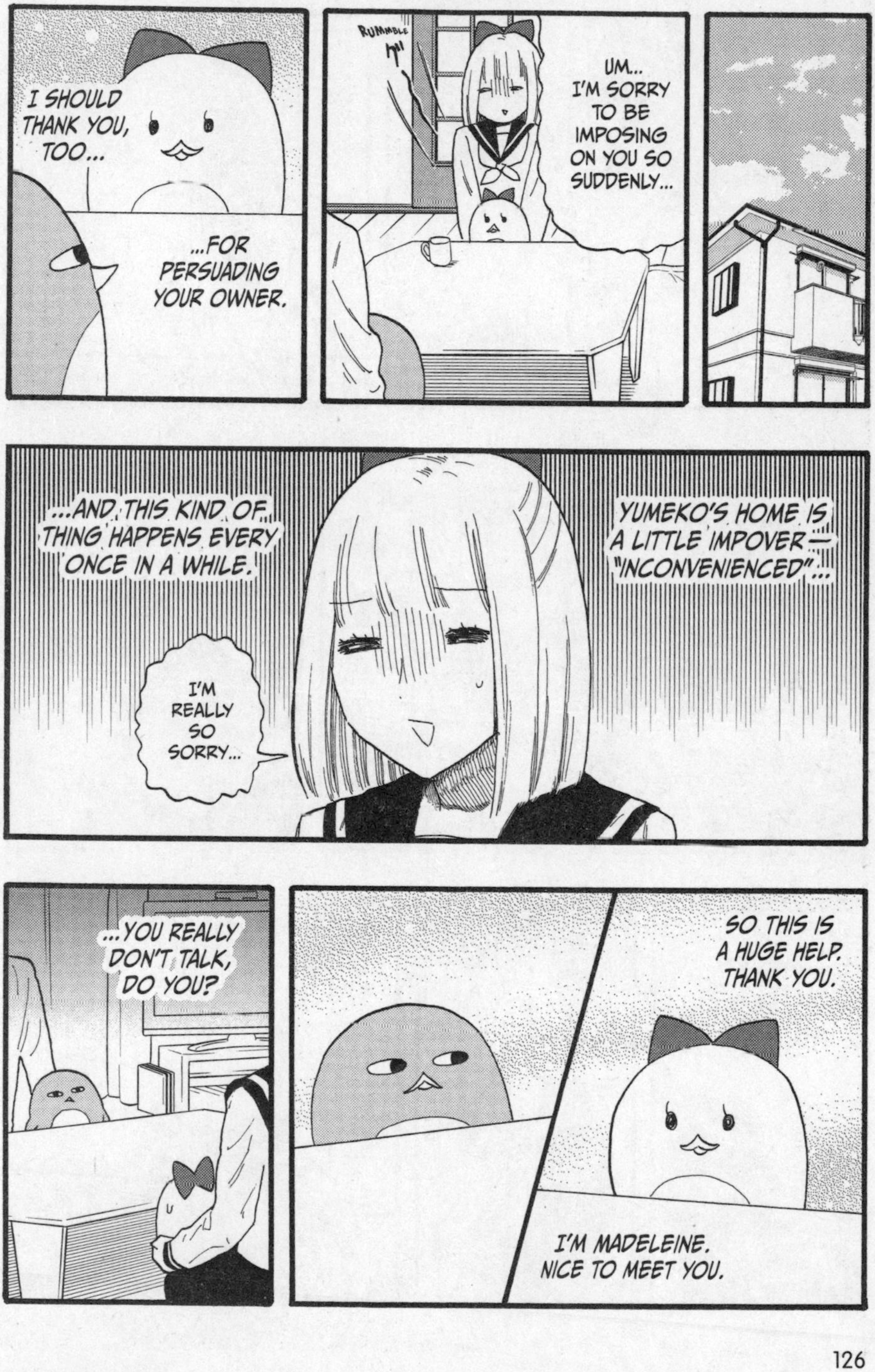

RUMMBLE
UM... I'M SORRY TO BE IMPOSING ON YOU SO SUDDENLY...
I SHOULD THANK YOU, TOO...
...FOR PERSUADING YOUR OWNER.
YUMEKO'S HOME IS A LITTLE IMPOVER— "INCONVENIENCED"...
I'M REALLY SO SORRY...
...AND THIS KIND OF THING HAPPENS EVERY ONCE IN A WHILE.
SO THIS IS A HUGE HELP. THANK YOU.
I'M MADELEINE. NICE TO MEET YOU.
...YOU REALLY DON'T TALK, DO YOU?

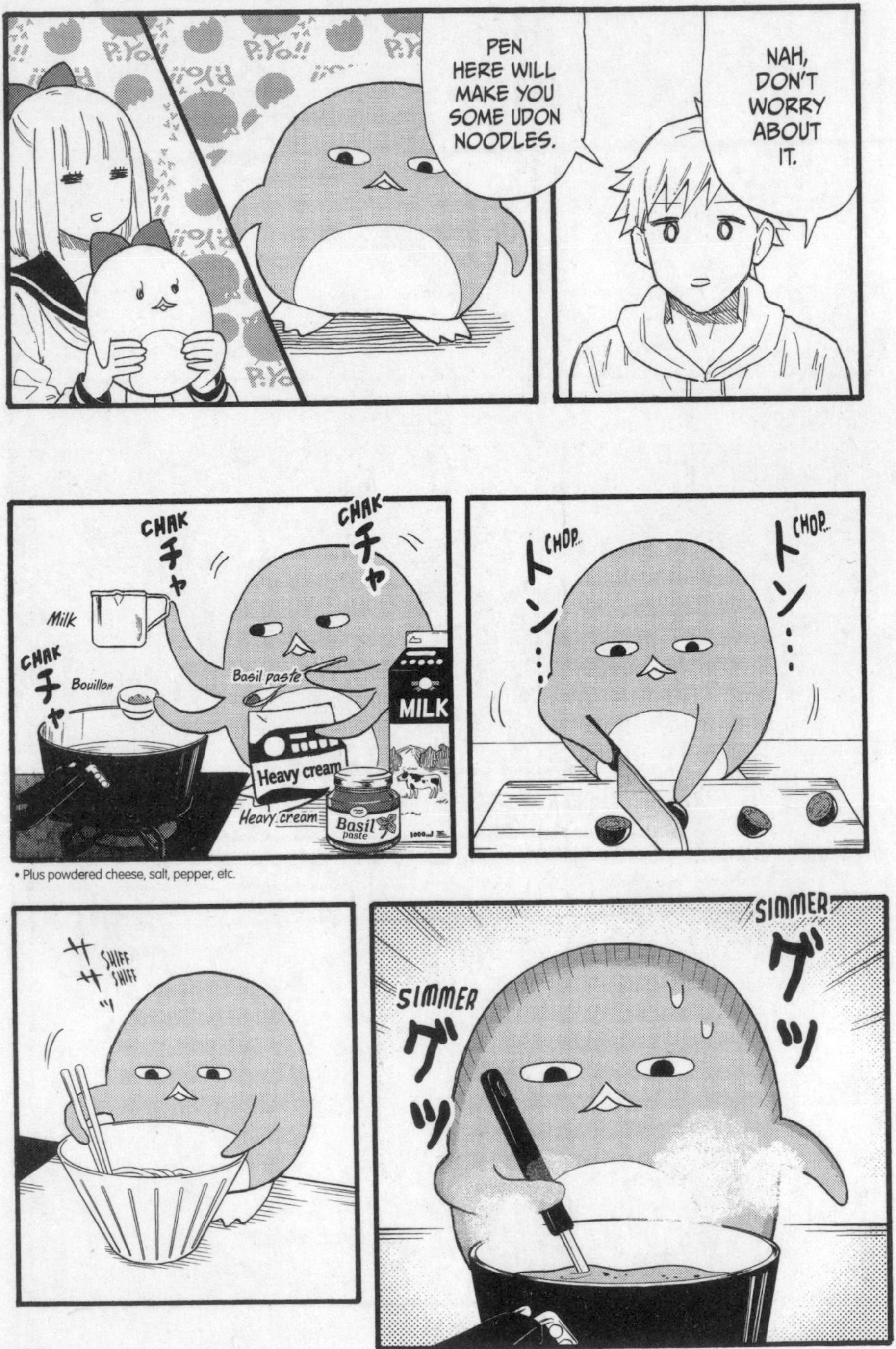
NAH, DON'T WORRY ABOUT IT.
PEN HERE WILL MAKE YOU SOME UDON NOODLES.
P.Yo!!
CHOP... トン…
CHOP... トン…
CHAK チャ
CHAK チャ
Milk
CHAK チャ
Bouillon
Basil paste
MILK
Heavy cream
Heavy cream
Basil paste
SIMMER グツ
SIMMER グツ
SHIFF SHIFF

• Plus powdered cheese, salt, pepper, etc.

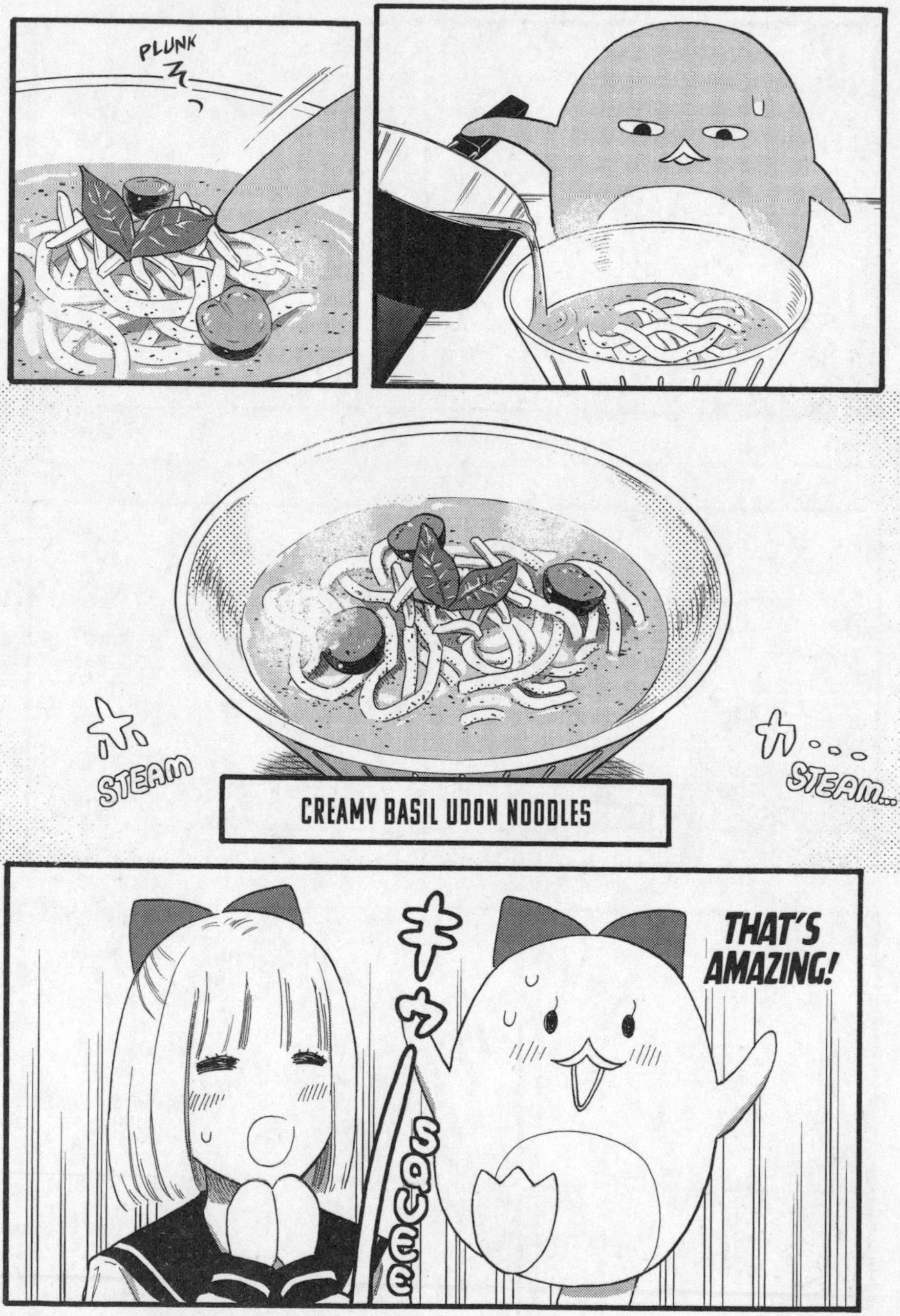
PLUNK
STEAM...
STEAM
CREAMY BASIL UDON NOODLES
THAT'S AMAZING!
SQUEE

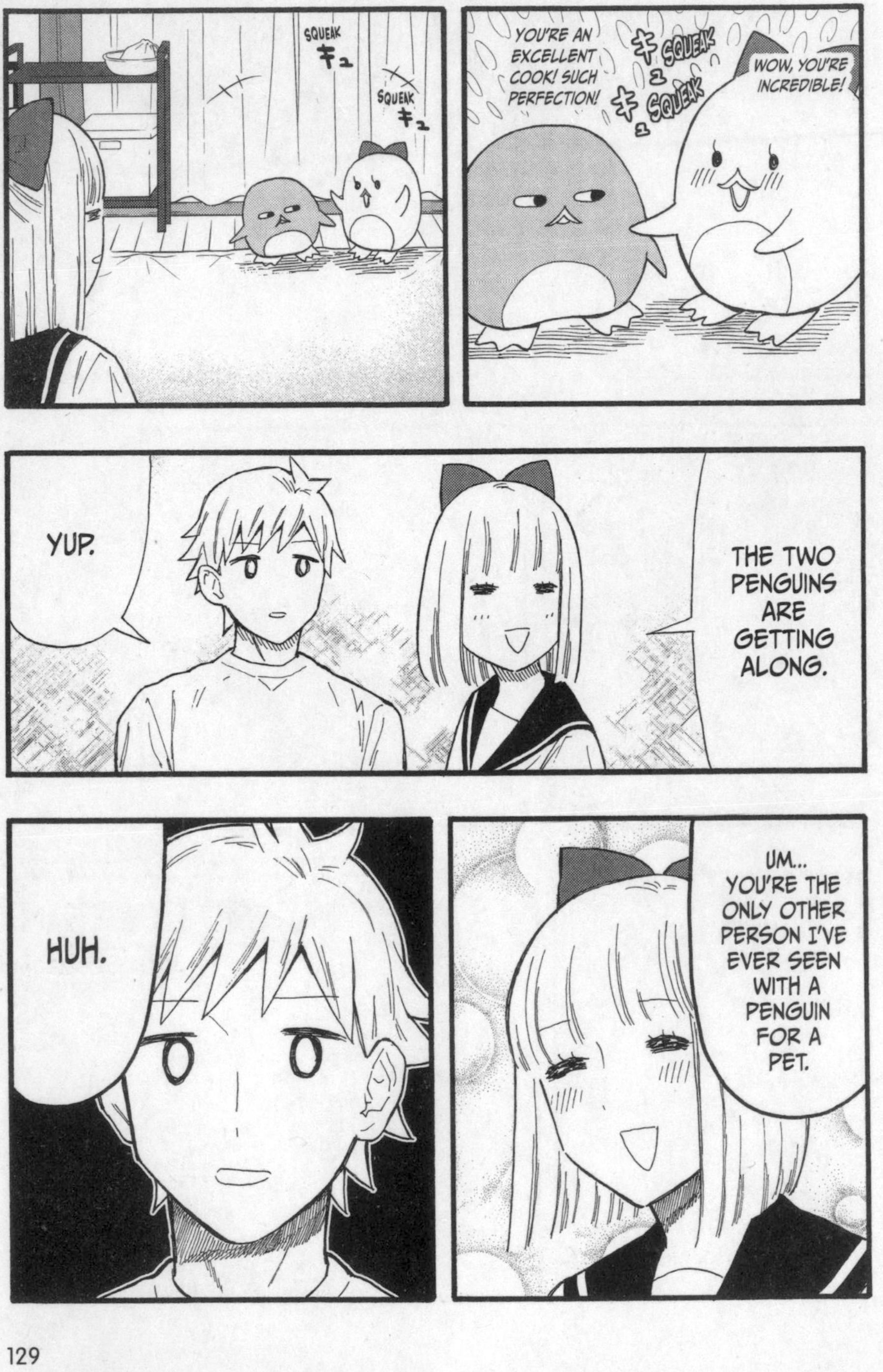
WOW, YOU'RE INCREDIBLE!
キュ SQUEAK
キュ SQUEAK
YOU'RE AN EXCELLENT COOK! SUCH PERFECTION!
SQUEAK キュ
SQUEAK キュ
THE TWO PENGUINS ARE GETTING ALONG.
YUP.
UM... YOU'RE THE ONLY OTHER PERSON I'VE EVER SEEN WITH A PENGUIN FOR A PET.
HUH.

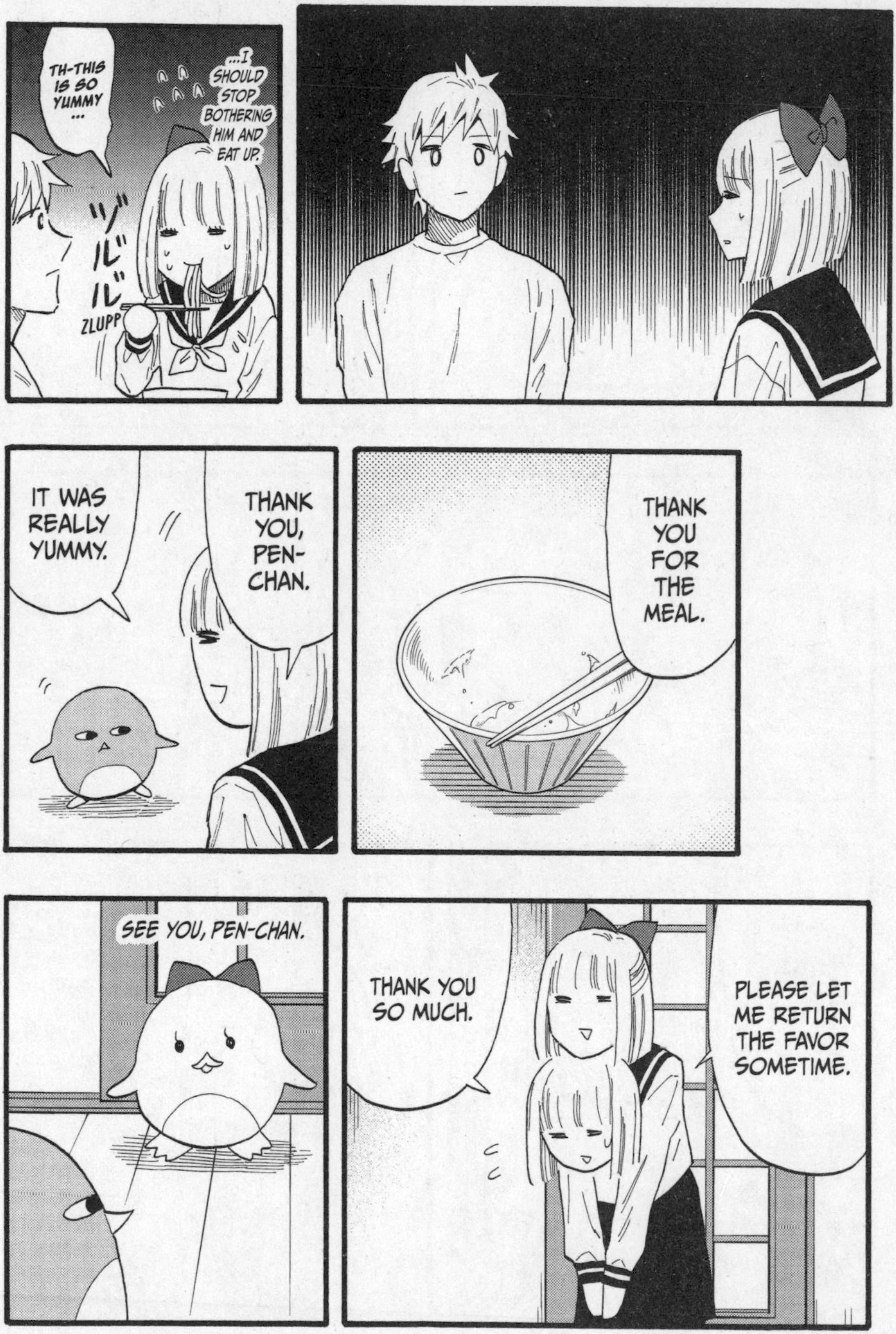
...I SHOULD STOP BOTHERING HIM AND EAT UP.
TH-THIS IS SO YUMMY ...
ZLUPP
THANK YOU FOR THE MEAL.
THANK YOU, PEN-CHAN.
IT WAS REALLY YUMMY.
PLEASE LET ME RETURN THE FAVOR SOMETIME.
THANK YOU SO MUCH.
SEE YOU, PEN-CHAN.

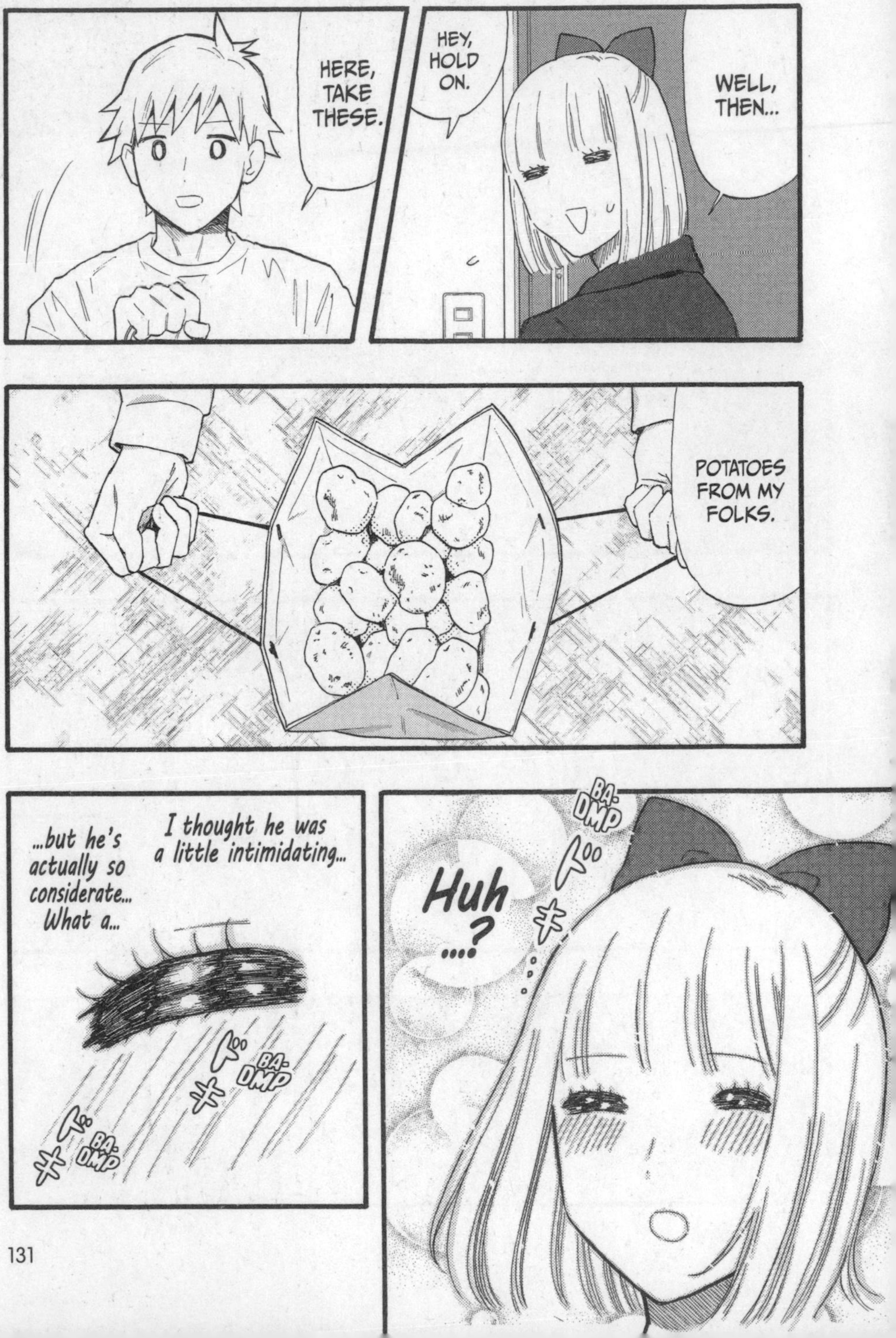
WELL, THEN...
HEY, HOLD ON.
HERE, TAKE THESE.
POTATOES FROM MY FOLKS.
BA-DOMP
ドキ
Huh ....?
I thought he was a little intimidating...
...but he's actually so considerate... What a...
BA-DOMP
ドキ
BA-DOMP
ドキ

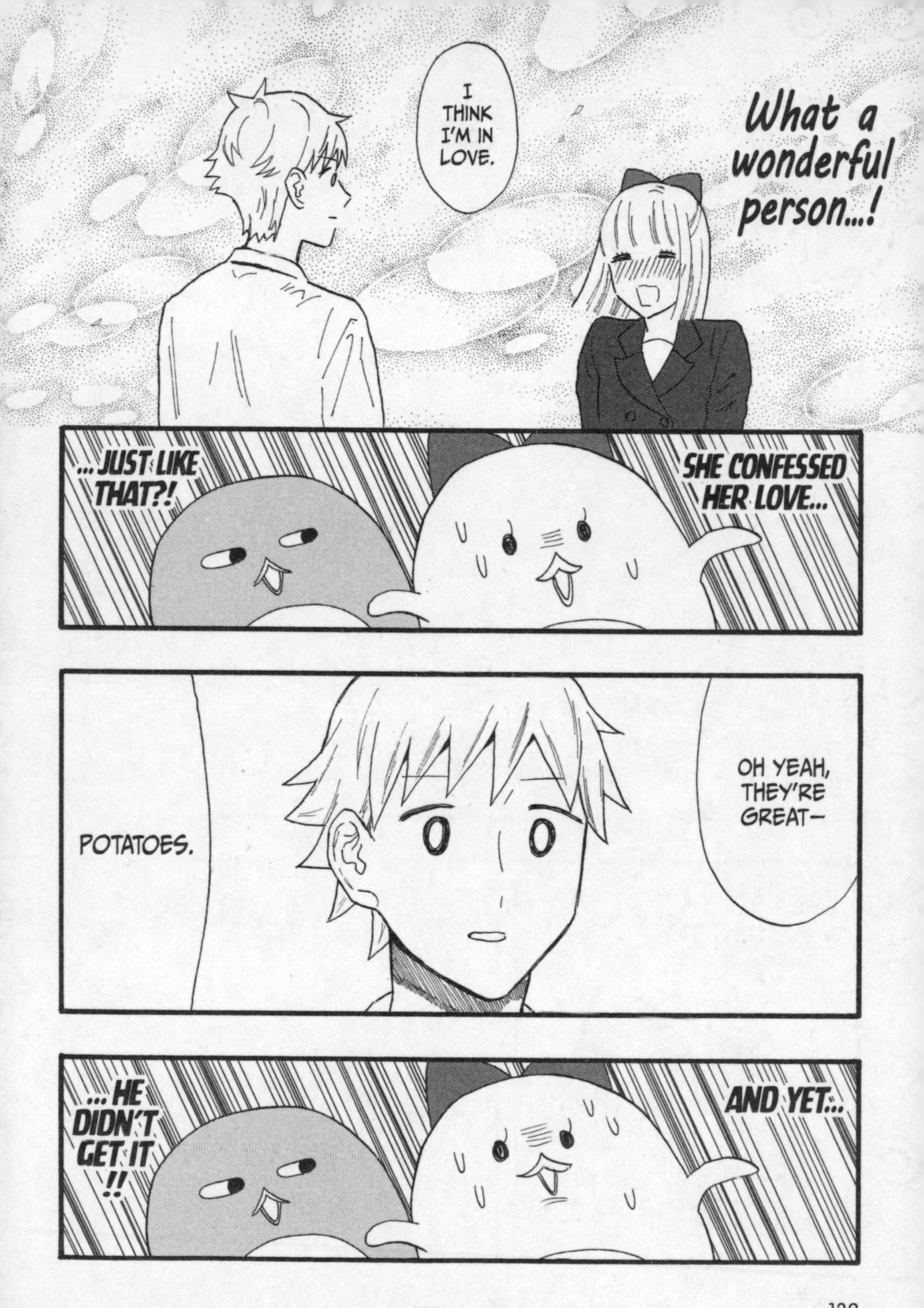
What a wonderful person...!
I THINK I'M IN LOVE.
SHE CONFESSED HER LOVE...
...JUST LIKE THAT?!
OH YEAH, THEY'RE GREAT—
POTATOES.
AND YET...
...HE DIDN'T GET IT!!

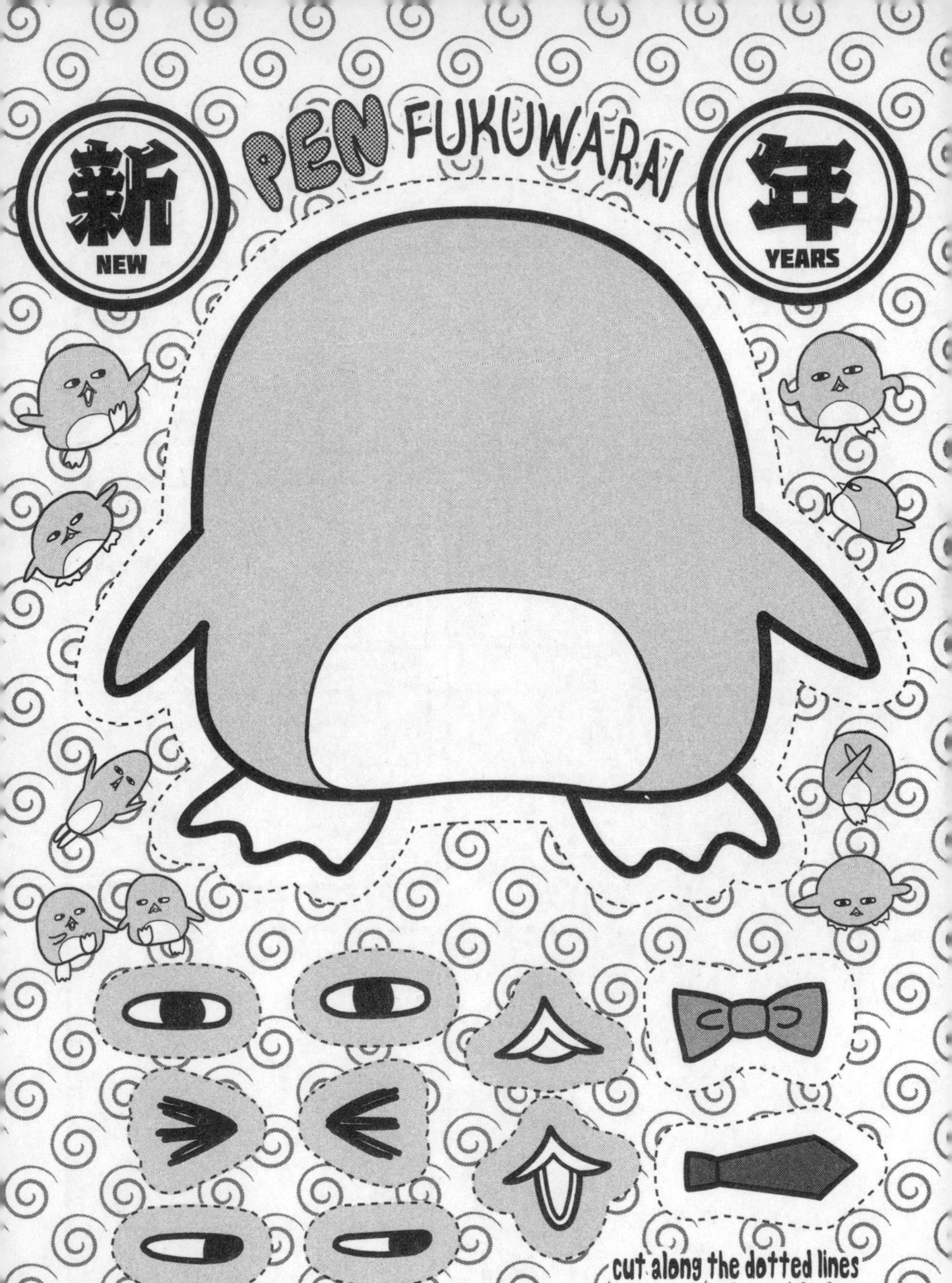
PEN FUKUWARAI
新
NEW
年
YEARS
cut along the dotted lines

Pen 13 The Penguin Gets Stalked by His Owner's Friend

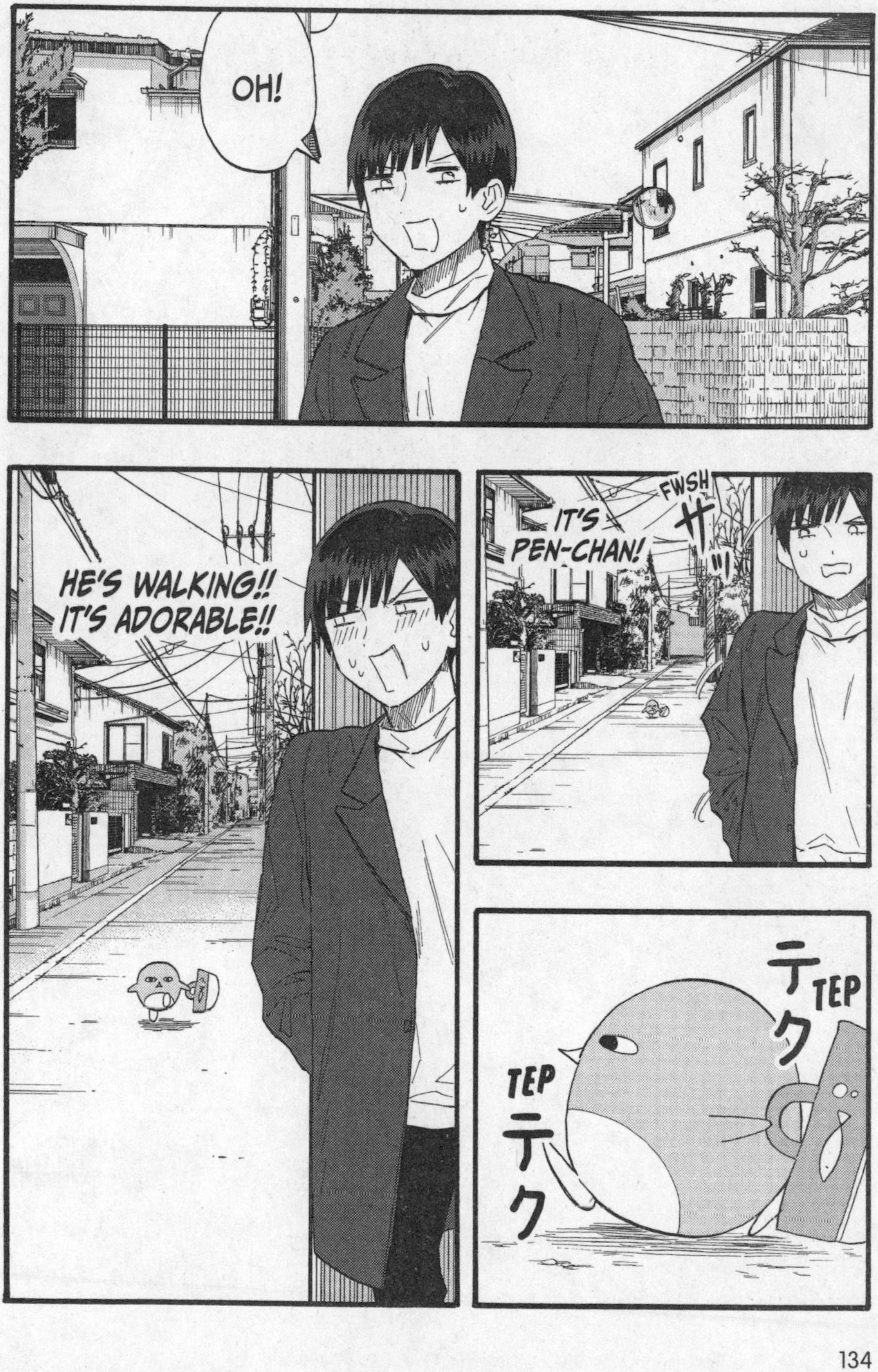
OH!
IT'S PEN-CHAN!
FWSH
テク TEP
TEP テク
HE'S WALKING!! IT'S ADORABLE!!

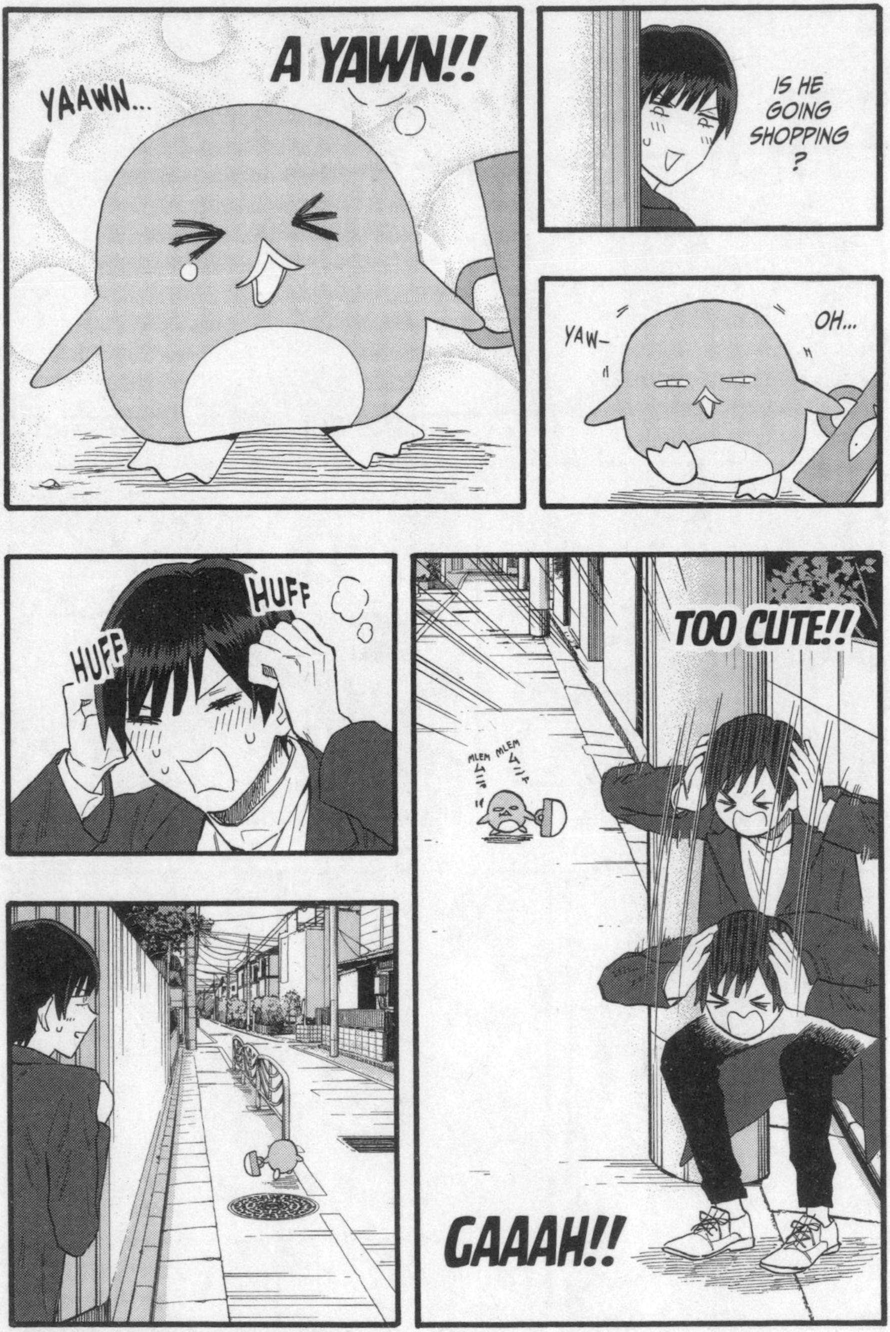
IS HE GOING SHOPPING ?
OH...
YAW—
A YAWN!!
YAAWN...
TOO CUTE!!
MLEM MLEM
GAAAH!!
HUFF
HUFF

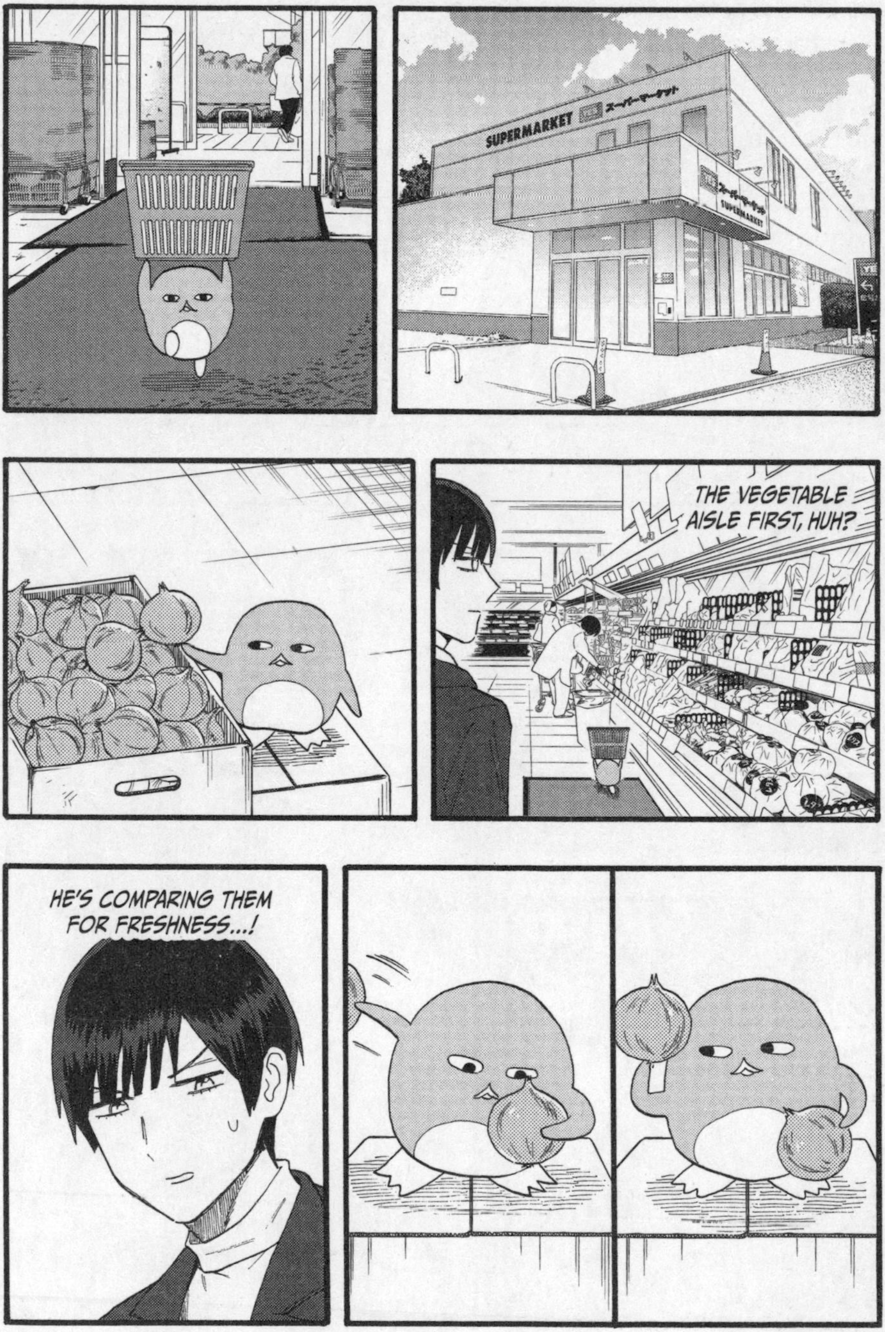
SUPERMARKET
スーパーマーケット
THE VEGETABLE AISLE FIRST, HUH?
HE'S COMPARING THEM FOR FRESHNESS...!

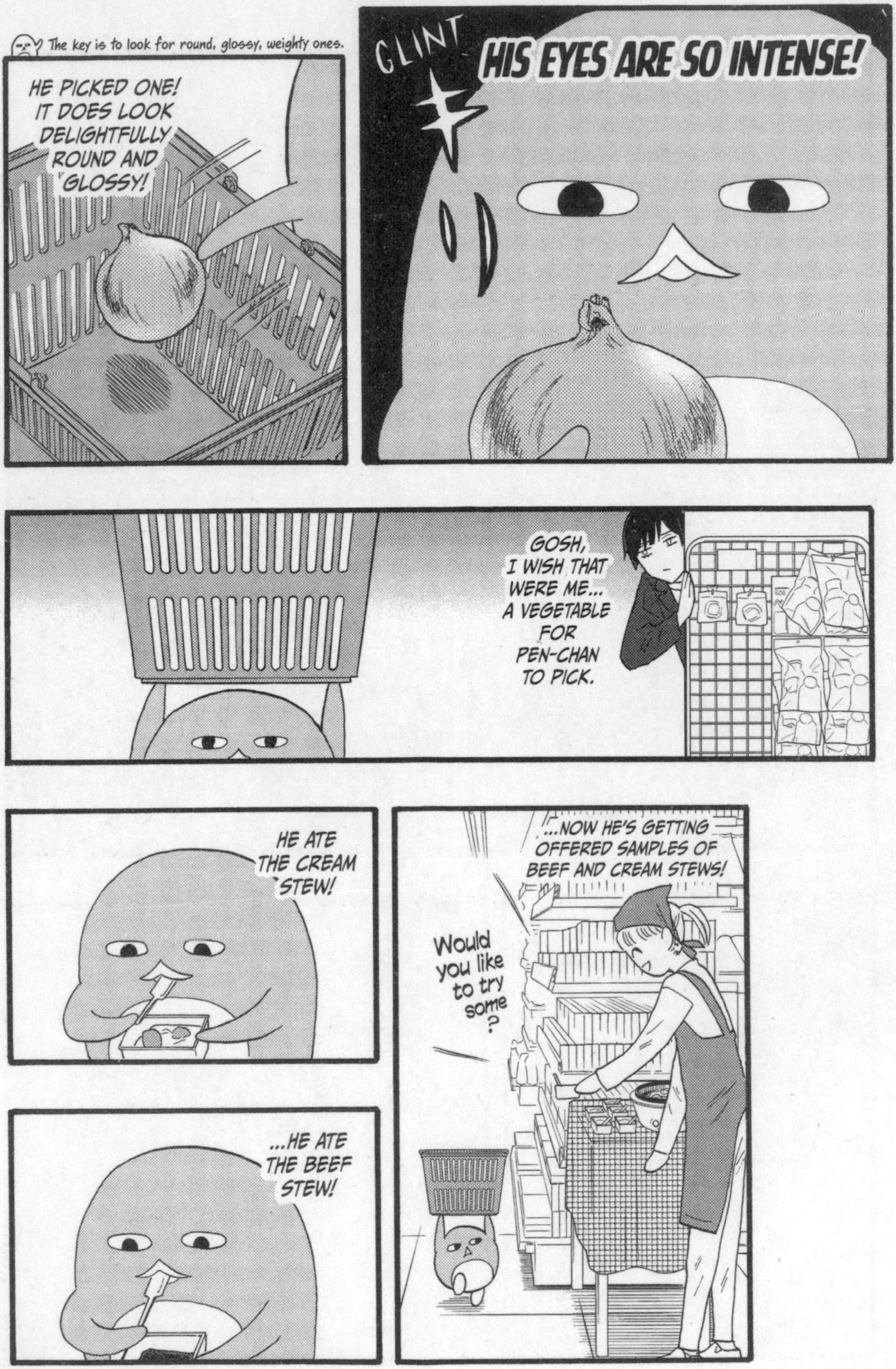
The key is to look for round, glossy, weighty ones.
GLINT
HIS EYES ARE SO INTENSE!
HE PICKED ONE! IT DOES LOOK DELIGHTFULLY ROUND AND GLOSSY!
GOSH, I WISH THAT WERE ME... A VEGETABLE FOR PEN-CHAN TO PICK.
...NOW HE'S GETTING OFFERED SAMPLES OF BEEF AND CREAM STEWS!
Would you like to try some?
HE ATE THE CREAM STEW!
...HE ATE THE BEEF STEW!

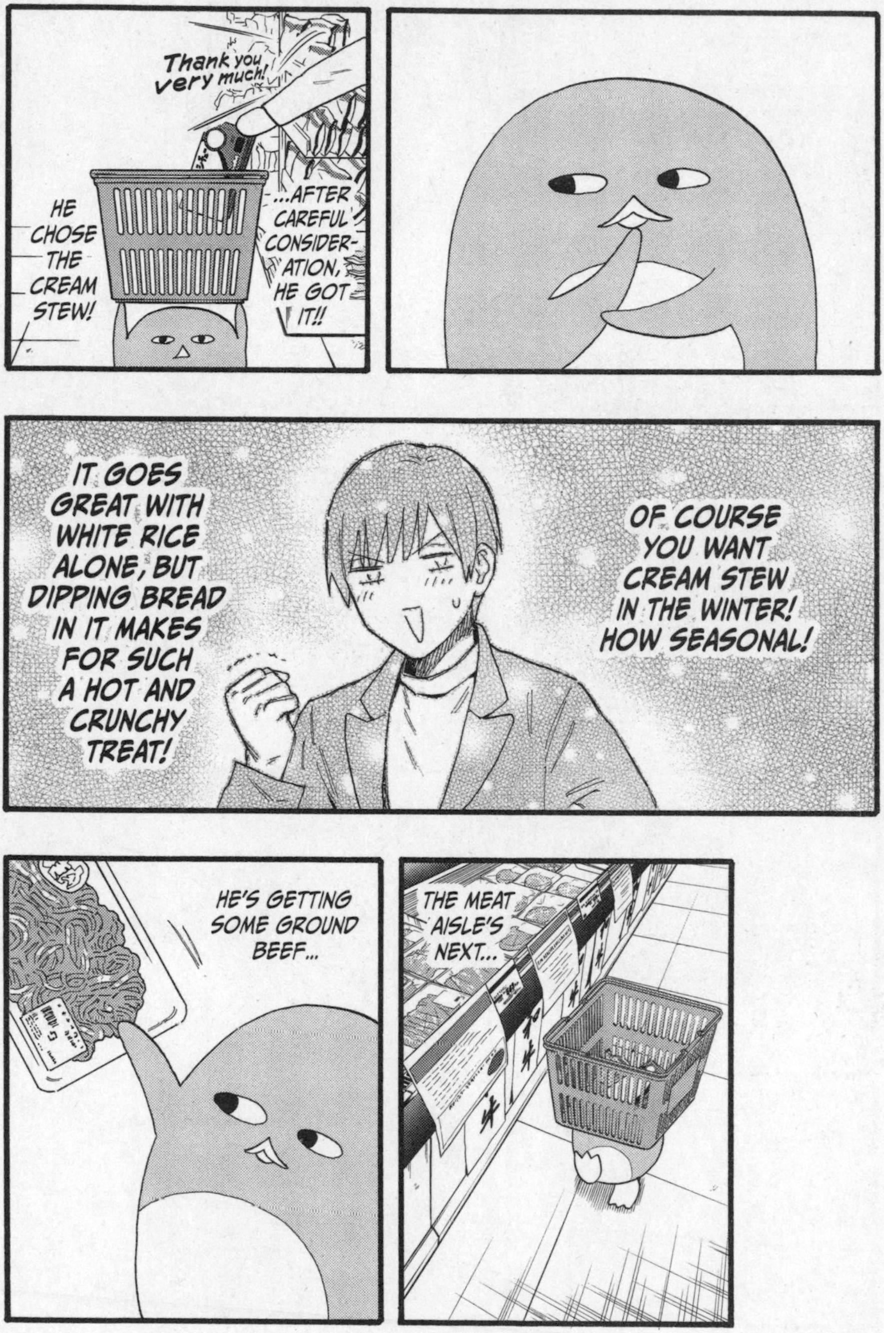
Thank you very much!
...AFTER CAREFUL CONSIDERATION, HE GOT IT!!
HE CHOSE THE CREAM STEW!
OF COURSE YOU WANT CREAM STEW IN THE WINTER! HOW SEASONAL!
IT GOES GREAT WITH WHITE RICE ALONE, BUT DIPPING BREAD IN IT MAKES FOR SUCH A HOT AND CRUNCHY TREAT!
THE MEAT AISLE'S NEXT...
HE'S GETTING SOME GROUND BEEF...

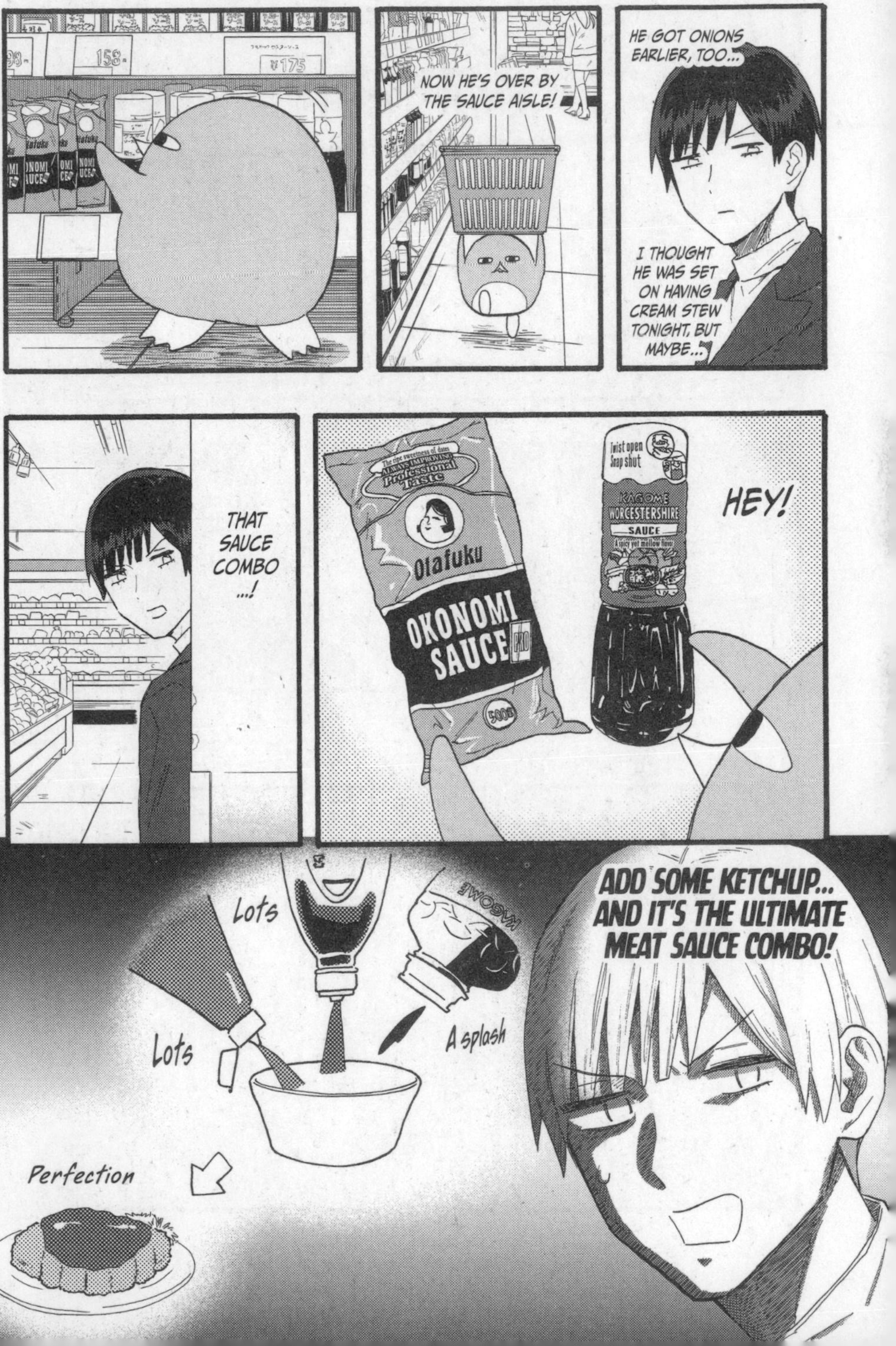
HE GOT ONIONS EARLIER, TOO...
I THOUGHT HE WAS SET ON HAVING CREAM STEW TONIGHT, BUT MAYBE...
NOW HE'S OVER BY THE SAUCE AISLE!
Twist open Snap shut
KAGOME WORCESTERSHIRE SAUCE
A spicy yet mellow flavor
HEY!
The ripe sweetness of dates
ALWAYS IMPROVING
Professional Taste
Olafuku
OKONOMI SAUCE PRO
500g
THAT SAUCE COMBO ...!
ADD SOME KETCHUP... AND IT'S THE ULTIMATE MEAT SAUCE COMBO!
A splash
Lots
Lots
Perfection

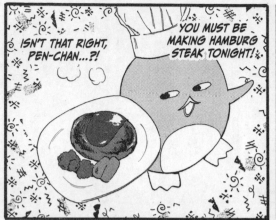

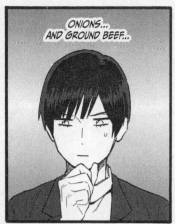

ONIONS... AND GROUND BEEF...
YOU MUST BE MAKING HAMBURG STEAK TONIGHT!
ISN'T THAT RIGHT, PEN-CHAN...?!
I WANNA EAT THAT, TOOOO...!
WHIRR
SHOOT, I FOLLOWED PEN-CHAN FOR THE WHOLE GROCERY TRIP...

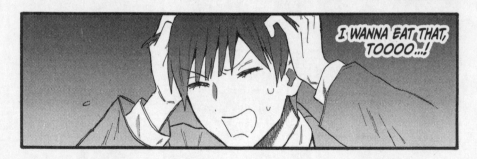

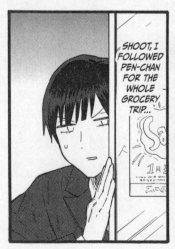

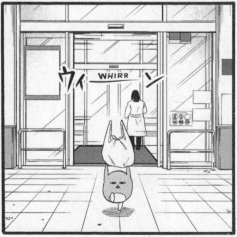

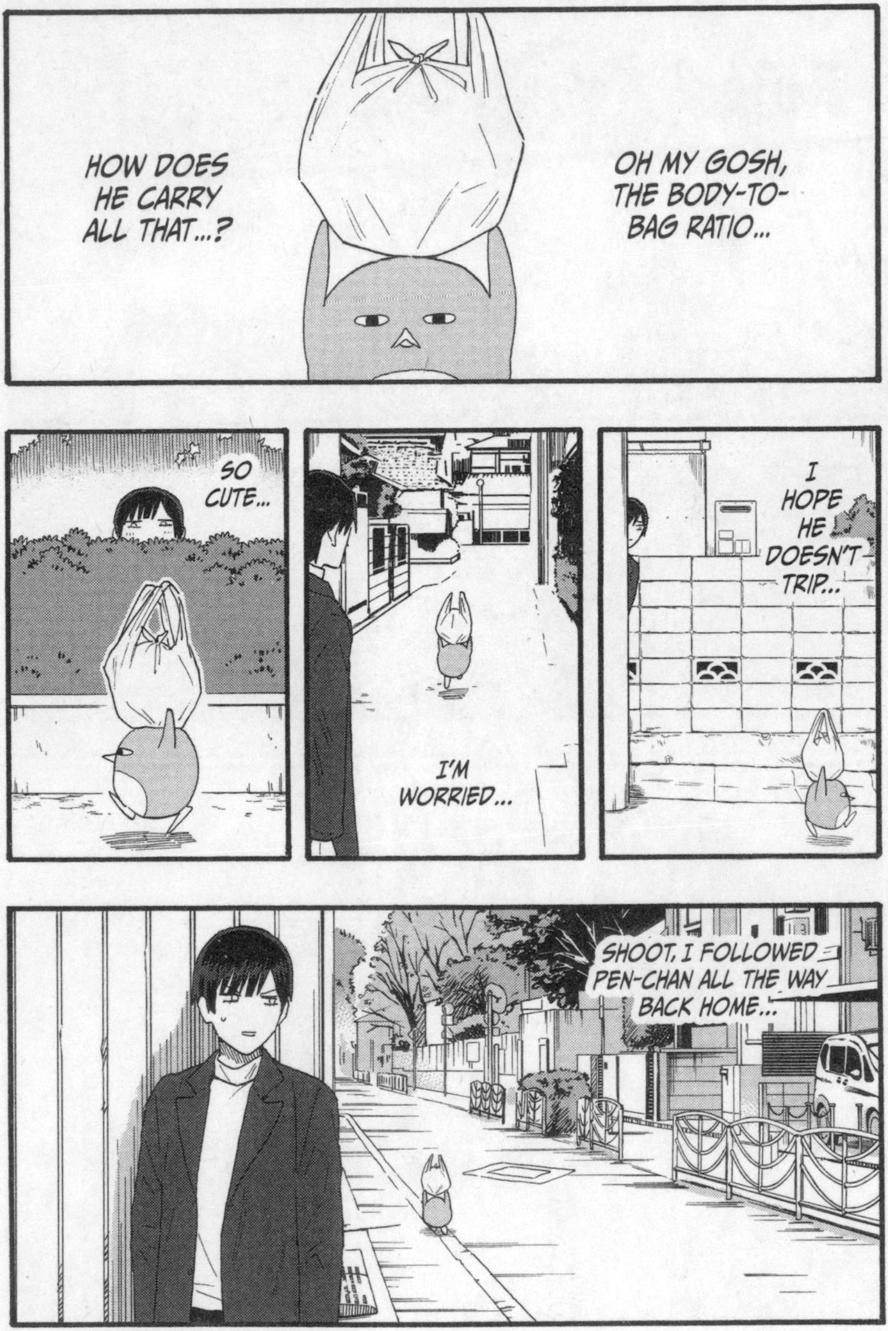
OH MY GOSH, THE BODY-TO-BAG RATIO...
HOW DOES HE CARRY ALL THAT...?
I HOPE HE DOESN'T TRIP...
I'M WORRIED...
SO CUTE...
SHOOT, I FOLLOWED PEN-CHAN ALL THE WAY BACK HOME...

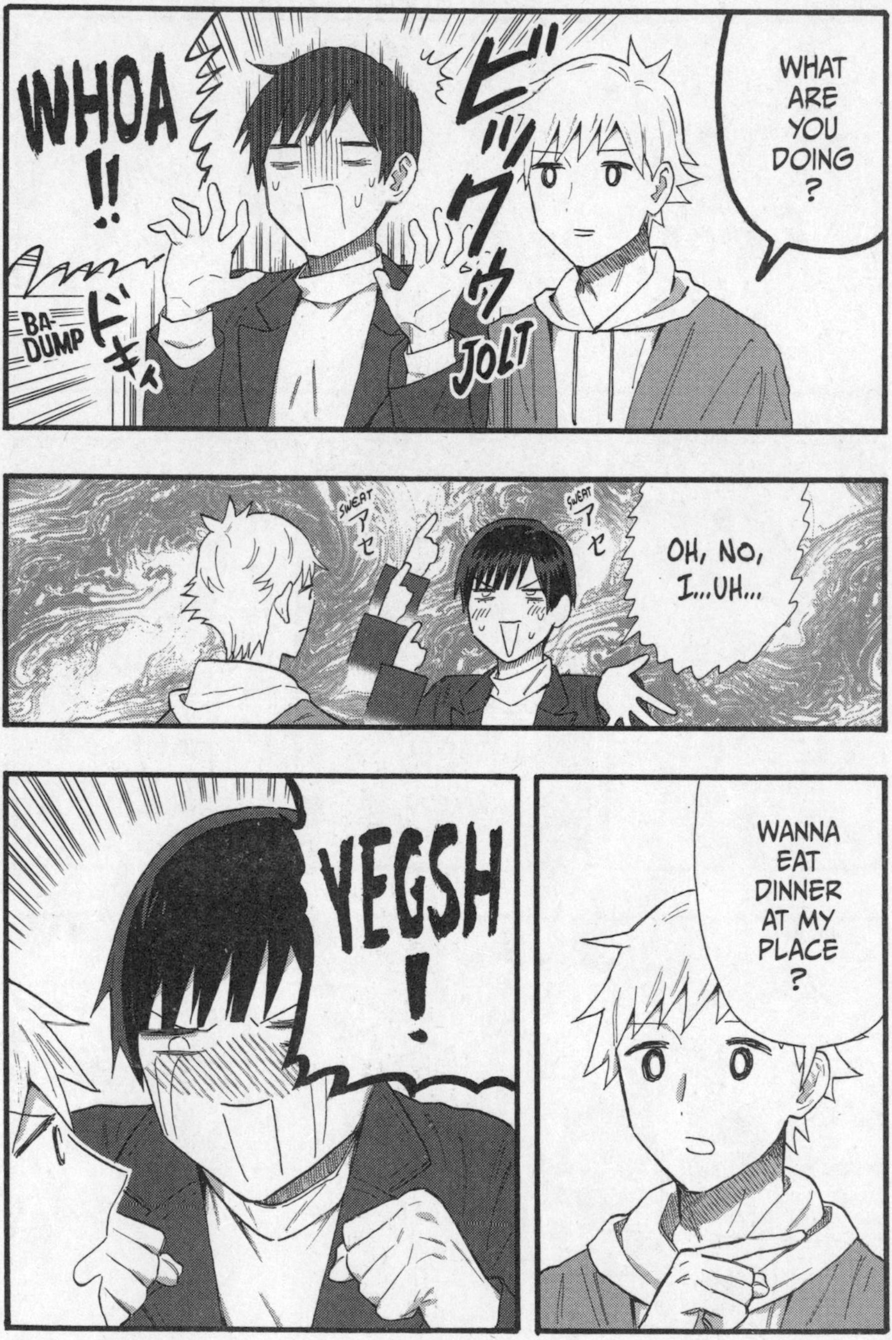
WHAT ARE YOU DOING?
ビクゥ
JOLT
WHOA!!
ドキィ
BA-DUMP
OH, NO, I...UH...
SWEAT アセ
SWEAT アセ
WANNA EAT DINNER AT MY PLACE?
YEGSH!

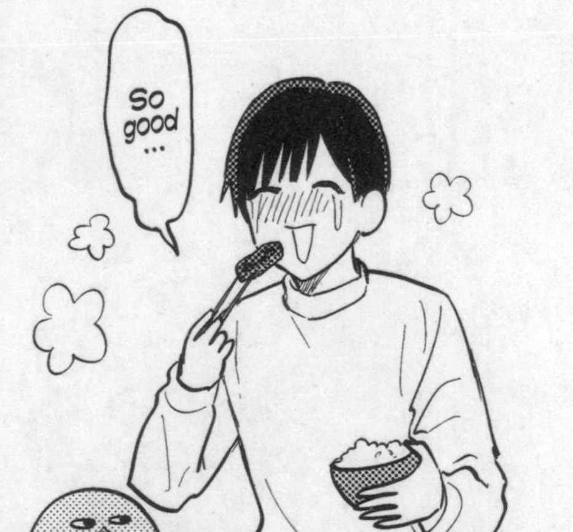
So good ...

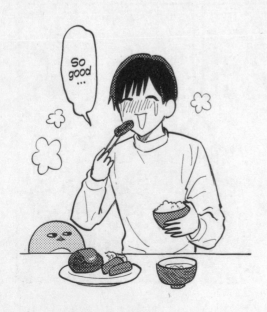

LAZE
ごろ
LAZE
ごろ
LIFESTYLE
WINTER PLEASURES
FLIP
ピラ
WHAT YOU NEED IN YOUR LIFE RIGHT NOW:
The World of Knitting
LIGHTWEIGHT AND WARM

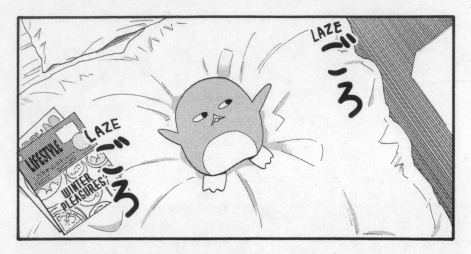

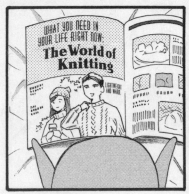

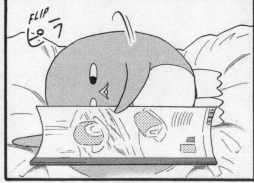

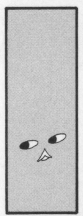

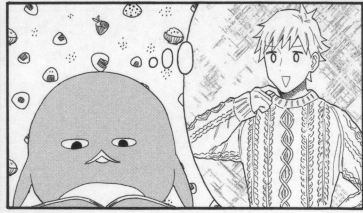

Pen 14 The Penguin Knits a Sweater for His Owner

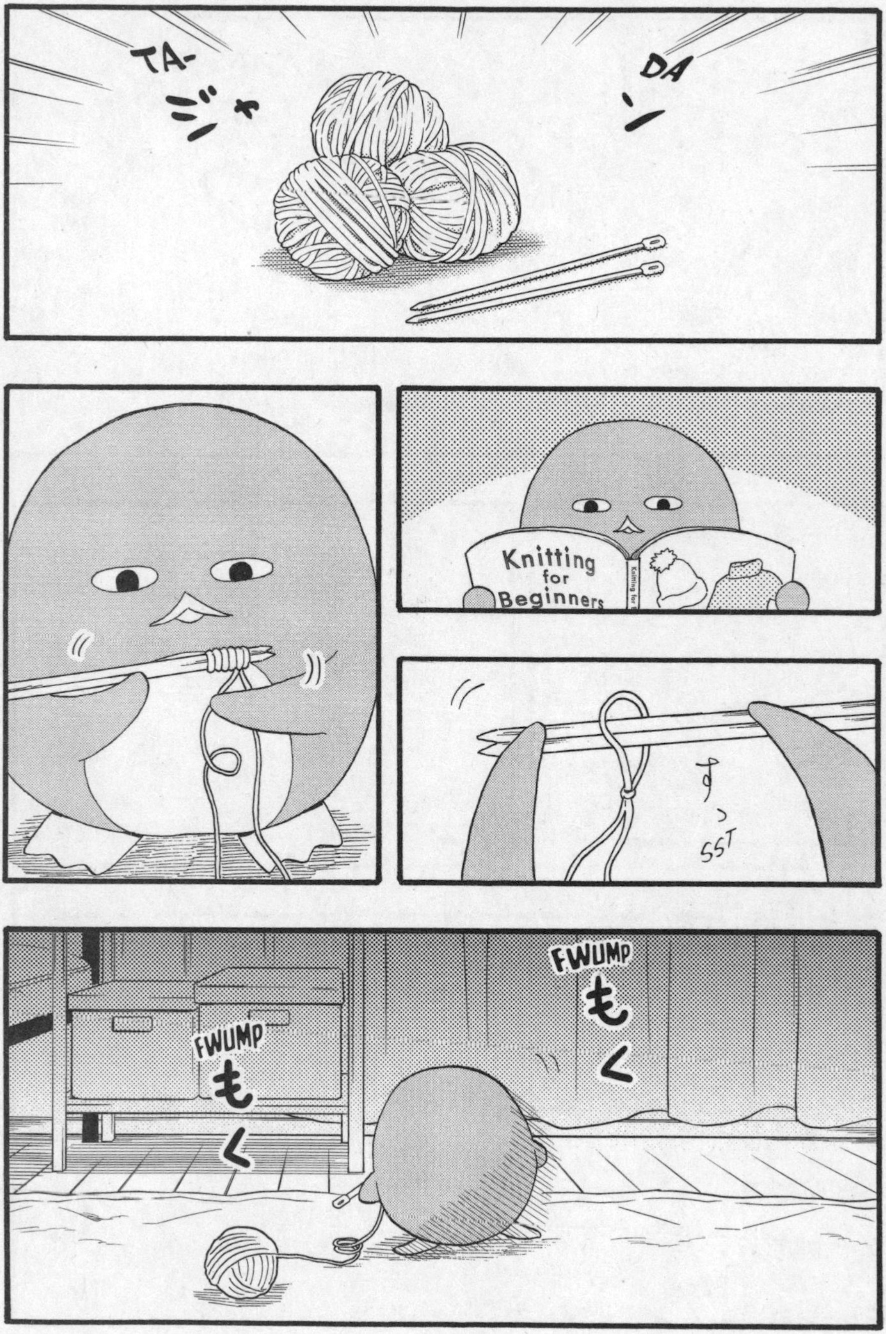
TA-
ジャ
DA
ン
Knitting for Beginners
すっ
SST
FWUMP
もく
FWUMP
もく

あみ
KNIT
KNIT
あみ
FLIP
パラ
FLIP
パラ
Knitting for Beginners
Easy tips for first-timers.
Q What should I do if I make a mistake?
A The best thing to do is to undo the stiches and do it over! There are a few tricks for fixing mistakes, but they can end u messing up your knitting instead. We don't recomm them for beginners.
Knitting for Beginners
Easy

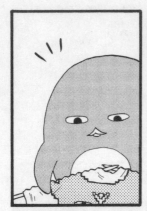

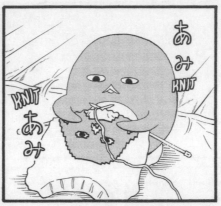

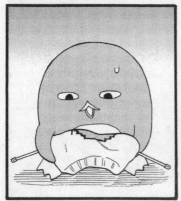

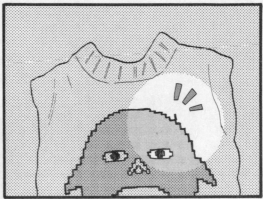

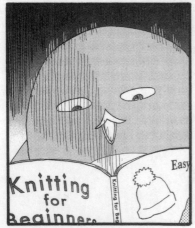

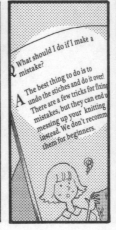

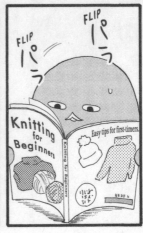

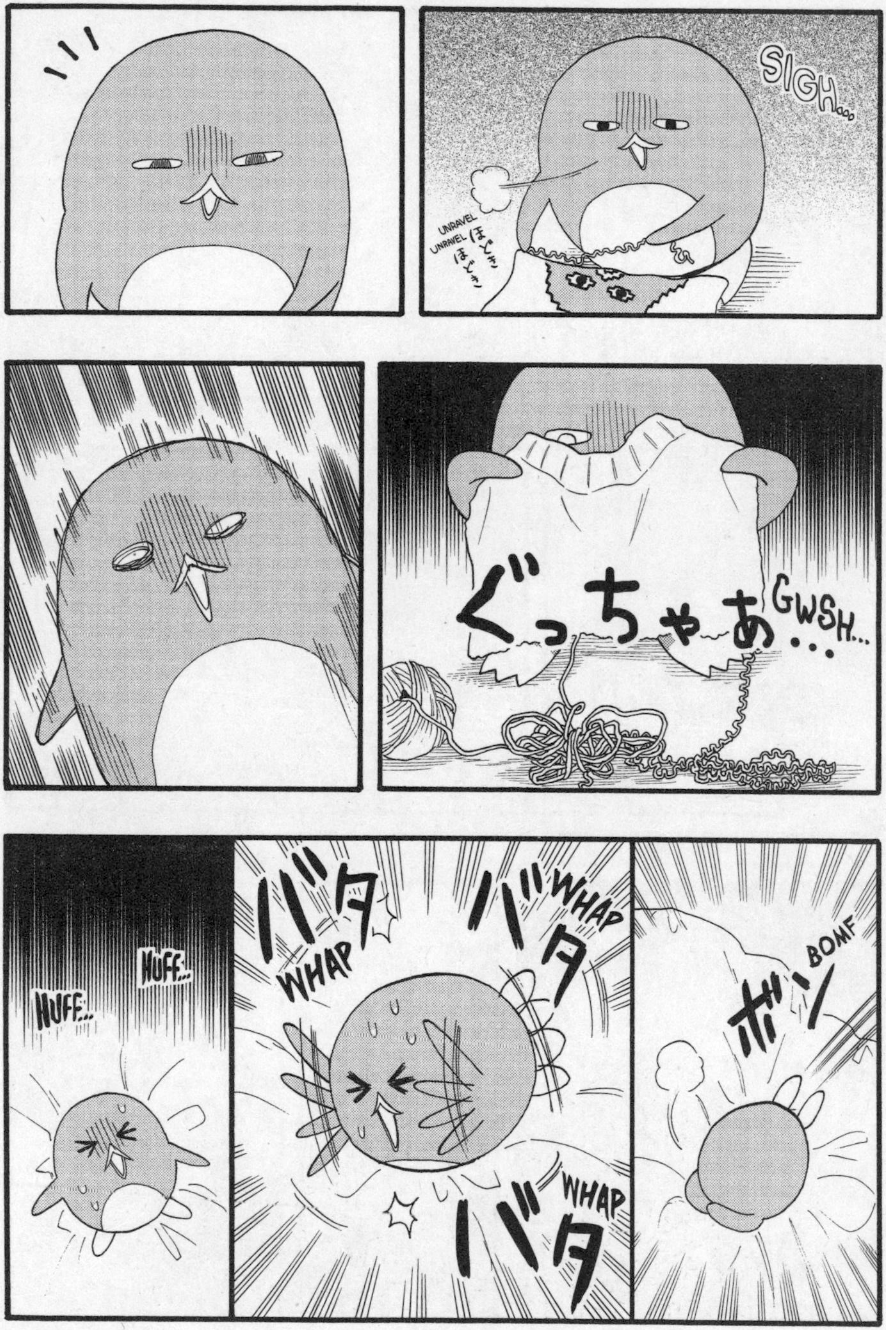
SIGH...
ほどき ほどき
UNRAVEL UNRAVEL
ぐっちゃぁ...
GWSH...
ボン
BOMF
バタ
WHAP
バタ
WHAP
バタ
WHAP
HUFF...
HUFF...

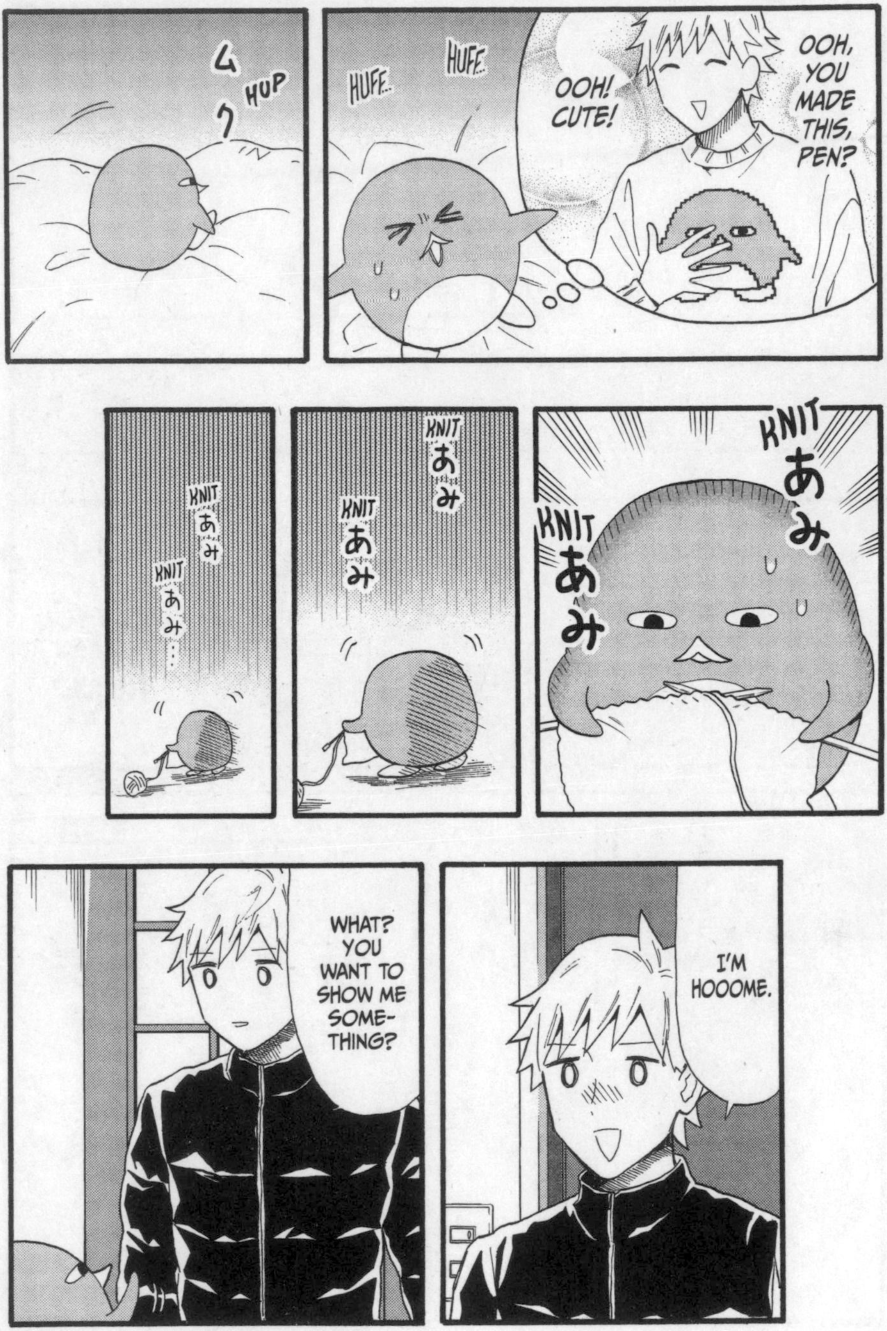
OOH, YOU MADE THIS, PEN?
OOH! CUTE!
HUFF...
HUFF...
ムク
HUP
KNIT あみ
KNIT あみ
KNIT あみ
KNIT あみ
KNIT あみ
KNIT あみ...
I'M HOOOME.
WHAT? YOU WANT TO SHOW ME SOME-THING?

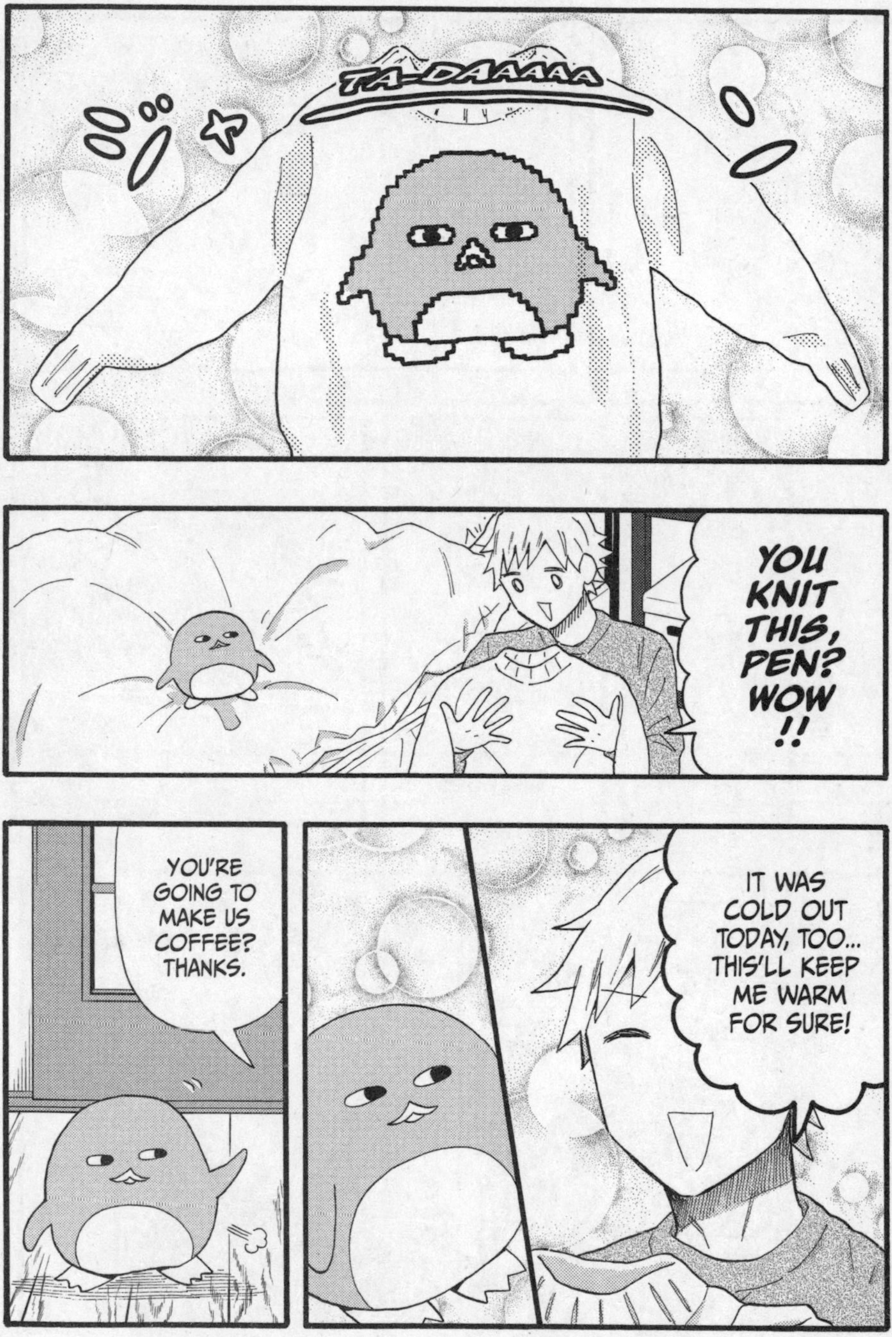
TA-DAAAAA
YOU KNIT THIS, PEN? WOW!!
IT WAS COLD OUT TODAY, TOO... THIS'LL KEEP ME WARM FOR SURE!
YOU'RE GOING TO MAKE US COFFEE? THANKS.

つんっ
THOCK
VWSH
WATCH OUT!!
BLAT

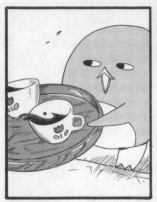

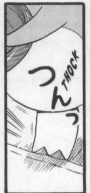

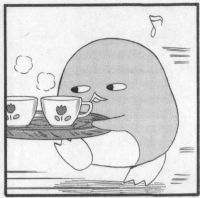

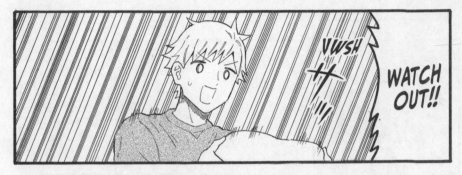

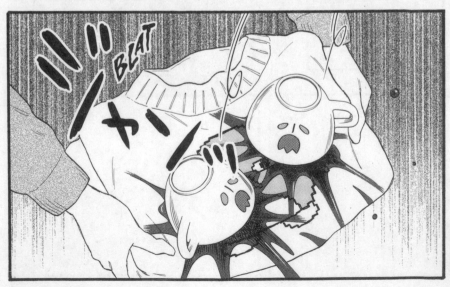

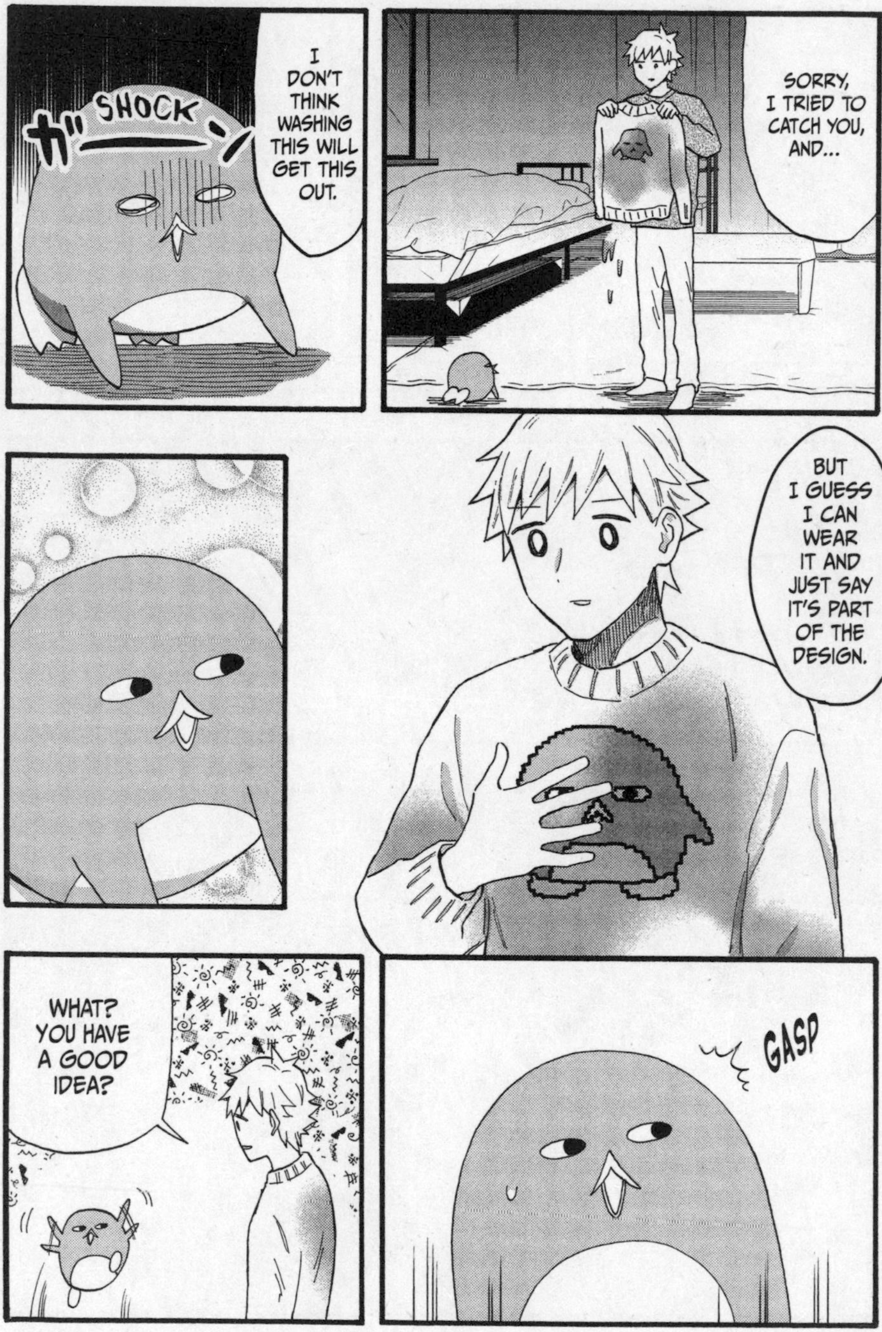
SORRY, I TRIED TO CATCH YOU, AND...
SHOCK
I DON'T THINK WASHING THIS WILL GET THIS OUT.
BUT I GUESS I CAN WEAR IT AND JUST SAY IT'S PART OF THE DESIGN.
GASP
WHAT? YOU HAVE A GOOD IDEA?

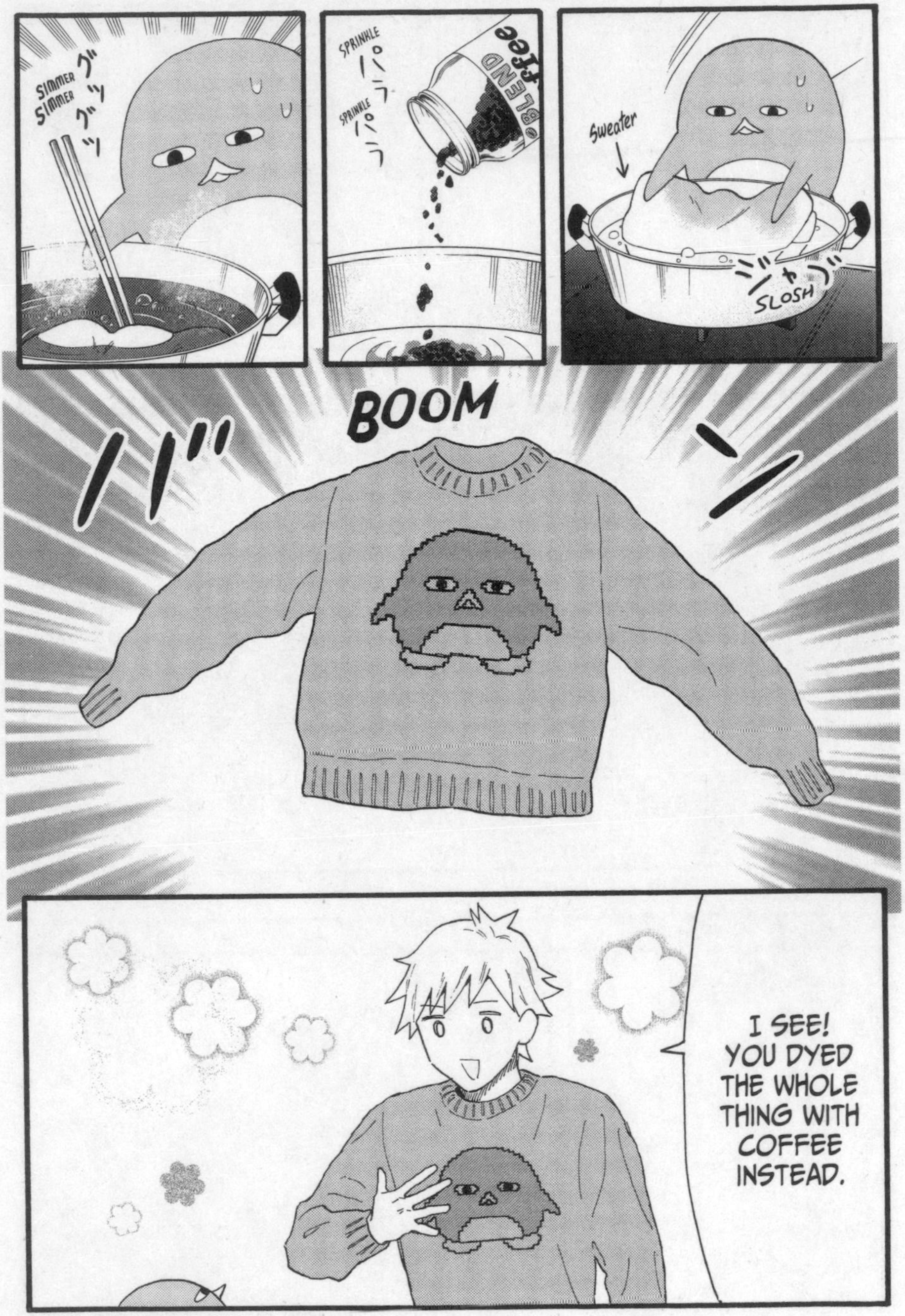
Sweater
SLOSH
SPRINKLE パラ
SPRINKLE パラ
SIMMER グツ
SIMMER グツ
BOOM
I SEE! YOU DYED THE WHOLE THING WITH COFFEE INSTEAD.

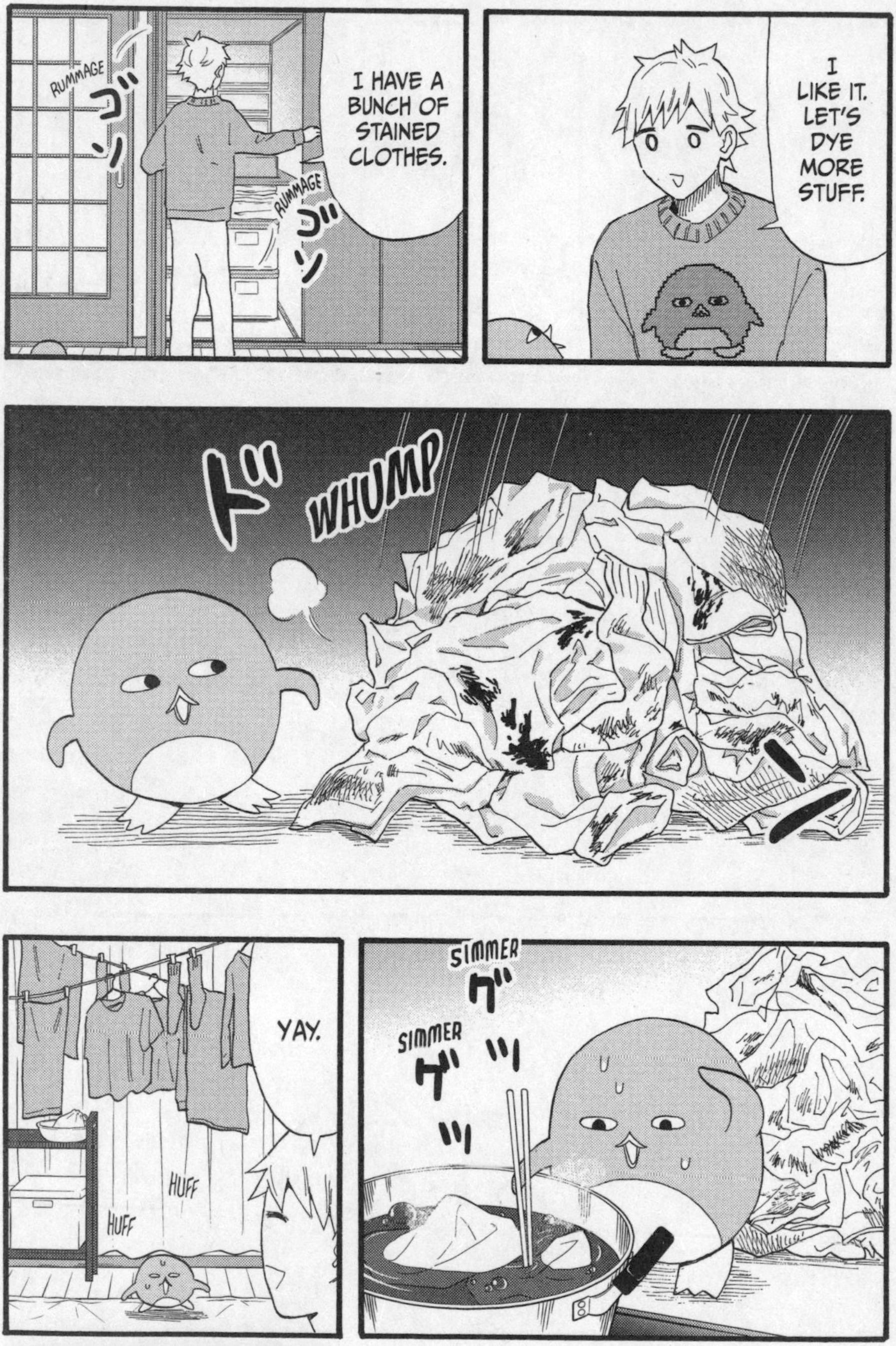
I LIKE IT. LET'S DYE MORE STUFF.
I HAVE A BUNCH OF STAINED CLOTHES.
RUMMAGE
ゴソ
RUMMAGE
ゴソ
ドッ
WHUMP
SIMMER
グツ
SIMMER
グツ
YAY.
HUFF
HUFF

TO BE CONTINUED IN VOLUME 2!

What's Really Important

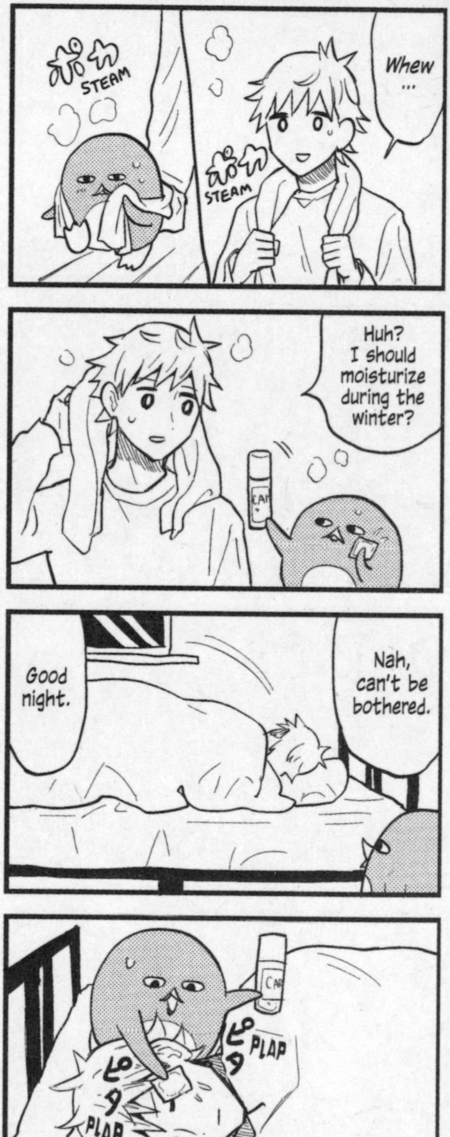
ポカ STEAM
ポカ STEAM
Whew ...
Huh? I should moisturize during the winter?
Nah, can't be bothered.
Good night.
ピタ PLAP
ピタ PLAP

Just-Picked and Fresh!

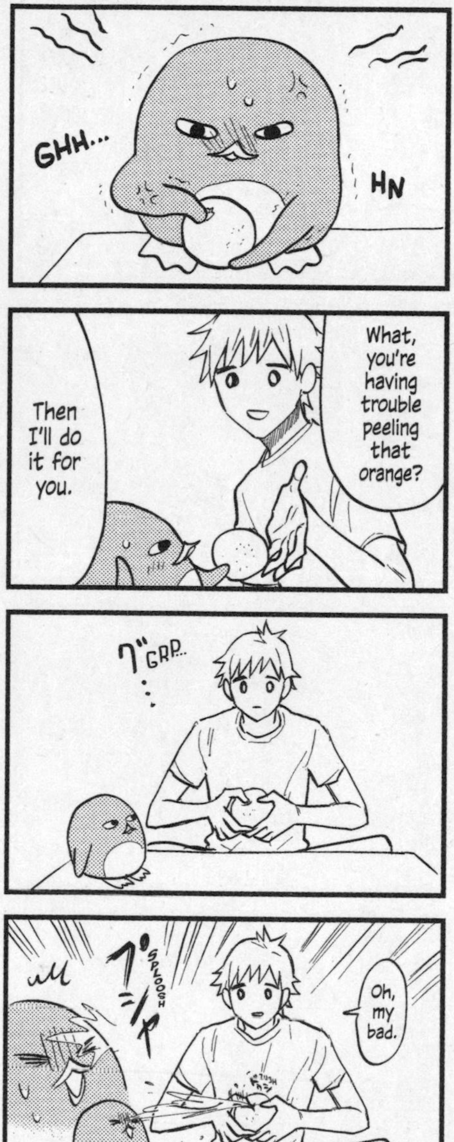
GHH...
HN
What, you're having trouble peeling that orange?
Then I'll do it for you.
グ GRP...
SPLOOSH
Oh, my bad.

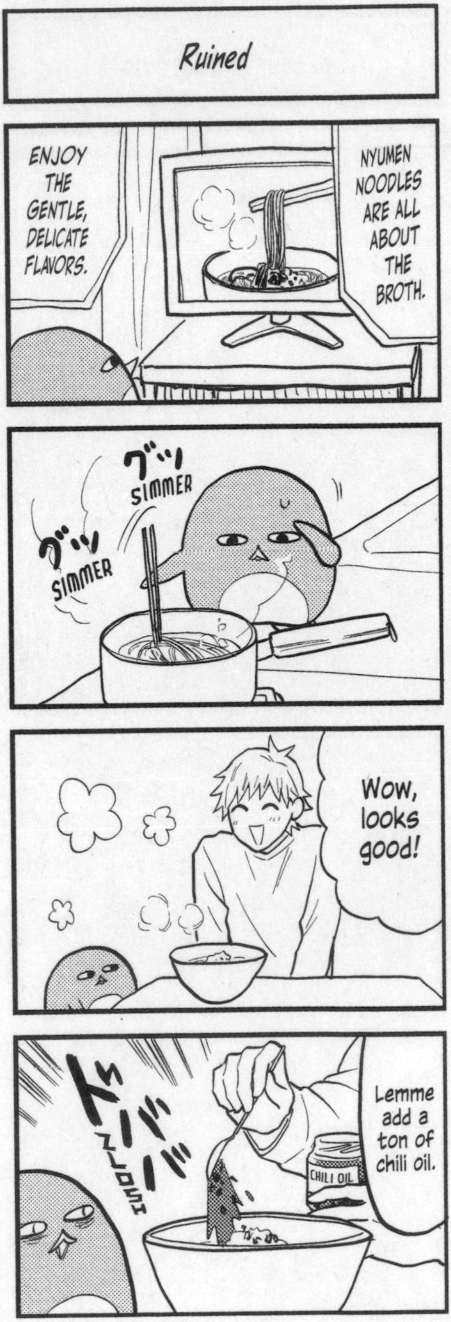
Ruined
NYUMEN NOODLES ARE ALL ABOUT THE BROTH.
ENJOY THE GENTLE, DELICATE FLAVORS.
グツ
SIMMER
グツ
SIMMER
Wow, looks good!
Lemme add a ton of chili oil.
ドバババ
SLOOSH
CHILI OIL

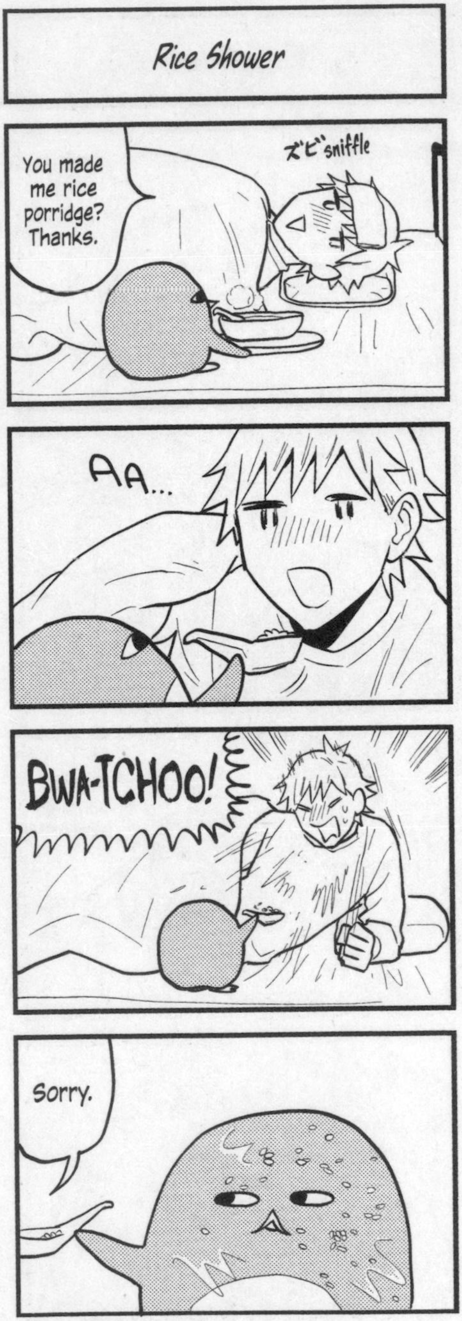
Rice Shower
ズビ sniffle
You made me rice porridge? Thanks.
AA...
BWA-TCHOO!
Sorry.

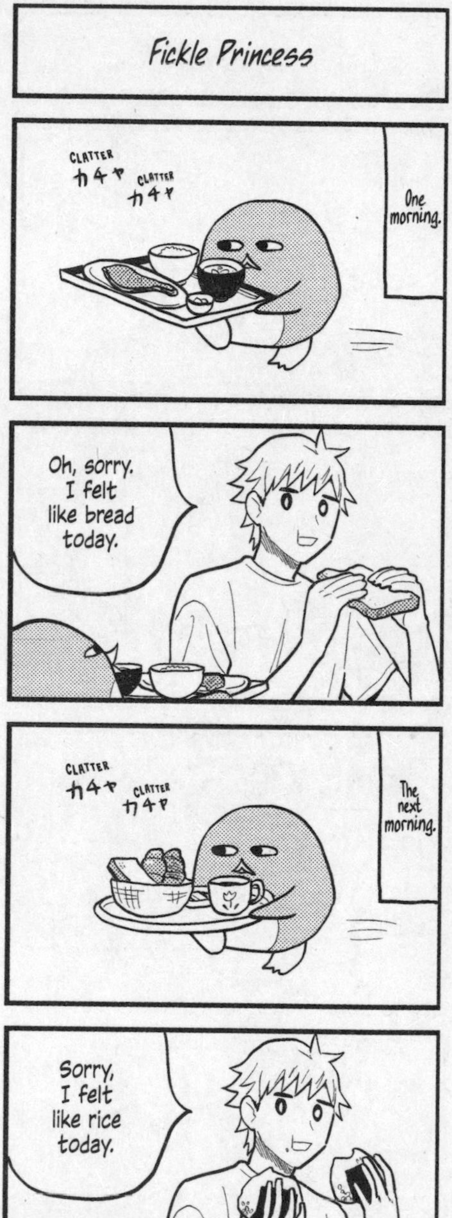
Fickle Princess
One morning.
CLATTER
カチャ
CLATTER
カチャ
Oh, sorry. I felt like bread today.
The next morning.
CLATTER
カチャ
CLATTER
カチャ
Sorry, I felt like rice today.

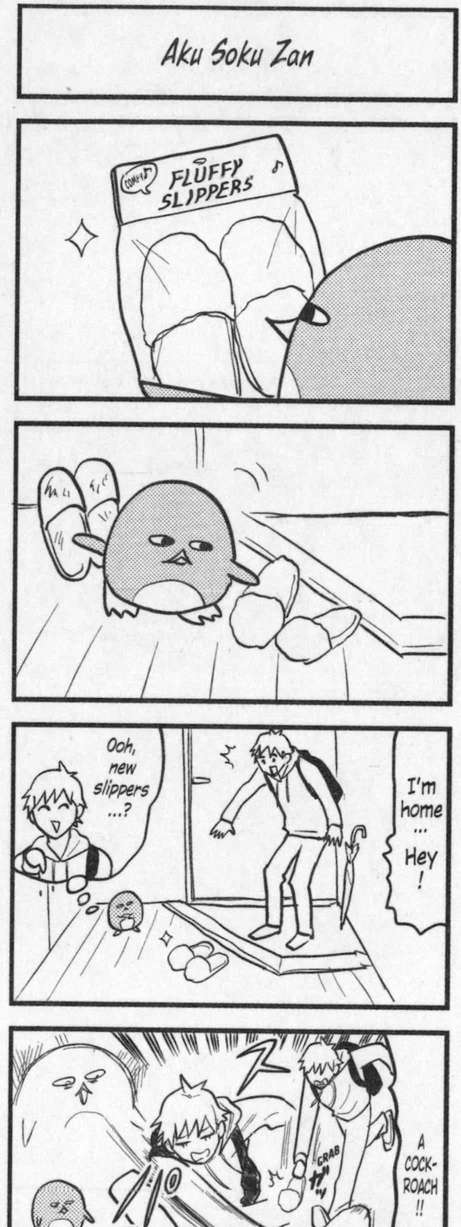
Aku Soku Zan
COMFY♪
FLUFFY SLIPPERS
I'm home... Hey!
Ooh, new slippers ...?
A COCKROACH!!
GRAB
SLAP!

Mirage

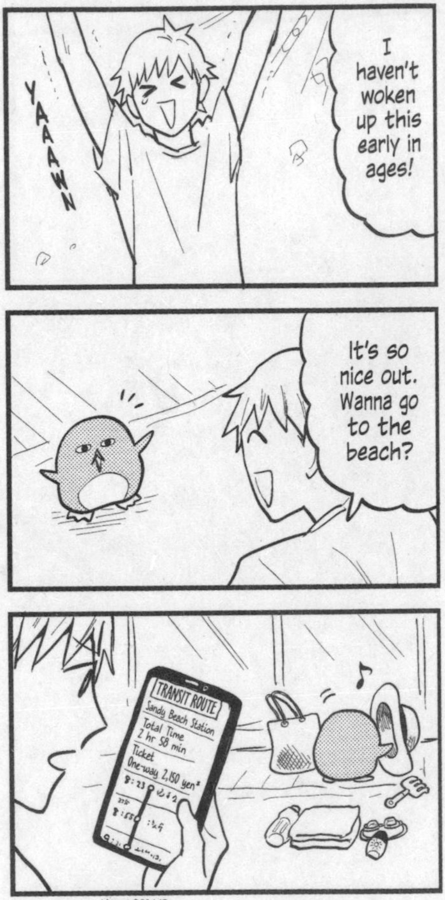
YAAAAWN
I haven't woken up this early in ages!
It's so nice out. Wanna go to the beach?
TRANSIT ROUTE
Sandy Beach Station
Total Time 2 hr 58 min
Ticket One-way 2,150 yen*
Forget it, I'm going back to sleep.

• About $21 US.

11 Years

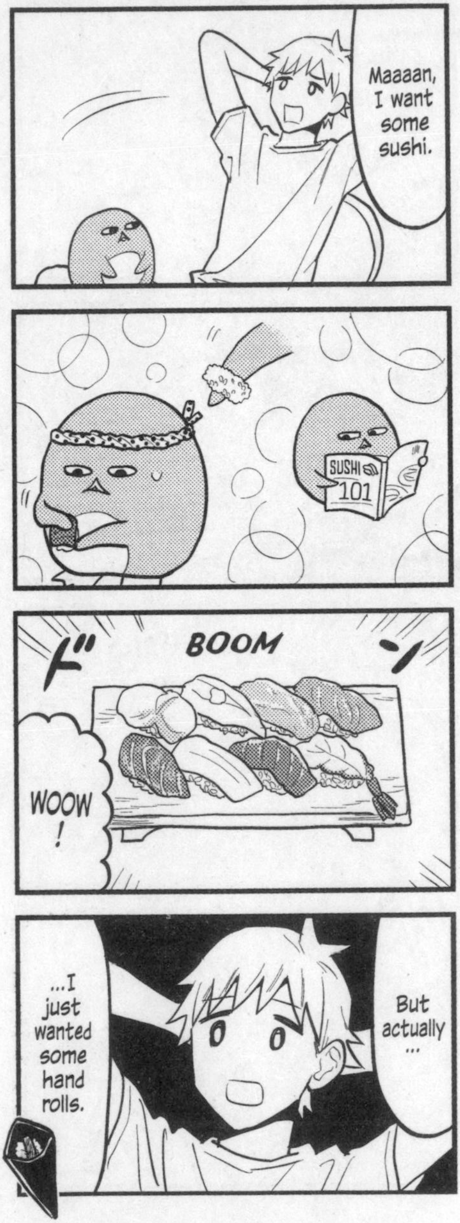
Maaaan, I want some sushi.
SUSHI 101
ド
BOOM
ーン
WOOW!
But actually...
...I just wanted some hand rolls.

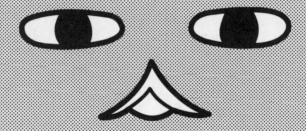

GUIN

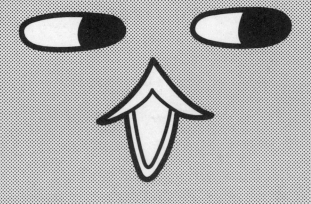

PEN.

Akiho Ieda
家田明歩

I feel so incredibly lucky that what started off as a random drawing got serialized, and now, in an unexpected turn of events, it is an actual book! So far, everything has been thanks to luck. It's true that "Life is Just a Miracle." I would really appreciate your continued support as I press on!

Translation Notes

pg 3

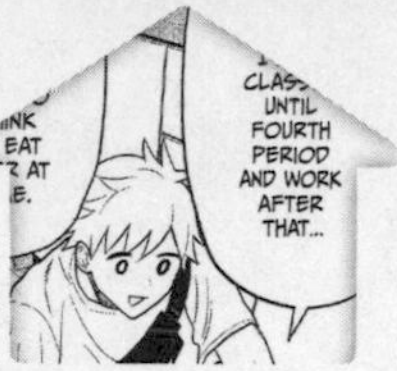
UNTIL FOURTH PERIOD AND WORK AFTER THAT...

FOURTH PERIOD

Class schedules at Japanese universities are split into "periods" that each last about an hour and a half.

pg 9

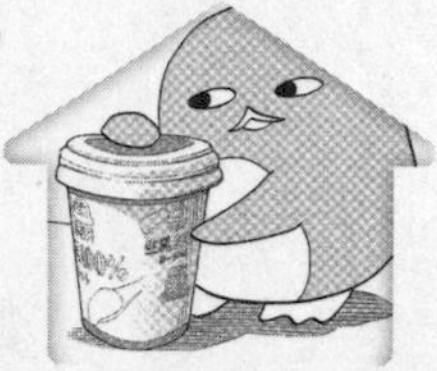

YOGURT

Pen-chan is using a process to help tenderize the meat.

pg 13

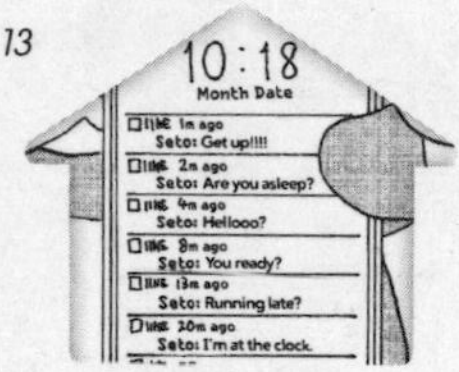
10:18
Month Date
IINE 1m ago Seto: Get up!!!!
IINE 2m ago Seto: Are you asleep?
IINE 4m ago Seto: Hellooo?
IINE 8m ago Seto: You ready?
IINE 13m ago Seto: Running late?
IINE 20m ago Seto: I'm at the clock.

IINE

A reference to LINE, the most popular free messaging app in Japan.

pg 14

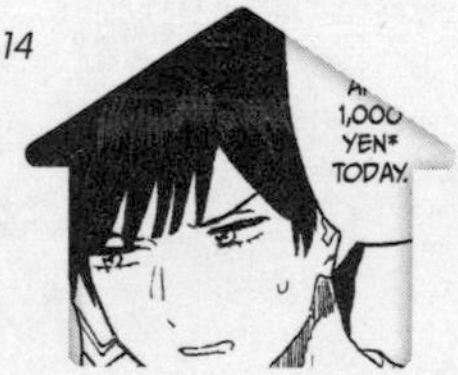
1,000 YEN* TODAY.

TICKETS ARE 1,000 YEN TODAY

Movie tickets are typically about 1,800 yen (approx. $18) for adults and 1,500 yen (approx. $15) for university students, but theaters occasionally have days when tickets are cheaper, often on the first day of the month.

pg 30

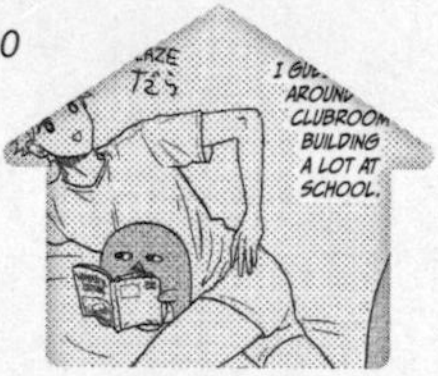
CLUBROOM BUILDING A LOT AT SCHOOL.

CLUBROOM BUILDING

Most Japanese universities, high schools, and junior high schools have a building with rooms designated for club use.

pg 37

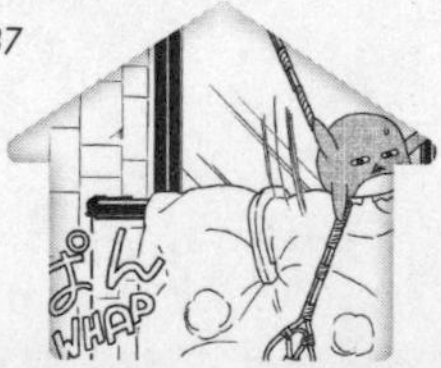
WHAP

SLAPPING THE COMFORTER

In Japan, comforters and futon mattresses are periodically aired out in the sun to supposedly prevent mold and mites. Traditionally, one would slap the comforter with a special stick to knock the dust out.

pg 45

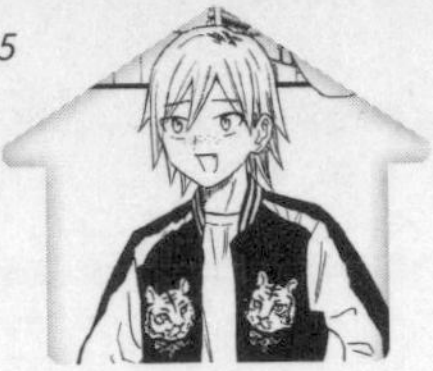

OTA IS FROM KANSAI

Ota embodies the classic Kansai character from Osaka, with a loud, cheery Kansai dialect and a tendency to butt in and call others out on things that don't make sense. His clothes often feature tigers or a capital "T" in reference to the famous Hanshin Tigers, Osaka's professional baseball team.

pg 45

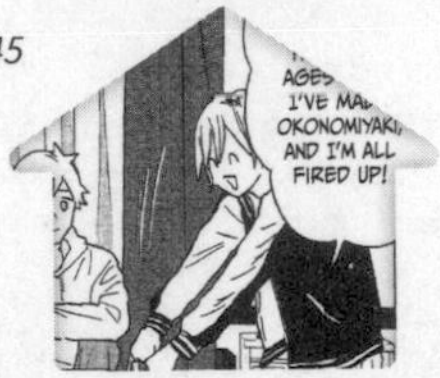
OKONOMIYAKI, AND I'M ALL FIRED UP!

OKONOMIYAKI

A savory pancake with a cabbage and batter base that is very popular in the Kansai region, particularly in Osaka and Hiroshima. *"Okonomi"* means "as you like it," and all kinds of ingredients can be added, from the classic pork or seafood, to other fare such as kimchi or avocado. The whole thing is usually topped with a sweet and savory *okonomiyaki* sauce, mayonnaise, and green nori seaweed flakes.

pg 47

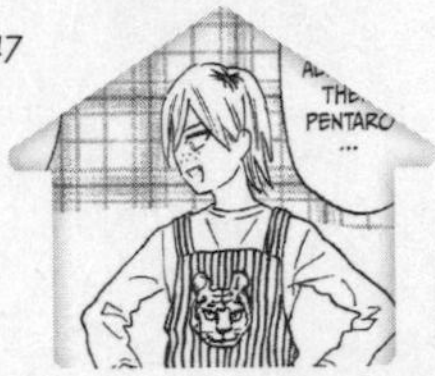
PENTARO ...

PENTARO

In Japanese, "-taro" is a common suffix in male names. While it is somewhat dated in today's terms, it is often playfully used in pet names or nicknames.

pg 87

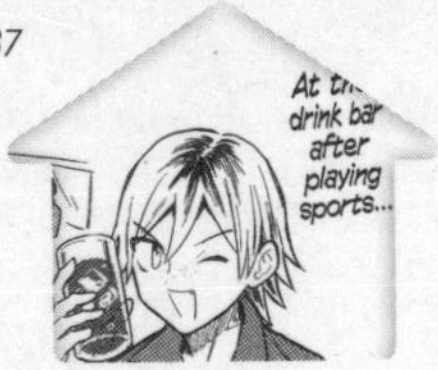
drink bar after playing sports...

DRINK BAR

A "drink bar" is a popular all-you-can-drink soft drink service (soda, juice, tea) at casual Japanese restaurants, where customers can help themselves to beverages of their choice from drink machines. Because you can choose how much you fill your cup, it's an unspoken tradition to invent your own custom mix of the drinks available.

pg 113

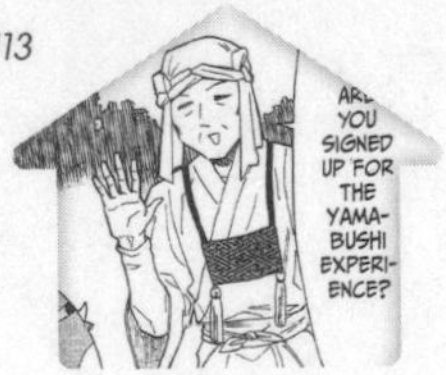
YOU SIGNED UP FOR THE YAMA-BUSHI EXPERI-ENCE?

YAMABUSHI

Yamabushi are ascetic mountain hermits who practice *shugendo,* a holy path on the quest for spiritual powers. Practitioners in training are expected to reply, "I humbly accept," to the instruction they are given. Here, Pen has been dragged into a weekend experience program designed for the public.

pg 127

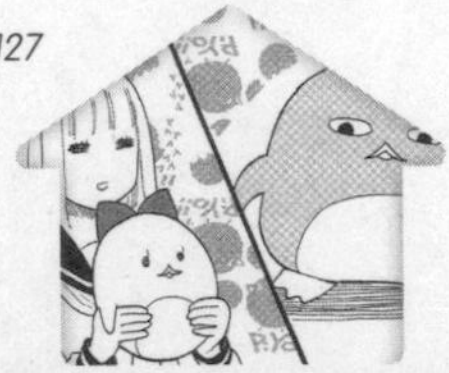

PIYO

In Japanese, "*piyo*" is the sound that little birds make—*cheep, cheep, cheep!*

pg 133

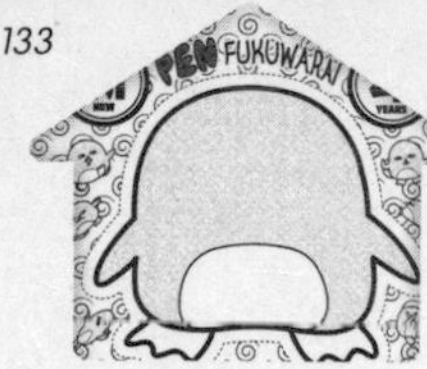
FUKUWARAI

FUKUWARAI

A traditional New Year's game for children where facial features have to be placed on a blank face while wearing a blindfold with hilarious results. The person closest to making a proper face wins, similar to the game Pin the Tail on the Donkey.

pg 156-159

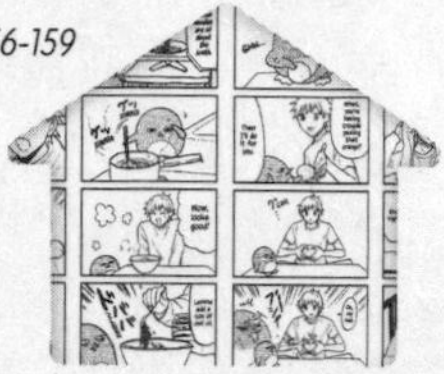

BONUS PENGUINS

Some of these comic strip titles are subtle nods and references. "Just-Picked and Fresh!" is titled "*Mokidate* Fresh!" in Japanese, a nod to the *Glitter Force* (JP: *Fresh Pretty Cure!*) franchise. "Fickle Princess" (JP: "Kimagure Princess") is the title of a Morning Musume song.

pg 157

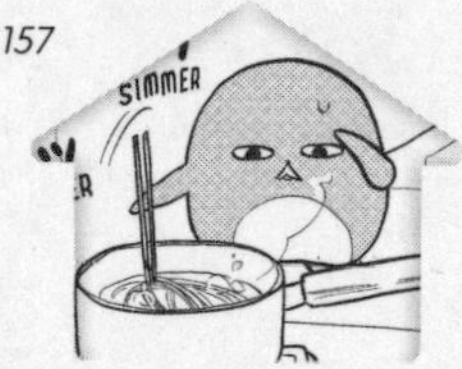
SIMMER

NYUMEN NOODLES

Very fine wheat flour noodles in a hot broth.

pg 158

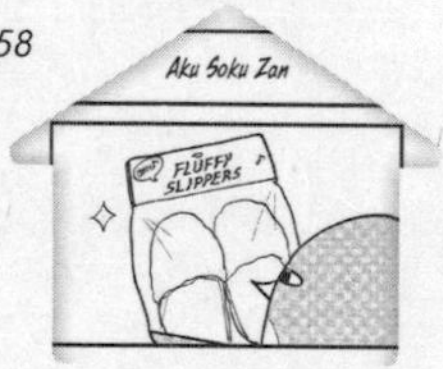
Aku Soku Zan
FLUFFY SLIPPERS

AKU SOKU ZAN

Meaning "swift death to evil," this is the character Hajime Saito's motto in Nobuhiro Watsuki's manga *Rurouni Kenshin.* Saito believes evil must be executed immediately and without question.

pg 159

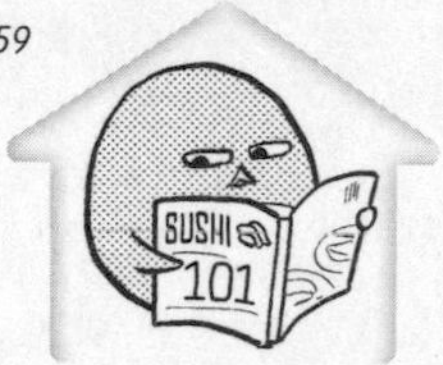
SUSHI
101

11 YEARS

There is a saying that it takes a total of 11 years of training to become a sushi chef: three to master cooking sushi rice, and eight to master the art of forming the sushi.

pg 162

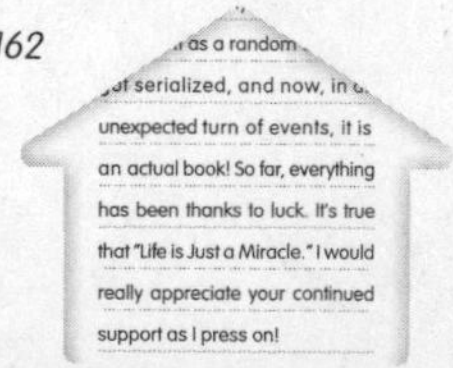
as a random
serialized, and now, in
unexpected turn of events, it is
an actual book! So far, everything
has been thanks to luck. It's true
that "Life is Just a Miracle." I would
really appreciate your continued
support as I press on!

"LIFE IS JUST A MIRACLE"

This is an opening song from the 2012 Japanese-Korean anime series *Pretty Rhythm: Dear My Future* about "Prism Star" idols.

Penguin
& House

The adorable new odd-couple cat comedy manga from the creator of the beloved *Chi's Sweet Home*, in full color!

Sue & Tai-chan

Konami Kanata

Sue is an aging housecat who's looking forward to living out her life in peace... but her plans change when the mischievous black tomcat Tai-chan enters the picture! Hey! Sue never signed up to be a catsitter! *Sue & Tai-chan* is the latest from the reigning meow-narch of cute kitty comics, Konami Kanata.

KC
KODANSHA
COMICS

Young characters and steampunk setting, like *Howl's Moving Castle* and *Battle Angel Alita*

Beyond the Clouds © 2018 Nicke / Ki-oon

A boy with a talent for machines and a mysterious girl whose wings he's fixed will take you beyond the clouds! In the tradition of the high-flying, resonant adventure stories of Studio Ghibli comes a gorgeous tale about the longing of young hearts for adventure and friendship!

Magus of the Library

Mitsu Izumi

MITSU IZUMI'S STUNNING ARTWORK BRINGS A FANTASTICAL LITERARY ADVENTURE TO LUSH, THRILLING LIFE!

Young Theo adores books, but the prejudice and hatred of his village keeps them ever out of his reach. Then one day, he chances to meet Sedona, a traveling librarian who works for the great library of Aftzaak, City of Books, and his life changes forever...

KC KODANSHA COMICS

The beloved characters from *Cardcaptor Sakura* return in a brand new, reimagined fantasy adventure!

RESERVoir CHRoNiCLE
TSUBASA
OMNIBUS
1
CLAMP

TSUBASA
WoRLD CHRoNiCLE: NIRAIKANAI
1
CLAMP

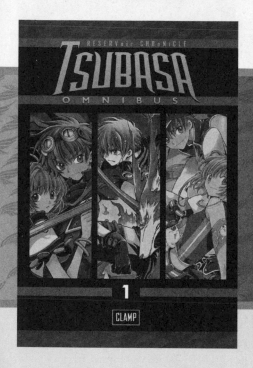

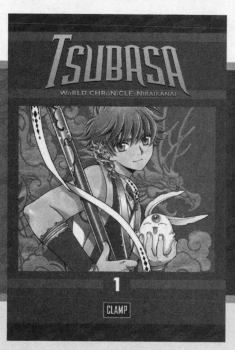

"[*Tsubasa*] takes readers on a fantastic ride that only gets more exhilarating with each successive chapter." —Anime News Network

In the Kingdom of Clow, an archaeological dig unleashes an incredible power, causing Princess Sakura to lose her memories. To save her, her childhood friend Syaoran must follow the orders of the Dimension Witch and travel alongside Kurogane, an unrivaled warrior; Fai, a powerful magician; and Mokona, a curiously strange creature, to retrieve Sakura's dispersed memories!

KC KODANSHA COMICS

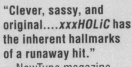

xxxHOLiC © CLAMP-ShigatsuTsuitachi CO.,LTD./Kodansha Ltd.
xxxHOLiC Rei © CLAMP-ShigatsuTsuitachi CO.,LTD./Kodansha Ltd.

Kimihiro Watanuki Is haunted by visions of ghosts and spirits. He seeks help from a mysterious woman named Yuko, who claims she can help. However, Watanuki must work for Yuko in order to pay for her aid. Soon Watanuki finds himself employed in Yuko's shop, where he sees things and meets customers that are stranger than anything he could have ever imagined.

KC KODANSHA COMICS

A SMART, NEW ROMANTIC COMEDY FOR FANS OF *SHORTCAKE CAKE* AND *TERRACE HOUSE*!

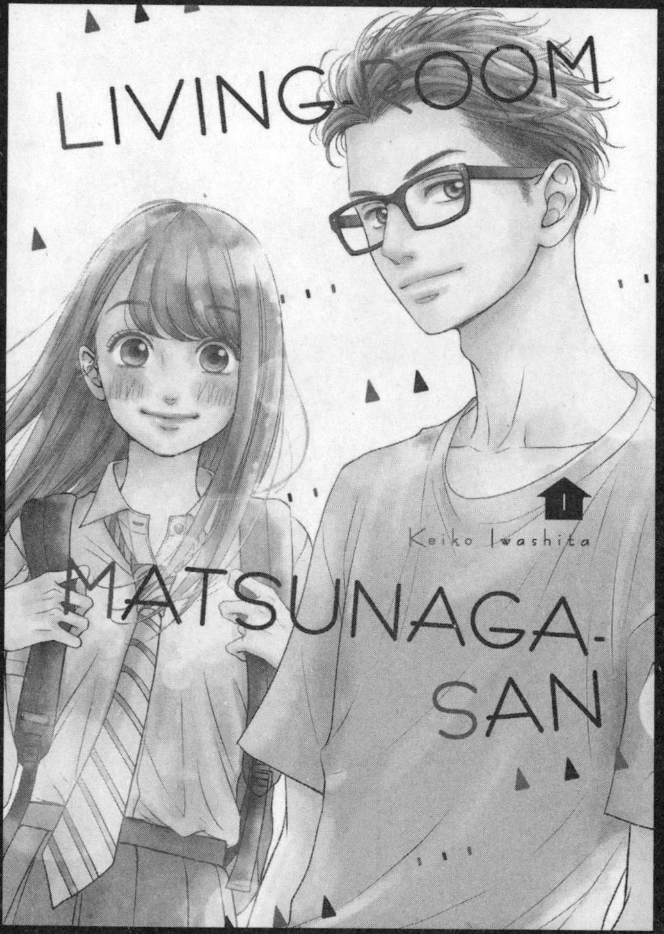
LIVING-ROOM
MATSUNAGA-SAN
1
Keiko Iwashita

A romance manga starring high school girl Meeko, who learns to live on her own in a boarding house whose living room is home to the odd (but handsome) Matsunaga-san. She begins to adjust to her new life away from her parents, but Meeko soon learns that no matter how far away from home she is, she's still a young girl at heart — especially when she finds herself falling for Matsunaga-san.

Princess Jellyfish

Akiko Higashimura

ALSO AN ANIME!

"One of the best manga for beginners!"
—Kotaku

Tsukimi Kurashita is fascinated with jellyfish. She's loved them from a young age and has carried that love with her to her new life in the big city of Tokyo. There, she resides in Amamizukan, a safe-haven for geek girls where no boys are allowed. One day, Tsukimi crosses paths with a beautiful and fashionable woman, but there's much more to this woman than her trendy clothes...!

Penguin & House 1 is a work of fiction. Names, characters, places, and incidents are the products of the author's imagination or are used fictitiously. Any resemblance to actual events, locales, or persons, living or dead, is entirely coincidental.

A Kodansha Trade Paperback Original

Published in the United States by
Kodansha USA Publishing, LLC, New York.

Publication rights for this English edition arranged through
Kodansha Ltd., Tokyo.

First published in Japan in 2020 by Kodansha Ltd., Tokyo
as *Pento House*, volume 1.

Original cover design by Airi Inoue (Nartis)

ISBN 978-1-64651-346-8

Printed in the United States of America.

1st Printing

Translation: Sawa Matsueda Savage
Lettering: Evan Hayden
Editing: Haruko Hashimoto
Kodansha USA Publishing edition cover design by Phil Balsman

Publisher: Kiichiro Sugawara

Director of Publishing Services: Ben Applegate
Associate Director of Publishing Operations: Stephen Pakula
Publishing Services Managing Editors: Madison Salters, Alanna
Ruse Production Managers: Emi Lotto, Angela Zurlo

KODANSHA.US

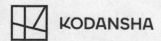

KODANSHA